"Carol Carter's *Majoring in the Rest of Your Life* should be on every college student's required reading list. The tremendous energy and concrete skills that fill the pages of this book promise to alleviate the fears many students have about finding a meaningful career upon graduation. Perhaps more importantly, this book places the college experience in the context of one's greater educational and professional journey, helping students see the long-term applications of the skills they are learning in the classroom."

—ADELINE AZRACK, *Public Health student, Youth Worker, Stanford University 2002*

"When I faced the daunting task of putting quadruplets into college I knew I could not do it alone. I reached out for any resources that could help me. Carol Carter probably does not know that she became my "literary" support system by helping the kids and I understand what lay ahead and offering tools to optimize the college experience and their years in starter-adulthood."

—SUZY KELLETT, *CPCC; Mother of 28-year-old quadruplets and Certified Life Coach*

"*Majoring in the Rest of Your Life* is your guide to connecting with who you are and what you want in life. In simple, straightforward language, Carol Carter takes the guesswork out of pursuing, reaching, and achieving your goals both in and out of college."

—DR. JOE MARTIN, *National Motivational Speaker, Real World University*

"Carol Carter has produced a synergistic, reflective, thought-provoking work that is a path to enlightenment for students, parents, educators and anyone who wants to do more with their life. She shares her journey with us, while teaching us how to experience our own journey. A MUST READ for everyone who wants to succeed, indeed excel, in the real world."

—JUNE A. BROWN, *Attorney/Entrepreneur & Professor, Olive Harvey College–City Colleges of Chicago*

"*Majoring in the Rest of Your Life* takes a holistic rather than a compartmentalized approach to the college experience of preparing for the future. So many students are almost paralyzed at the thought of planning for their future. This book offers valid, manageable steps to help students break through their emotional inertia and move forward with confidence."

—SUSAN IZUMO, *Counselor, Moorpark College*

"I felt as if a counselor was talking to me instead of me reading advice out of a book."

—EMILY DERR, *student, Syracuse University*

"Carol Carter goes beyond the *process* of college and career success—she teaches students to integrate who they are as people into that process. She helps students learn about the tools they need to make college/career choices that are in tune with their abilities and their emotions. Carol puts the people into the process—a powerful combination."

—MJ HUEBNER, *My College Options*

"I just completed the most important book of my life; by the grace of God I found the book while stumbling through my roommate's bookshelves. I now want to take responsibility for my own life by redefining, revising, and most importantly by taking action toward future accomplishments."

—CJ ANGELO, *Entrepreneur, Atlanta, GA*

"Knowing your options when it comes to financial aid is an integral part of college for most students. This book tells you how to get started!"

—GARY LEWIS, *Financial Aid Director, Colorado Mountain College*

"I was inspired by the first-hand accounts and how many students went through the same things I did! This book was instrumental for the motivation I needed to finish my last two years of college."

—JUSTIN BEATTIE, *Commercial Real Estate Broker, San Diego, CA*

"I remember well the scary feeling of being in college for the first year! This book helps to explain what makes college so overwhelming at times and how to successfully overcome these challenges."

—PETER OLSEN, *graduate, St. Olaf College*

"This book has so much useful information that everyone needs to succeed."

—WILSON NGAI, *student, Colorado State University*

"*Majoring in the Rest of Your Life* gives insight on relationships, racism, and dealing with the issues that come with leaving home for college."

—LAUREN GREEN, *student, Lane Technical College Preparatory High School, Chicago*

"The book's advice on getting to know professors in their field of interest and the importance of campus involvement helps students develop contacts that can open doors to future career success and allows them to feel more connected to their school."

—TIM NORDBERG, *M. Div., Executive Director, Hope for the Family Ministries*

"All most interviewers want to talk about during an interview is what graduates did *outside* the classroom. *Majoring in the Rest of Your Life* gives expert advice on how to achieve an optimal college experience, which will demonstrate a graduate's potential to employers."

—KATIE DOOLEY, *Career Consultant, First Services in Chicago*

"Successful networking is crucial to developing your professional personality and having success. I learned that if I maintain healthy relationships at work it will be easier to advance my career. The parts in this book about networking and emotianl intelligence helped me to understand this!"

—LIZ DOLE, *student, Ohio Wesleyan*

"This book is an invaluable resource for young and old alike to identify the tools they need to become prepared for major decisions in their lives. I would not be where I am in the college process without it!"

—BEN MOWER, *student, Juan Diego Catholic High School, Draper, Utah*

"Much of the information found in the book has given me a good foundation about what to look for and what questions to ask as far as careers are concerned."

—STEPHANIE PROKSCH, *student, Regis University*

"*Majoring in the Rest of Your Life* creates a basic outline for an ideal way to get through college."

—ANGELA CRYAN, *student, Central Michigan University*

"This book will serve as an excellent resource as I round out my senior year of college."

—SERENITY ATKINSON, *student, Montana State University*

"One can find information in bits and pieces from seminars or counselors, but having it all condensed into this book in a very clear and understandable way is comforting . . . I feel like having this information will give me an edge on my competition when I go out to find an internship or job."

—MARTTA MCGLYNN, *student, Syracuse University*

"*Know thyself* is the first principle for coping with the present and planning for the future. The case study approach in Carol Carter's book allows each reader to build a composite image of a productive self."

—FRANK T. LYMAN, JR. *Ph.D., retired Teacher/Educator, University of Maryland, College Park; Educational Consultant, K–12*

MAJORING IN THE REST OF YOUR LIFE

CAREER SECRETS FOR COLLEGE STUDENTS

FOURTH EDITION

Carol Carter

LifeBound

DENVER, COLORADO

For my parents, John and Mary, and my brothers, David, Scott, Craig, and Kent, who have always provided the balance between being demanding and being supportive.

LifeBound
1600 Broadway
Suite 2400
Denver, Colorado 80202
www.lifebound.com

Copyright © 2005 by Lifebound, LLC

ISBN 0–9742044–2–0

10   9   8   7   6   5   4   3   2   1

Printed in the United States of America.

contents

foreword

As you embark on your college career, think about the most you can learn from this experience, not the least you can learn or the most you can do to "get by." Find your edge. Stretch yourself. Go outside of your comfort zone. Try things you have never tried. Assert yourself and your ideas. Connect with people who are different from you. Ask yourself what you have in common with people from all walks of life, not just people who see the world the way you do. Find the professors who will really challenge you, not the ones who are most likely to "give" you an A. You are your own scorekeeper now, so be sure you measure up to your own highest level of integrity, self-worth, and self-respect.

When you can, lead. Lead in class with your questions. Lead outside of class in the organizations you join. Lead with your ideas. Lead with your heart as well as your head. Lead with your convictions. Vote. Speak up. Play a role. Get an internship. Make a difference. Pay attention to your passions and your interests; work as hard as you can to develop them to the fullest. Pay attention to your weaknesses. They need not become your strengths, but you don't want them to be liabilities. So persist with the things that are hard for you and you will see that, over time, you can manage them and integrate them with the things that you do best.

Finally, connect with people who motivate and inspire you. Find role models whom you value in your friends, peer leaders, professors, and business contacts. Ask yourself how you can be of service to others and how you can use your unique abilities to help others learn and grow through your everyday actions, not just your service work.

You are creating your life. College is the chance to plant the seeds. Your life is your garden and this is your chance to get the tools and skills to tend it well for the rest of your life.

Stephen E. Loflin
Executive Director, National Society of Collegiate Scholars

note from the student editors

With my graduation rapidly approaching, I look forward to what is to come: graduate school and the beginning of a new career. However, in the midst of my preparation for the next phase of my life, I've found myself looking back and revisiting the past four years.

There is a reason people say college is the best four years of your life. Where else will you find so many opportunities to try new things, meet new people, and belong to a community? Looking back at my freshman year, I can remember how overwhelming everything seemed—in spite, and because of, so many fantastic opportunities. College is full of new beginnings. Living away from parents, taking serious responsibility for your own education, meeting people, and becoming involved means you are suddenly beginning an adult life.

Use this book as a guide for your college experience, and let it teach you about all the opportunities that are available to you. Not everyone will be able to do everything, but with each class, club, and internship, you are becoming the person you will eventually be in work and in life. Take what you can from this book and use it to find your way; make your years in college the fullest that they can be, and they *will* be the best years of your life. —*Jessie Meeks*

Having worked with this book for several months, I've grown close to the lessons and the experiences of other students. Like me, you'll discover new things about different people in different places, and isn't that what going to school is all about anyway?

Doors previously invisible to you will be revealed as you read this book. I was encouraged not only to *see* the doors, but to approach them and turn the knobs. You may feel a little frightened by what you see as the doors swing open, but don't waver. Your future is bright, and this book will give you the ideas and the direction you need to have a productive and fun four years in college. —*Dylan Lewis*

introduction

"dear freshman . . ."

M ajoring in the Rest of Your Life can help you choose a career
and give you specific suggestions to get you from your freshman to your senior year and on to the job of your dreams. It makes
no difference whether you've already selected a career. Just keep
your mind open. All that's necessary, really, is for you to commit
yourself to getting a good education, setting career goals, and then
working to reach them.

for example?

M ark Garrety graduated from the University of Washington
with a history degree and a 3.9 grade point average. Four
months later he still hadn't found a job.

Sharon Heider partied through four years at the University of
Georgia. She was a marketing major with mediocre grades.
Everybody loved her. Now she's a bank teller. People still love her.
But she's unhappy and thinks her degree should be bankable for
more than $20,000 a year.

José Rodriguez is a senior at Northwestern. He's made good
grades, worked part-time in the library, and served as campus coordinator for the United Way. What will he do after graduation? José
has no clue. Law school, maybe.

Then there's you. You're browsing through these pages wondering why you should read this book. Will it really help you get a job
once you're out of school?

Yes. It will help you analyze your interests and decide what you
do and don't like in and out of school, and it will give you advice on

how to get from your first freshman class to your first job. By reading this book and taking action, you'll be one giant step closer to the job you want—the job that stimulates you, motivates you, challenges you, and inspires the best in you. The job that is invigorating as well as rewarding.

But that's what everybody wants, you say. True, but it's not what everybody gets. Why? Because most of us are ill prepared in two areas: self-awareness and planning. Put simply, you must first know what you want and then devise a strategy that will enable you to get it. These skills aren't typically taught in college. They are common-sense secrets that one learns readily on the job. But they can be learned in school. In fact, if you learn them early, you'll have an enormous advantage once you're out working.

Second, few people in college bother to get good advice. They fail to realize that there are all kinds of people whose perspectives on college, jobs, and life can greatly benefit them. This book gives you lots of examples of how people in college and at work continue their education, build their skills, and enjoy themselves. You'll see that there are many different methods to achieve success. And you'll learn how to develop relationships with people: how to get help from them and how to give help yourself.

Third, this book will show you not only how to recognize opportunity but also how to *act* on it. Seizing the moment is as important as thinking things through. You'll learn how to make your pipe dreams real.

More important, you will learn to recognize your own unique potential. This is not a way of looking at the world that puts you at the top by placing everybody else at the bottom. On the contrary, it is a way to understand that everyone can succeed.

You will take this knowledge and experience and put it to work for you. You will learn to overcome the fears and doubts that limit your ability to go after what you want. Bottom line: you will learn to tap your own internal resources and talents.

So remember, the only person you have to compete with is you. You know the dialogue between your ego and alter ego: one says, "Go for it!" while the other screams, "No way, I'm scared!" You'll learn to bring these two sides into line so that YOU can really work for YOU.

Okay, you say. I'm ready. But maybe I don't know what I want to do.

No problem. This book will help you define your skills and interests so you can choose a career. Maybe you screwed up in high school. Okay, college is a clean slate. Maybe academics aren't your strong suit. Well, you can strengthen your weak suit and finesse your strong ones into a winning hand. (The classroom isn't the only proving ground.) Maybe you've never held a job or joined a club. All right, you can start now.

You'll use this book throughout your college career. So the earlier you read it, the better. If you're a freshman, great. If you're a senior, that's fine too. It will teach you valuable business lessons that will help you in your first job.

job skills

Each chapter in *Majoring in the Rest of Your Life* will help you both in college and out. The "tools" for success are categorized below, but you will learn their true meaning in the context of real-life situations in school, and later at work. For now, just take note of each skill.

If you master these skills in college, you will have a greater chance of succeeding scholastically. Think of the categories below as life skills. Though few people are adept at all of them, becoming good at some of them is a significant accomplishment. Decide which skills you have. Then think about the ones you want to work on and develop over the next few years.

1. Write Your Own Success Story
Planning/Organizing. The ability to define specific points of action for yourself and others, which will allow you to set priorities and get or complete a job—or achieve a goal—successfully.

2. Discovering Who You Are and Emotional Intelligence
Problem-Solving/Analytical Skills. The ability to analyze and identify problems, determine their causes, and make suggestions for resolving them. The ability to take positive action.

3. Futures and Options

Creativity/Innovativeness. The ability to let your mind wander; to discern larger patterns and relationships; to see the overall as well as the detail-filled picture.

4. Take the Plunge

Drive/Energy. The sheer energy to get the most out of your courses and your professors while balancing your work and activities. The ability to be productive over long hours; to go above and beyond what is required.

5. Being on Your Own

Continuous Improvement. The ability to commit yourself to life-long education and continuous personal improvement through stretching your mind, learning new skills, and embracing change.

6. Stand Up and Be Counted

Teamwork. The ability to work with others toward a common goal; to be supportive of their ideas and to focus on the goals of the group.

People Management. The ability to work with a group by helping each member to set and define personal and group goals; to delegate responsibility and to give constant credit to those who participate.

Leadership. The ability to influence others in a positive, motivating way; to command attention and respect.

7. The Real World

Commonsense Smarts. The ability to know how things work in the "real world"; to know instinctively what to do in different kinds of situations.

8. Intern We Trust

Independence/Tenacity. The ability to be unconventional; to take a stand on something you firmly believe in, but which may be unpopular with a larger group.

9. Windows on the World

Personal Adaptability. The ability to adjust quickly to any situation, group of people, or environment; to use past experiences to measure new ones and respond nondefensively to criticism.

10. Networking

Communication. The ability to articulate your thoughts well, both on paper and orally; to speak effectively one-on-one as well as in groups.

11. Paperwork

Marketing Yourself. The ability to make a clear and convincing presentation to those whom you want to persuade.

12. Your Third Degree

Interpersonal Skills. The ability to talk openly and freely with others; to put them at ease with you and to exude confidence and enthusiasm.

13. You're Hired!

Stress Tolerance. The ability to cope in stressful or discouraging situations; to keep things in perspective.

14. Outlooks and Insights

Results/Remaining Goal-Oriented. The ability to set measurable and attainable goals and to be motivated by the challenge of achieving them.

At the end of each year, refer to this list. Where have you made progress? Where do you need to improve? What specific goals will you set to help you improve?

1

write your own success story

I find that the harder I work, the more luck I seem to have.

—THOMAS JEFFERSON

We have an extraordinary leverage in influence—individually, professionally, and institutionally—if we can only get a clear sense, a clear conception, a clear vision of the road ahead.

—JOHN NAISBITT, IN *MEGATRENDS*

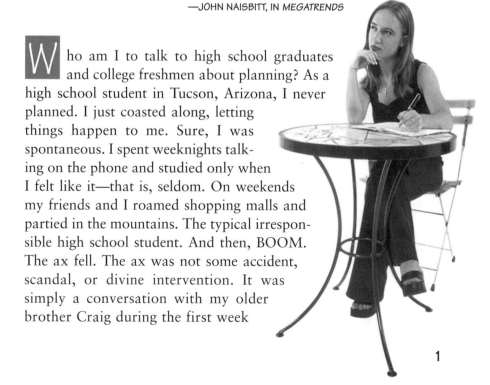

Who am I to talk to high school graduates and college freshmen about planning? As a high school student in Tucson, Arizona, I never planned. I just coasted along, letting things happen to me. Sure, I was spontaneous. I spent weeknights talking on the phone and studied only when I felt like it—that is, seldom. On weekends my friends and I roamed shopping malls and partied in the mountains. The typical irresponsible high school student. And then, BOOM. The ax fell. The ax was not some accident, scandal, or divine intervention. It was simply a conversation with my older brother Craig during the first week

1

of my senior year in high school. Our talk changed the course of my life.

At seventeen I was intimidated by my four older brothers. I saw them as bright, motivated, and respected achievers—the opposite of me. Whenever one of them asked me about what I was doing or thinking, I'd answer with a one-liner and hope he'd soon leave me alone.

This conversation with Craig was different. He didn't give up after five minutes, despite my curt, vague responses.

"Carol, what are you interested in?"

"I dunno."

"What do you think about all day?"

"I dunno."

"What do you want to do with your life?"

"I'll just let things happen."

Craig persisted. His voice grew indignant. He criticized me for talking on the phone, for spending too much time at pep rallies and

rock concerts, for not studying, for not challenging myself. He pointed out that I hadn't read an unassigned book in three years. He asked if I intended to approach college in the same way I approached high school—as one continuous party. If so, he warned, I'd better start thinking of a career flipping burgers because no respectable employer would ever take me seriously. He asked me if that was what I wanted to do with my life. He cautioned that out of laziness and lack of planning I would limit my options so narrowly that I would never be able to get a real job. I had wasted three years of high school, he said. College was a new start, since employers and graduate schools seldom check as far back as high school for records. He advised me to quit making excuses, decide what I wanted, and plan how to achieve it. My only limitations would be self-imposed.

Craig left my room, sermon completed. I didn't speak to him before he flew back to New York that afternoon to finish his senior year at Columbia. I hated him for interfering in my life. He made me dissatisfied with myself. I was scared he was right. For the first time, I realized that "typical" was not necessarily what I wanted to be.

The next day, still outraged but determined to do something, I went to the library and checked out six classics: *Pride and Prejudice* by Jane Austen, *The Great Gatsby* by F. Scott Fitzgerald, *A Farewell to Arms* and *For Whom the Bell Tolls* by Ernest Hemingway, *A Portrait of the Artist as a Young Man* by James Joyce, and *Sister Carrie* by Theodore Dreiser. Then I wrote down in a notebook a few goals that I wanted to accomplish. They all seemed boldly unattainable: Earn straight A's (previously I had made B's and C's); study every week including one weekend night; keep reading classics on my own. If I couldn't make it in my senior year of high school, why should I waste time and money on college? I'd beat fate to the door and begin my career at the hamburger stand immediately.

Three weeks later, I got a letter from Craig. He knew how angry I was with him. He told me our conversation hadn't been easy for him either, but that if he hadn't cared, he wouldn't have bothered to say anything. He was right. I needed that sermon. If I didn't come to terms with my problems, I would never be able to move from making excuses to making things happen.

I worked hard and got results. The second semester of my senior year, I made all A's (except for a B in physics). I finished the six classics, and others as well. I started reading newspapers and magazines. I had to move the *Vogue* on my nightstand to make room for *Time*, *Harper's*, and *Fortune*. I found I could set goals and attain them, and I started to realize that I wasn't so different from my brothers after all.

To my utter astonishment, I discovered that for the first time, I enjoyed learning. My world seemed to open up just because I knew more about different kinds of people, ways of thinking, and ways of interpreting things that I had previously assumed to be black-and-white. (If you are a shy person, joining a club and getting to know—and actually like—a few people whom you had originally perceived as unfriendly or uninteresting may astonish you as much as my newfound appreciation for learning astonished me.)

The summer before college, I thought about what I wanted to do with my life, but I couldn't decide on a direction. I had no notion of what I wanted to major in. What to do . . . what to do?

I turned to Craig, a phone call away in New York City. He told me not to spend my first year of college worrying about what I wanted to do. The main priority was to learn as much as I could. College, he told me, was my golden opportunity to investigate all kinds of things—biology, psychology, accounting, and philosophy. He told me I'd become good at writing and critical thinking techniques—skills that would help me learn any job after graduation. And though I could continue to expand my educational horizons throughout life, college was the best opportunity to expose myself to the greatest minds and movements of our civilization.

Craig also warned me that being a scholar, though important, wouldn't be enough. (He had just graduated from Columbia as a Phi Beta Kappa, but since he hadn't gained any real-world experience in college, it took him several months to find his first job.) To maximize my options upon graduation, I would have to do three things:

1. Learn as much as possible from classes, books, professors, and other people.
2. Participate in extracurricular activities.
3. Gain real-world experience by working part-time and landing summer internships.

If I did these three things reasonably well, Craig assured me, I could choose from a number of career opportunities at the end of my senior year. And even if I only did two of the three full-force and one half-speed, I'd still be in good shape. Making an effort in each area and having a modest outcome were attainable goals. That way I could balance my college experience and open options for the future.

Craig advised me to look ahead and develop a plan of action for each of my four years of college. He told me that foresight—the ability to consider the bigger picture beyond short-term challenges and intermittent goals—is invaluable in most jobs; it distinguishes outstanding people from the rest of the pack.

This book is designed to be for you what Craig was for me—my adviser during college. The following chapters will provide you with guidelines for success by asking you to examine yourself, set goals, and believe in your ability to achieve them. It will give you specific examples of how to get things done. It will also introduce you to all kinds of people, all of whom followed their own varying, yet similar paths toward their goals. Most important, you'll learn that everyone—including YOU—has his or her own set of skills, abilities, passions, and unique talents to tap. Finding the career and lifestyle that allow you to cultivate and nurture them is one of the most important secrets of success.

Additionally, you will uncover ideas to structure your college years and beyond. These ideas will no longer be secrets of success; they will become tools for building a rewarding future. Use this book to your advantage, but also enjoy it. While you explore this book, you will discover new things about your world and your life. The stories are written to help you understand the achievements and experiences of other students just like you! Take advantage of these stories, they'll help you mold life's decisions. In addition, the activities and questions at the end of each chapter are designed to help you grow into adult life while you learn more about yourself. The future is in your hands and the world full of opportunities. Only you can take the steps needed for success, and these lessons will point you in the right direction.

so take action!

A good way to start is to assess your shortcomings and strengths. As I've already told you, one of my shortcomings in high school was not learning all I could from my classes and teachers. Your shortcoming may have been that you focused entirely on your studies without developing many outside interests or activities. Someone else may feel that he concentrated so much on an outside activity—such as training for a particular sport—that he had no time for studies or friends. What was your major shortcoming in high school?

Now think about three things:

1. What pleased you in high school?
2. What could you have done better?
3. What do you want to improve on in the future?

Identifying these areas will help you strike a good balance during college. Once you get in the habit of analyzing past experiences, you will have a clearer notion of what you do and don't want in the future. That's important.

Whether you are a high school senior, a college freshman, or a college senior, the next thing you must do is decide to take action. Don't worry if you don't know what you want to do. Just commit yourself to the process. If you do, you'll eventually find out which careers might be best for you and how you could best prepare for them.

To recap, here are the priorities:

1. Gain knowledge.
2. Participate in activities.
3. Get real-world experience.

making it happen

L uck is the residue of design," said Branch Rickey, known as the Mahatma for his strategic methods as a team owner and general manager in baseball. He developed the farm system in which the minor leagues are organized. His plans of action took a handful of disjointed teams in faraway cities and banded them into an organization that has left its mark on American culture.

Nothing happens magically. If you want to be a success, you are going to have to take personal responsibility for your life. Why do some graduates get twenty job offers and others receive none? Although successful people may appear lucky, in fact they illustrate the maxim "Luck favors the prepared mind."

Joe Cirulli agrees. He is the owner of the successful Gainesville Health and Fitness Center in Florida. Early in his life, exercise was a priority, an essential part of his day. So he followed his interests and put his talents to work by starting his own health club. While many other clubs have folded around him, he has experienced enormous success—his membership continues to grow, and he is able to keep his club filled with the best equipment and the most knowledgeable professionals.

When Joe was twenty, he worked as an assistant manager and a sales representative for a health club. One of his responsibilities was to train new sales representatives for the club. He worked hard to prepare them for their jobs only to have to compete with them once they were trained.

He remembers talking with the vice president of the company about his frustration. The vice president, a person Joe respected, advised him to keep on putting his best efforts into his work. "Right now you may not see the benefit of your hard work, but one day you will."

Joe followed his advice. Less than five years later, his skills at training people in the health-club industry paid off—he was able to put his expertise to work at his own club. "Knowing how to motivate employees to do their best, to care about the quality of their work, and to care about our customers has had an enormous impact on the success of my own company."

Joe believes the secret to his success is giving 100 percent of himself in everything he does. "Success is the culmination of all your efforts. There are thousands of opportunities for people who give their all."

How do you arrange to have the most options when you leave college? Plan, develop foresight, and take charge of your life, and you will become one of the lucky ones. Most important, decide that you want to succeed—and believe it.

Charles Garfield, a clinical psychologist who has spent his career studying what motivates people to superior effort, says that the drive to excel comes primarily from within. Can "peak performances" be learned? Yes, says Garfield. High achievers are not extraordinarily gifted superhumans. What they have in common is the ability to cultivate what the German writer Johann Wolfgang von Goethe termed "the genius, power, and magic" that exists in all of us. These achievers increase the odds in their favor through simple techniques that anyone can cultivate:

- Envision a mission.
- Be result-oriented.
- Tap your internal resources.
- Enlist team spirit.
- Treat setbacks as steppingstones.

These are skills that this book is going to teach you.

first things first

The first thing to keep in mind when planning: accept the world the way it is. Your plans should be based on a realistic assessment of how things are, not on some starry-eyed vision of how they should be. You can dream, but there's a happy medium between cold reality and the pie in the sky. That's why you must be open to opportunity. Indeed, you must create it. Although you can't change the hand you were dealt, you can play it as wisely as possible. That's what this book is about. So start today. Start now.

The more questions you ask now, the better prepared you'll be in four years. You don't want to be stuck in a boring job or wondering why you can't find work.

Are you going to make mistakes? I hope so, unless you're not of the human species. Making mistakes is the process by which we learn. And whenever we're disappointed by the outcome, we need to maintain a positive attitude, log the information—and keep going. The key is to learn from your mistakes without letting them slow you down.

discover who you are

DEFINING YOUR INTERESTS, ABILITIES, AND GOALS, AND UNDERSTANDING EMOTIONAL INTELLIGENCE

Know thyself. —INSCRIPTION, TEMPLE OF DELPHI

To thine own self be true. —SHAKESPEARE

Y ou've been told that it pays to find out everything you can about the colleges you're thinking of attending and the jobs they might lead to. But it's also worthwhile to do some serious research into the subject that can make or break your college experience: *yourself.*

Phil was a pre-law freshman. After spending six months talking to law students and attorneys, he made a great discovery: he realized that he didn't want to be a lawyer. No area of law intrigued him. He disliked spending hours in solitary research, and law didn't accommodate his strengths—working with groups and developing programs. So Phil switched his major to English and his minor to history. Today he's in business for himself as an international marketing consultant. And he loves his work.

If you don't know yourself, you'll make uninformed decisions. My college friend Mary was an accounting major because she knew she'd be employable. She was right. But she soon discovered that she hated working with numbers, and after just two years, she quit accounting. So long, general ledger.

I recently had dinner with Mary. She's living in New York and writing for a food-and-wine magazine. We talked about the internal struggles that prompted her to make a career change. Now she's crazy about her job and regrets only that she didn't invest the time and energy in college to determine her interests. "College students shouldn't opt for a career because it will be easy to find a job," Mary says. "'Easy' can equal 'uninteresting' and 'unfulfilling' if you don't have a passion and interest for the work itself. Pursue what will be rewarding in the short term *and* the long term."

Cathy Hudnall agrees. After five years as a secretary at Wells Fargo Bank in San Francisco, she was invited to join the bank's junior officer training program. Realizing she had a true interest in and aptitude for banking, she enrolled in the American Graduate School of International Management. "Find out while you're in college what makes you tick," says Cathy, who is now a senior manager and vice president at the Bank of Canada.

"Nothing great was ever achieved without enthusiasm," said Ralph Waldo Emerson. You want to be enthusiastic about your job so that you will do it well and enjoy it. In order to do that, you must first take some time to analyze what it is you like to do.

An honest and complete self-appraisal is your first step toward choosing the right career. By asking yourself critical questions, you'll be way ahead of most of your classmates—leagues, fathoms, kilometers squared. *Way* ahead.

the three Ds

W hich of the following describes you best?

- **Drifter.** Life just happens to you, often in ways decidedly unfriendly or random.

- **Dreamer.** You have wonderful plans for the future but can't always realize your dreams. Your favorite line is borrowed from Scarlett O'Hara, of *Gone with the Wind* fame: "I can't think about it now. I'll think about it tomorrow."

- **Doer:** You have the confidence, the vision, and the persistence to make your goals come together. You plan, act, and achieve.

Most people are some combination of the above. Maybe you've been a *Drifter*. In this chapter, you'll be able to graduate to *Dreamer* as you explore your interests, abilities, and passions. The rest of this book is devoted to becoming a *Doer*.

Does this mean that drifting and dreaming are not important? On the contrary. One of my best friends, Madeline, aptly reminded me that a balance of drifting and dreaming is necessary. "All doing squashes the learning, pain, and growth that dreaming and drifting inspire," she wrote. "Success is balance. It is reading well, thinking deeply; having the wisdom to see the broader picture; knowing the importance of friends and family; taking the time to marvel at a sunset, a small child, or an older person."

MY TWO CENTS   *How Do I Apply It?*

Kelly Carson, University of Kansas

All my life, I've had this amazing passion for languages. Ever since I was little, I have gobbled up books like candy, raiding my parents' bookshelves and coming home from the library with big stacks of new things to read. But, somehow, I knew that simply reading wasn't enough, that there was something missing. On my first day of Spanish in 8th grade, all of the pieces seemed to fit together—I was a linguist to the core. Ever since that point, I have been enrolled in Spanish classes—and have loved every day of it! People sometimes laughed or were surprised that I was already so certain that I had found what I loved—but it didn't matter. After every time someone asked how I would make a living studying Spanish, or told me I was much too young to know what I wanted to do with my life, I would go to my next Spanish lesson and know that my feelings were right.

So, I loved Spanish and I did well in it, but where to go from there? My junior year of high school, I decided to approach my Spanish teacher and ask her how I could get more involved in Spanish in the community. She was delighted by my request, and I soon found myself helping teach ESL (English as a Second Language) in an underprivileged elementary school three days a week after classes. The opportunity to teach English to children who spoke Spanish banished any doubts I had about wanting to pursue a career in the language. I loved working with the kids, seeing their faces light up when they caught a new concept or learned a new word, watching them open up in their other lessons because they could communicate with their classmates. I felt truly privileged to be a part of it. Of course, this wasn't all I did in high school: I was in the top 5 percent of my class, the drum major for my marching band, actively involved in our theater program, first chair piccolo and flute in our Symphonic Winds, president of Curriculum Council, and a National Merit Finalist—but I always knew that Spanish was somehow my destination.

When I started my college years on a full scholarship at the University of Kansas, I knew I wanted to continue teaching ESL, so I stopped in at the Center for Community Outreach (a renowned "volunteer clearinghouse" on campus that places students all over Lawrence according to their interests) and asked what I could do to help. After a few days, I found myself presented with a new and interesting challenge: teaching ESL to a 22-year-old woman. At first, I was intimidated—what if she didn't like me, or I couldn't understand her, or I wasn't a good enough teacher, or . . . the list of worries goes on. Even as these thoughts swirled through my head that first day as I walked up the stairs to her apartment, I knew that everything would be fine. After Diana overcame her initial shyness, she began to make great progress in learning English, and we became good friends. We went salsa dancing together; I came to her daughter's birthday parties; and many more experiences exposed me to her culture, her friends, and her cooking. To this day, I still teach Diana twice a week, and we still love sitting together after the tutoring is done, chatting and laughing together.

My friends from school loved hearing my stories about my adventures with Diana, and soon people began asking if they could start tutoring, too! I began putting my friends into contact with Diana's friends who wanted to learn English, never knowing just how much that small beginning would grow. I began to see that there was a huge number of people in my town desperate to learn English, and just as many language students wanting to get out in the community, practice their speaking skills, and just plain have fun. With this in mind, I approached the Center for Community Outreach yet again, with the idea to create a program to provide ESL tutors to children and adults in Lawrence. Six months later, that "small idea" has grown into Project Bridge, an ESL tutoring organization that I coordinate at KU with over 30 members and growing by the day!

Throughout all of these experiences, I have one lasting goal: to pursue my passions and dreams, and to make the world a better place along the way. This ambition has never led me wrong: every day I find something new to be passionate about, to be excited for, and I can see the differences I'm making in other people's lives along the way. Perhaps this is what the high school and college years are really about: not just having the perfect SAT score or being student council president or joining the best fraternity or sorority, but being able to find what you love, to remain true to your passions, and, most of all, to make a difference.

finding a balance

A balance of drifting, dreaming, and doing will help you define and achieve what you determine is most important in college, in work, and in life. So how might you go about "discovering" yourself further? Here are four suggestions:

1. Keep a journal.
2. Survey yourself.
3. Keep asking questions.
4. Overcome obstacles.

1. Keep a Journal

Throughout college, keep track of your plans, deeds, fears, and dreams. Write down goals for yourself and then reread them after six months. Which have you achieved? Which do you want to pursue now?

Your journal is your secret companion. Write in it every day, through good times and bad. Share your expectations and aspirations, your disappointments and fears. Write about the world as you see it. Be blunt and blatantly honest. After a month, begin rereading your journal. It will reveal interesting patterns. You'll see a definite progression, and that's rewarding.

Pam Zemper, vice president and director of marketing at Security Pacific Executive Professional Services, says that she has always kept lists—they are her form of journal writing. Her lists remind her of activities she wants to try, subjects she wants to learn, ways she wants to grow. "As I go back and review my lists over the years, I can see how certain dreams tie together. My lists give me a framework out of which I formulate my goals and then my plans."

2. Survey Yourself

Answer the following questions as honestly as you can. After all, no one else is going to see your answers unless you want them to. These questions should help you evaluate your high school experience and define your college goals. They will also help you get a handle on your strengths and weaknesses, key elements in the process of self-discovery. Periodically, throughout your life, you'll find it helpful to look back at what you've done so that you can get perspective on what you want to do as you go forward. Later in the book, you'll have a chance to look ahead and dream about what kinds of things you want to do. Now look back and reflect for a moment.

HOW I SEE MYSELF

1. In high school, I felt most proud that I

2. I feel most disappointed that I did not

3. The most important thing I learned in high school was

4. I developed confidence by

5. The teacher who had the greatest positive influence on me was

6. In high school, I was motivated by

7. The five things I enjoyed most were

8. The five things I enjoyed least were

9. The five things I found most interesting were _____

_____

_____

10. My biggest disappointment was _____

_____

11. My greatest success was _____

_____

12. The most difficult thing I've had to do is _____

_____

13. In high school, I considered myself _____

_____

14. My friends would describe me as _____

_____

15. If I could change one thing in my life, it would be _____

_____

16. I am angered by _____

_____

17. I would describe myself as the kind of person who _____

_____

18. The thing I would most like to change about myself is _____

_____

19. My philosophy of life is _____

_____

20. <u>One thing I would like to improve is</u>

MYSELF AMONG OTHERS

1. <u>The kind of people I most like to be with are</u>

2. <u>I most admire my fellow students and teachers who</u>

3. <u>The kind of people I find it most difficult to be around are</u>

4. <u>The person who has had the most influence on my life has been</u>

   <u>because</u>

5. <u>The character traits I most like in people are</u>

6. <u>The ones I dislike most are</u>

7. <u>Given a choice between being with others or being by myself,</u>

   <u>I usually choose to</u>

   <u>because</u>

Keep in mind that self-discovery requires continual reexamination. As your perspective and ideas change, you'll find yourself revising your earlier lists. With each revision you will move closer to your goals, both in the short and long term. Don't worry if you can't answer all of these questions now. You'll have plenty of time in the next few years to explore different areas that interest you. These answers will serve as your information base when the time comes to evaluate your career path.

3. Keep Asking Questions

Don't be complacent and accept everything you read and hear. Find out if things make sense. We've all heard the slogan "Question authority." Let it serve as a gentle reminder.

Challenge friends, parents, and teachers in discussion. Learn opposing viewpoints and continually question your beliefs. Practice putting yourself in other people's shoes. Continue to develop your critical-thinking skills. Ask yourself what you're doing, why you're doing it, and how you can do it better.

Dick Christensen, a community psychiatrist and an assistant professor at the University of Florida, was torn between pursuing a career in medicine and working as a priest in the inner city. One of the strategies he used to help him make a decision was to talk with people and ask them questions.

"Perhaps the most valuable experiences of my college years were the opportunities I found to spend time with people who were doing what I was considering," he explains. "I spent time with people who had returned from the Peace Corps, I listened to physicians talk about their experiences in medicine, and I saw firsthand what it was like for a person to live and work in the inner city as a priest. My college years afforded me the luxury of time, even in the midst of academic demands, to approach others with life questions that could only be answered by life experiences."

4. Overcome Obstacles

Everyone has insecurities and shortcomings. It's a fact of life. However, we don't like to explore our dark sides. We usually keep them locked up tightly inside. Left unattended, our insecurities are manifested as fear; and the more you try to run from fear, the more it will dominate your life. Think of the dilemma as an intellectual puzzle to be solved. Turn the puzzle around in your mind, looking at it from as many angles as possible. Be comforted by the fact that you do have a choice: you can be courageous and deal effectively with your fears.

The first step toward overcoming your fears is identifying them. Complete the following statements honestly.

WHAT ARE YOU AFRAID OF?

1. Very few people realize that I am afraid of _____

_____

2. When I am alone the thing that frightens me most is _____

_____

3. When I am with other people the thing that frightens me most is ____

_____

4. I'm embarrassed when _____

_____

5. My greatest fear about college is _____

_____

The next step is to accept these fears. That's right. In order to overcome your fears, it helps to embrace them. Here's an exercise that will help. Imagine that each of the five situations above came true and that you were forced to confront your fear. Answer the following questions for each:

1. Describe the scene in detail. _____

_____

_____

2. What happened? _____

_____

3. What does it feel like? _____

_____

4. What were you thinking? _____

_____

5. What could you have done to make the anxiety more tolerable? _____

_____

_____

Aside from fears, other obstacles will surely get in your way. Maybe you think you're not smart enough because of that IQ test you took in fourth grade. You were having a bad day; it happens. Maybe you believe that you're incompetent because you didn't ace the SATs. Relax. Remember, even Einstein flunked at least one critical exam.

Einstein is not unique, at least not on that score. Robert Sternberg, a noted Yale psychologist, has done extensive research on IQ tests and intelligence. He has noted that intelligence is a composite of several factors. Many of these—including motivation and the capacity to adjust to change—are difficult to measure accurately using a written test. If you do score well on aptitude tests, don't rest on your laurels. Your brain is not a bank. It cannot pay the rent, nor can it pay for the Himalayan odyssey you're hoping will get you away from home for the summer. Stretch your natural talents by coupling your intellect with determination and a commitment to action.

winning against all odds

There are other obstacles much more formidable than genius or the lack of it. Jackie Fitzgerald, the national sales manager for Sunlover Clothing Products, supported her family while attending Villanova University in Pennsylvania. She had begun college as a pre-med student because her mother had always wanted her to be a doctor.

"I didn't have the financial support from my family that most students have," Jackie recalls. "After I decided I didn't want to be a doctor, I lost all emotional support from my mom." This, Jackie says, was the greatest obstacle she had to overcome.

She learned how to encourage herself when no one else was there to cheer her on. With her many commitments, Jackie learned time management and self-reliance. These skills enabled her to graduate with honors as a sociology major and psychology minor, and later to be enormously successful in business. "It's better to graduate with a solid education in a field you love than to pursue a career in an area you're not passionate about."

For Jill Goldfarb, things were worse. During the first week of her freshman year at the University of Michigan, her mother died of a stroke. Jill dropped out of school for the fall semester and worked at a department store before returning to school in the spring. In March, her father died suddenly of a heart attack.

"I survived because I had to," says Jill, who immersed herself in her studies and extracurricular activities. Her hard work and dedication were perhaps the greatest tributes she could pay to her parents. Remarkably, Jill graduated with a degree in management information systems with a 4.0 average.

If you're starting college under a difficult (or even tragic) circumstance, don't let a disadvantage deny you success. There is truth to the old adage that adversity breeds character. Learn the difference between situations that you can and can't control. Set your sights on a goal that you can achieve, and then go for it. Throughout life, each of us encounters obstacles and challenges on a regular basis. It's how we deal with these challenges, and what we make of them, that determine our true success.

emotional intelligence

W hen you dare, your dreams, goals, and inspirations keep you looking ahead and moving forward. How you balance those ambitions with the setbacks and happenstance of everyday life shows how "emotionally intelligent" you are. Emotional intelligence also emerges from how gently you handle the dreams and hopes of others, as well as your own. Finding the strengths and weaknesses in your emotional intelligence, you discover whether you need to make sacrifices to achieve discipline in use of your time. And, without losing your underlying focus, you want to attend to spontaneous moments in your life. You never know.

What Is Emotional Intelligence?

Feelings are a wonderful part of being alive. What would life be like without love, joy, and excitement? What if you could never enjoy the first snowfall of winter, a fun evening with your closest friends, or the welcome feeling of returning home on your breaks from school? Of course, there's the down side too—breaking up with your partner, failing a test, having your computer break down, and so on. But there's more to life than working, eating, and sleeping.

The way you handle your emotions is crucial to your success in life. Emotional intelligence is the ability to know what you and those around you are feeling—and to handle those feelings skillfully.

In 1995, Yale scholar Daniel Goleman released his groundbreaking book *Emotional Intelligence,* which brought this new thinking to light. Goleman contends that the mystique of a high IQ has led us to ignore emotional savvy, which can be as vital in determining the course of our lives. He argues that EQ may be even more important for success in life than IQ.

The Impact of Emotions

Stress is everywhere—in our personal relationships, our jobs, our finances, our social standings. Do you cringe when you're expected to address a room full of people? How do you respond when you sense a friend is feeling nervous or lonely? These are the kinds of emotionally charged situations where a high IQ won't solve anything for you. Goleman explains that although you may be highly intelligent with bookish endeavors, a lack of self-control or an impersonal demeanor can actually sabotage your career and personal relationships.

"The brightest among us," he writes, "can be emotional morons." Take the case of Jason Haffizulla, a Florida high school student who dreamed of entering Harvard Medical School. He had so many A+ grades in so many courses that his grade point average was 4.614, well above a straight A. But one day, when his physics teacher gave him a B on a quiz, Jason lost control and stabbed the teacher with a kitchen knife. The consequences of his impulsive actions will affect the rest of his life.

In addition to there being no insurance against acts of passion, a brainy IQ lends no warmth or social grace to a person's character. Emotional intelligence leads to greater drive, self-discipline, caring, and cooperation.

Managing Stress

Stress is one of the most pressing concerns of our time. According to the American Medical Association, up to 90 percent of all visits to doctors are for stress-related ailments. A highly stressful life can lead to health problems as simple as tight muscles or as serious as heart disease and cancer. Learning to de-stress is an essential skill for maintaining your emotional equilibrium. Fortunately, there are a number of ways to manage our reactions to stressful events.

Facing Insecurities

Consciously or unconsciously, all of us have felt that we must meet certain arbitrary standards to attain self-worth. Failure to do so threatens our security and significance. This results in a fear of failure and can lead to obsessive behavior.

"The more insecure people are, the more desperate they are to have control," says Howard Rankin, clinical psychologist and director of the Carolina Wellness Retreat in Hilton Head, South Carolina. "If you can't get it in one area, you try to get it in another." Eating disorders like anorexia nervosa are another distorted form of control, he says—a way to compensate for feeling powerless.

You may feel overwhelmed and helpless. You may obsessively play over in your mind again and again how you could have performed better on a test or handled an argument better. Learning from your mistakes is certainly noble, but uncontrolled rumination only burns up precious emotional energy that could be used for other tasks. When you catch yourself obsessing, stop and remind yourself that while you could have done better, you've learned from that situation and it's time to move on. Say this to yourself several times a day, if necessary. This kind of positive self-talk will help you put things in perspective.

The key to the control teeter-totter is accepting that there are some things you simply cannot control. Diseases strike, your favorite team loses, and you can't be perfect at everything. Hard work does pay off, but in some cases it's best to let go. Remember, it's not all up to you.

Even though you can't control certain events, you can control your reaction to them, says psychologist Nancy Schlossberg, professor emeritus at the University of Maryland and author of *Overwhelmed: Coping with Life's Ups and Downs.* "Even if you can't control the earthquake, you can control how you deal with it," she says. "You have to acknowledge the loss, grieve, refocus the camera, and possibly reshape the dream." The ability to let go is a critical step toward fortifying your emotional intelligence.

Managing Difficult Emotions

Ruby Bridges, a shy little girl from New Orleans, accomplished an astonishing feat. In the fall of 1963, she became one of the first African Americans to integrate into an all-white school. It was a monumental task for anyone, especially for a six-year-old kindergarten student. Every day a federal marshal accompanied Ruby to school because she had to pass through a gauntlet of outraged citizens as she entered the building. The angry mob shouted abusive chants at her. One of the protesters even brought a black doll inside a baby's coffin and thrust it in Ruby's face in an effort to intimidate her.

Robert Coles, a child psychologist, came upon these harrowing incidents every day on his way to work and was deeply disturbed by the venom directed at this child. He had also studied the coping skills of children in stress, so he offered to help Ruby cope with her trauma. With her parents' permission, Dr. Coles began meeting regularly with Ruby to determine if she was emotionally holding up under the pressure, and if so, how.

He couldn't have been more surprised by his research. Ruby wasn't only coping—she was thriving in spite of the difficulties. At the close of his sessions with her, Dr. Coles notes, "Having something to believe in protected Ruby from psychiatric symptoms and gave her a dignity and a strength that is utterly remarkable."

The story of Ruby Bridges epitomizes what we mean by exercising emotional intelligence in the face of difficulties. Ruby's emotional resiliency helped to keep her strong. You too can face the stresses of college life, and beyond, when you channel your emotional energy toward a meaningful purpose.

The Good News About Difficult Emotions

Although emotional suffering feels like an unwelcome intruder, every difficult emotion has the potential for developing your emotional intelligence. Instead of denying or repressing negative emotions, realize that feelings like stress, anger, and sadness provide the training ground for developing healthy coping mechanisms.

Although you may find it hard to be content when you're confronted with a problem, a measure of contentment is possible as you learn to manage adverse emotions constructively instead of allowing them to control you. Consider Derik Baker, a sophomore at Columbia University in New York City. While playing football during his freshman year, he seriously injured his knee and could not return to the game. "All through high school I dreamed of playing football in college," he says. "Then everything was shattered."

Derik overcame his disappointment with the support of his family and friends. "I called my mom a lot, especially after rehab workouts, because I'd feel so discouraged," he says. "She listened and reminded me that even though I couldn't play football, I was at a top-notch school and that I had a lot to be thankful for." He also drew emotional strength from his friends. "Just being with my friends, even if we weren't talking about what happened to me, helped. They made me feel accepted."

Derik Baker also feels intellectually inferior to his peers. "Coming from a small public school in a small town, I wondered, 'Do I have the ability to go to school here?' I mean, the kids here are so amazing." Derik says that the classes at Columbia are highly interactive and students must orally present their ideas and thoughts in group settings—something Derik felt uncomfortable with. "At my high school we never did that. We just took in information from the teacher. All I got out of a book was the information that I read. When we read a book in my humanities class [at Columbia], we discuss it, and I almost never add to the discussion. When the other students read the book, it stirs up thoughts and they make connections. If I do speak my mind, I feel like I do it on a lower level than my classmates. I think I may always struggle with this feeling of intimidation, but I've learned how to cope with it."

One way Derik copes is by improving his writing skills so that the work he turns in compensates for his lack of class participation. He has also met with his professors to explain why he doesn't fully participate in the discussions and to ask for their advice.

Derik reminds himself that even though he may not think as critically and analytically as his peers, he is rich in life experiences. "I have a few more life experiences being middle class and working. A lot of them haven't played sports and most come from wealthier families than mine. In casual talk, my friends may come up with something from a poet. A lot of what they're saying sounds academic, whereas I talk about something that has happened in my life. I think that's a kind of smart, too."

Fueling Motivation

Without motivation, almost nothing would get done. Motivation is the force that propels you to complete assignments and accept new challenges. Imagine dragging yourself through every task with only a half-hearted effort. Not only would important work go undone, but life would get pretty boring.

Motivation is most often fueled by enthusiasm. Although some people may seem to be born with a sunnier disposition, you can develop the enthusiasm to make you happy and successful. Enthusiastic people typically show greater peace of mind, higher self-esteem, a stronger sense of well-being, and even better physical health. This leads to increased success in school and in the workplace.

Here are a few ways to add enthusiasm to your life:

- *Engage in activities that you enjoy.* Make a list of the top ten things you enjoy doing and do at least one of them a week, suggests Erik Olesen in *Mastering the Winds of Change.* "Studies have found that people who do more of what they enjoy rate their lives better within six months," he says.

- *Associate with enthusiastic people.* "Enthusiastic people have an energy that you can't help but be affected by," says Harold Bloomfield. "Being around them can make you feel upbeat and positive."

- *Seek inspiration.* Look for books, movies, art, or music that has a positive effect on you. Sometimes you can find a character in a story or a few lines of a song that you identify with—feed off this energy and use it to enact positive changes in yourself.

- *Take on a new challenge.* Make it a priority to learn something new or engage in an activity that you find challenging. Your enthusiasm for this activity will spill over into other areas of your life.

- *Give yourself a pep talk.* "Try telling yourself to be more upbeat and enthusiastic, and you may be surprised to find how well it works," Olesen says. He suggests visualizing yourself in a particularly enthusiastic moment. "Remember what it felt like, and the feeling may come back."

- *Develop optimism in the face of setbacks.* When you experience a setback at school or work, you may automatically think, "I'm a failure." Instead of generalizing like this, think of the isolated event. Maybe you didn't get an A this time, but that doesn't mean you never will. Work toward next time instead of dwelling on past setbacks.

Social Skills

The ability to put people at ease is undoubtedly one of the hallmarks of emotional intelligence. You maintain mental and social poise by skillfully handling emotional reactions in others. One of the most difficult emotional reactions you will ever have to contend with in other people is anger, particularly anger vented toward you. Learning to resolve conflict constructively is key to developing your emotional intelligence. "How we work through our differences, to a large extent, determines our whole life pattern," writes David Augsburger in *Caring Enough to Confront.*

One principle to keep in mind when settling a dispute is expediency. For example, when you know that someone is upset with you, don't wait for them to come and make amends. Make an attempt to reconcile as soon as you know there's a problem. When you ignore the problem, your silence is often interpreted by the other party as rejection, and feelings of rejection tend to fuel anger. Most people want to resolve a conflict as much as you do, but maybe they just don't know how. Believe the best in other people, and that's what you'll usually get.

When trying to resolve a conflict, begin your message with the little word "I," as in "I feel frustrated that you didn't ask me before borrowing my computer." Avoid remarks that begin with the word "you," which can sound like an accusation, as in "You always do that." Rather than belittling the person you're at odds with, focus on reaching an agreement.

Healthy relationships are essential in life. To be an emotionally intelligent human being, you need to make people a priority. Relationships will not thrive if they are third or fourth on your "to do" list. Although this will require a commitment of your time, energy, and resources, it's important to keep relationships with other people alive. Schedule a lunch date with a friend or take your nieces and nephews for a walk. Even simple activities like that will strengthen your relationships and enhance your social skills.

your EQ in action

The coping skills you will need to live in our frenzied, competitive world will require more than just a high IQ. Learning to cope with life's complexities demands the full engagement of your emotions. It also means learning to take care of yourself. At the core of emotional intelligence is the ability to live at peace with yourself and others. Being at peace with yourself doesn't mean overlooking your deficiencies— instead, offer yourself the same forgiveness for mistakes and the courage to improve that you hope others will extend to you. From there you're off to a good start toward success and happiness.

3
futures and options

I don't know what I'd like to do. That's what hurts the most. That's why I can't quit the job. I really don't know what talents I may have. And I don't know where to go to find out. I've been fostered so long by school and didn't have time to think about it.

—CHICAGO PHONE RECEPTIONIST, QUOTED IN STUDS TERKEL'S *WORKING*

There is a job, and a future, waiting for you, as long as you really want to work. There are opportunities galore, as long as you make the effort to seek them out. There are tested ways to success in the job market.

—ROBERT O. SNELLING, SR., IN *THE RIGHT JOB*

Consider a typical freshman's nocturnal musings on what it means to use the career planning and placement center:

The career planning and placement center is a secret building in the middle of campus, where seniors are escorted at night, blindfolded, for initiation into inescapable careers. Jobs are assigned on the basis of alphabetical synergy, a scientific technique developed in California during the mid-seventies.

29

Alphabetical synergy pairs career and candidate by matching the first letter of the student's last name with the first letter of a career. For example:

Michael Crosby: double major in economics and physics.
Career selected by Alphabetical Synergy:
Crosby . . . c . . . CHEF . . . c . . . CRAPS PLAYER . . . No, wait a minute—
*****************CONTRACTOR***********************
!!!!!!!!!!!!!!!!!!!!!!!!!!!!!!!!

Still blindfolded, Michael is given a burlap sack containing the tools of the trade: hammer, nails, hard hat, and keys to the trailer that will be his new headquarters, along with a map specifying its exact location at the construction site in Death Valley, California.

Then he wakes up, screaming.

The moral of this nightmare? Simple. Don't be afraid to investigate your career center. It won't hurt you in the light of day. Don't wait until three days before graduation and expect to nail down the perfect job. Go early—during your freshman and sophomore years—to gather information about the fields that interest you. Career centers have a wealth of materials including books, company files, videos, and names of contacts. Trained career counselors are a valuable resource: they can help you get that summer internship, help you write your resume and prepare for the interview, or lend an ear as you talk through postgraduate job possibilities. Take advantage of this service.

Most placement centers offer interest surveys. Take them. These inventories are a good place to begin figuring out what you want to do.

One such test, the Strong-Campbell Interest Inventory, compares the responses of the test taker to those of professionals in various occupations. You can get an idea of the careers people with similar interests have chosen, pointing you toward jobs you may not have considered. The inventory also helps you identify your natural learning style, which can be a good thing to know before you spend years and thousands of dollars on a program that may not fit your style. If Strong-Campbell results tell you that you are more of a practical learner, for example, you'll want a short program focused on specific skills. That way you'll be able to walk away with a degree you can use immediately to further your career. On the other hand, if you find you are more of an academic type, you may be happier in a longer course of study. (Even if you risk becoming an eternal student.) In any case, it's important that you meet with a career counselor who can help you interpret the results of the tests you take.

"But don't rely solely on standardized tests," says Tim Dalton, a senior at Columbia University. "Many students who seek career guidance think they can just fill in the boxes, stick numbers into a computer, and then get a printout on the career they should pursue. The tests are a starting place—you must look within yourself for the answers."

Sometimes these tests can be off target. Anne, a friend of mine who is an editor, completed a survey that indicated she could be a dental hygienist—a job in which she has no interest! Like a hygienist, however, Anne does enjoy working quietly by herself or with a small group of people. The moral? Consider the broader interest profile as well as the specific job suggestions.

Cyrus Vesser, who worked for twelve years before returning to school to get his doctorate in history, says that brainstorming helped him choose his career. "The self-assessment tests and group discussions provided by my university were useful," says Cyrus. "Five years of wrong leads can be avoided by self-examination and experimentation in areas which spark your mind."

Many students fear they won't get a job after graduation. They consider only a few of the thousands of possible professions from which to choose. Students who don't know what they want to do frequently accept jobs they hate, or for which they're unsuited.

That's not how you want to spend your career, or your life. You can do better than that. Use your imagination! *There are thousands of jobs available.*

Your first step? *Relax.* You are going to get a job in the career of your choice, even if you currently have no idea of what you want to do.

Your second step? *Explore* the careers available to you—by reading, interviewing people, investigating your career center. Realize how many options you have.

Your third step? *Commit yourself* to the process of discovering what you want to do.

Your fourth step? *Chart* your possible career path(s) by listing:

1. *What you have done* (your previous volunteer and work experiences, such as having a part-time salesclerk position at the Gap clothing store)

2. *Where you are now* (your current volunteer or work experiences, such as doing summer volunteer work for the Humane Society)

3. *Where you want to go* (other experiences you need to plan for now, such as preparing to interview with an honorary society on your college campus for the purpose of developing your leadership skills)

Your fifth step? *Take action.*

Chapter 2 dealt with those characteristics that are unique to you. It asked you to identify both your strengths and your weaknesses and encouraged you to conduct an introspective look inside yourself. Now let's focus on what you can do with your newfound understanding of yourself in the professional world. In your journal, label a section "Personal Inventory Assessment" and devote at least one page to each of the following categories: interests; talents; skills; likes and dislikes; goals, values, and ambitions. Be sure to fill everything in. Don't worry if some of it doesn't make sense. Your thoughts will develop after you have a chance to reflect on your initial responses.

INTERESTS

I am curious about

I question

I'm concerned about

I'm fascinated by

I like to think/read/write about

TALENTS

I am good at these kinds of activities (physical, intellectual, creative, social, religious, etc.): _____

People compliment me on _____

People encourage me to _____

SKILLS

Specific skills (such as public speaking, car maintenance, word processing, etc.) I have: _____

Skills I want to learn: _____

LIKES AND DISLIKES

About people—their characters, habits, shortcomings, influences, etc.

Likes	Dislikes

About working environment—indoors or out, with people or alone, small company or large, etc.

Likes	Dislikes

GOALS, VALUES, AND AMBITIONS

I like:

I want to accomplish:

When I die, I want to be remembered for:

In life, I value these things most:

Contributions I want to make to the world:

Things that give me peace of mind:

survey your qualities

B elow are some essential characteristics every career seeker needs, regardless of what the inventory says. Take stock. Which characteristics best describe you? Which least describe you? How might you improve your weak areas before you graduate? If you analyze these things yourself, you'll be well prepared for your first salary review when your manager tells you what you've done well and where you stand to improve. You can't become better at something if you don't know what you need to improve.

Supportive	Long-term vision
Decisive	Sense of humor
Follow-up	Winning attitude
Organized	Ability to separate the trivial from
Ethical	the important

Sets and keeps high standards   Pays attention to detail

Confident, but not cocky   Able to manage stress

Fair   Even-tempered

Honest   Works well with all kinds of people

Keeps promises   Sets goals

take the next step

After you've completed your self-assessment inventory, analyze your responses. What are you learning about yourself? Is a pattern of what you'd like to do beginning to emerge? You don't have to draw any permanent conclusions now. The important thing is that you've identified your skills and interests.

What's so important about that? What's important is that you can use this knowledge to select your career options. Many people spend years in unrewarding careers before they realize that their jobs do not utilize their skills and interests. Consider the frequency of the midlife crisis as evidence. You are learning a different path—and you haven't even graduated from college yet.

ask the right questions

You have surveyed your skills and interests. Now it's time to examine the specific characteristics of different career options. Turn to Appendix F and review "A Look at the World of Work." You'll notice that the chart is grouped according to profession. Three categories—"Job Requirements," "Work Environment," and "Occupational Characteristics"—are listed across the top.

Look first at the "Job Requirements" category and select the characteristics that best describe you. Find the professions that require these characteristics to see which interest you. Then let this chart trigger questions such as the following:

1. What training would I need in the next four years to prepare myself for the types of jobs that interest me?

2. Under the "Work Environment" category, which of the conditions appeal to you? If you're not sure, then you might want to visit a few different workplaces and get a feel for the atmosphere.

3. What about the occupational characteristics? Are there plenty of jobs in your area of interest? Will the industries that interest you grow over the next few years?

These are important questions. Finding out the answers will help you make informed decisions. Keep these questions in mind as you read the chart. Remember, you don't have to know all the answers right now. The purpose of the chart is simply to jump-start your thinking about career possibilities. For now, all you need to do is start a running list of four or five areas you might be interested in. Over the next few years you'll explore these interests, narrow your focus, and eventually choose a career.

learn to reason

Why do we accept what we believe? Reasoning provides an answer. To reason is to understand the underlying motives and logic of our beliefs. Lex Kaplan began college thinking that he wanted to be a lawyer. Originally from Englewood, New Jersey, Lex majored in journalism. As president of his college political magazine, he fell in love with reporting and writing. He enjoyed it so much that when he graduated he freelanced for *The Phoenix*, a Boston periodical. He used his writing experience there to help him land a job at *The New Yorker* doing fact checking and writing "Talk of the Town" pieces. But after a year he feared that being a journalist would make him a dilettante—a writer without a specialty. So, without reasoning, he reverted to his pre-freshman beliefs and enrolled in law school. He quickly realized his mistake. While he was a hard worker, he discovered something about himself at law school.

"I found out I wasn't a fighter," he says. Competition on campus for corporate jobs was fierce. Lex found himself disliking both the competition and the idea of corporate law, which to him "seemed like a form of death." This time, Lex used his experiences in considering his next career move. He knew he wouldn't be happy as an attorney. So he turned down a job with a law firm in New York and decided to combine all his skills by starting up his own magazine.

Throughout your college and working careers, you will continually have to (1) come up with your own ideas and (2) convince others of their validity. Once you've reached a decision, opinion, or point of view, get used to defending it both orally and in writing. You'll feel more confident, even among your toughest critics, when you back up your claims.

You probably have ample opportunity to practice that skill now. For example, let's say your parents don't approve of the major you've chosen; they don't think you will make enough money from it to earn a living. When you have carefully thought through the decision yourself, you can more clearly articulate why you chose as you did. Even though your parents still may not agree with you, at least they will respect the reasoning behind your judgment.

Lex gave a star performance in the art of persuasion when he came up with a novel idea for a magazine that would fill a void in the market. He gave a seven-page proposal to an acquaintance he knew was interested in investing in the arts, and the man gave him $50,000. During the year that followed, Lex enthusiastically pitched his concept to writers, friends, and investors. Within the year he had (1) convinced some of his former colleagues at *The New Yorker* to work for his magazine, called *Wigwag*; (2) contracted articles from a number of known authors like Alice McDermott, Ralph Ellison, and Richard Ford; and (3) raised $3 million. All this he did from his two-bedroom apartment in New York, making the most of his "cold" phone calls and "blind" visits. Because Lex Kaplan believed in his project, so did many others.

MY TWO CENTS   *How Do I Apply It?*

Dylan Lewis, University of Colorado–Denver

My life has been a series of options, different roads leading different directions, all with separate stops and detours. By recognizing these exits and the destinations to which they lead, my life has become meaningful, interesting, and entertaining. I can see the forgone paths clearly in life's rearview mirror, and as I continue to let my abilities and experiences lead the way, I am able to peer through the fog that conceals my future. My future, of course, is uncertain, but the choices I make now will pave my life's road smooth and straight.

After high school, I had no idea what I wanted to do and definitely had no idea of who I was. I had been accepted to a mediocre four-year college as a transfer student because I had finished my freshman year at a community college during my senior year in high school. I thought I was prepared for college. My grades had been good, but I was in no way ready for real college classes. Since I had some experience with college curriculum, I registered for upper division classes, but I was less than prepared and quickly dug a hole I couldn't free myself from. The ladder out was formed of the most difficult decision I would ever have to make. My father gave me a series of options, none of which included another semester at school. I considered my options, and instead of attempting to negotiate with my father, I surprised him and chose the most difficult option, physically and mentally. I decided to join the United States Marine Corps.

I served four years, working as an Air Traffic Controller. I helped build a house with Habitat for Humanity. I volunteered for stage security at a charity rock concert. I learned about courage and respect. I gained life experience. I did something none of my friends did. I was willing to fight and die for the people of my country. I grew and I matured. I made great friends and forged lifelong contacts. I completed my tour honorably, was awarded and discharged, so I went back to school.

I come from an educated family. My father works as a college administrator and my mother as a teacher, both of them with post-graduate degrees. All of my uncles have earned either a Ph.D. or M.D. One grandfather is a successful businessman, and the other is an architect, so I guess you could say there is some pressure to succeed. My pressure, in this sense, is not ridden with anxiety because I trust I will make the right life decisions. However, I am neither a pre-med student, nor pre-law, engineering, or business, nor do I wish to be a college professor or a teacher of any kind. I chose something no person in my family has ever chosen to study formally. I thought about what my interests are and how I can incorporate them with a lucrative career. My choice of major will not bring the highest paying salary, but I trust it will bring me happiness and success. I will graduate with a degree in English. Critical reading and writing are my passion and hopefully, my career will be closely related.

So, here I am, 26 years old, a veteran, a soon-to-be college graduate with a great outlook on life. I chose to become a better person. I chose to join the Marines. I chose to return to college and graduate. In the future, I will make other choices, but none will be as important as the choices I've made since leaving high school. I have made the life I want to live, not by comparing to my relatives or friends, but by having the courage to take charge of my identity and my future. Every choice made will have rewards and consequences. I have reaped many rewards and suffered few consequences, but in order for my fortune to continue I must continue to look ahead, eyes towards the future and my mind on the goal.

doing the right thing for the right reasons

You came to college with a certain set of preconceptions, and you are also probably very aware of your parents' expectations. It is important to understand how these influences affect your decisions and to evaluate what is important to you—what really interests you. "Don't let somebody else persuade you to enter a career based on their idea of what's right, or practical, or that you can always fall back on," advises Nancy Wingate, a journalist and freelance writer who majored in English in college. She knew she didn't want to teach, but she wasn't sure exactly what she would do with an English degree. She did know that if she worked hard and kept pursuing her interests, she would find work that satisfied her.

"Everyone kept asking me, 'but what are you going to do with a degree in English?' I would just smile and say, 'I don't know, but I know I'll find something.' Sure enough, my first job (still during college) was as a part-time editorial assistant; my first full-time job was as a television producer—both jobs I absolutely loved!"

Steve Fort, an engineering supervisor at the Lockheed space facility in Florida, was motivated by money. "Quite frankly, my biggest goal in college was to get a well-paying job. I was rather single-minded in my pursuit of money because I thought money would lead to the good life. Now I wish I had spent more time considering what it was that I enjoyed rather than what would make me the most money."

"Too often, freshmen lean toward whatever will bring in the most money right after graduation," muses Mary Hopkins, a graduate student and editor of *The Daily Texan,* the student newspaper at the University of Texas. "The job market fluctuates more than it used to; top-paying jobs one year may drop out of sight the next. And at the end of a life, what does it matter how much something paid compared to how much you were able to contribute to the world?"

Mary makes an important point: People are motivated by different things. For some, money isn't nearly as important as finding fulfillment in their work. It's not that they don't want money altogether. It's just that if they must choose between a career that promises a good salary but isn't work they care about and a lower-paying job that promises work they love, they'll choose the latter. In fact, there's a trend in this country called "voluntary simplicity," meaning people are scaling down their lifestyles and "getting back to the basics." That's why discovering what matters to you is so key. You aren't only choosing a major, you're choosing a lifestyle.

Even after you're established in your career, you will periodically need to evaluate what is motivating you and decide if your work is taking you in directions that are important to you. Cruce Stark was a professor in the English department at the University of Delaware. His career was moving along as he planned. He was doing all the right things—writing solid, scholarly articles and getting published. On a yearlong sabbatical in Latin America, he realized what he really wanted to do at that point was to write a novel.

"During that trip I started asking questions about what I really wanted," he says, "about what I'd think about my life when nobody would be there except me to think about it; or when it truly wasn't going to matter what anybody else thought. Would I be happier when I was looking back at seventy if I'd been a success in my profession, with a string of highly regarded critical works, or would I like myself better if I tried to write fiction and failed? But of course I knew I wouldn't fail. If I worked as hard as I intended to, I'd have to succeed."

Cruce worked on his fiction writing for years before he got his first novel published. During that time, the senior people in his department at the university kept suggesting that he return to doing what he knew how to do. When his novel *Chasing Uncle Charley* was published, it received rave reviews from the *New York Times* and *Publishers Weekly*. As a result, he was promoted and was assigned to teach courses and lead workshops in creative writing.

"My basic realization was that, for better or worse, I was stuck with myself—so that's what I'd better get in touch with," he says. "Trying to satisfy anything or anybody else was going to leave a very important part of me very empty. Most of us spend too many years worrying what our lives will look like from the outside, as though it were some kind of movie for somebody else to see. It may come with age, but sometimes it finally breaks through—nobody's standing in line buying tickets to watch."

dream on

Now that you've defined your interests, skills, and goals, it's time to focus on the job that will incorporate them. What would you like to do if you could do anything? Really, truly, outlandishly . . . anything. Imagine the sheer delight of finding the career that taps your passion and allows you the privilege of being paid for doing it!

Francie Berger's childhood dream was to build Lego models for a living. Being a practical child, she assumed that no one would pay her to play, so she decided to become an architect. When Francie entered Virginia Tech's architecture program prepared to pursue a career in architecture, she had no idea that her childhood fantasies were about to come true.

During her freshman year, a toy designer gave a guest lecture in one of her classes. After hearing him speak, she decided to approach him about interning for him. Through her internship she developed a mentoring relationship with the toy designer, who encouraged her to approach Lego about creating a model design department in the United States. At this point, Lego had a manufacturing and sales plant in the United States, but all the models and designs were made in Denmark.

For her senior project, Francie designed a model Lego farm that included fourteen buildings and vehicles—she even drew up the plans and projected the costs. She then presented her project to the director of special events at Lego. "I never doubted that I would per-suade them to create this job for me," she says. "My dream was going to come true. As a kid I didn't think this kind of job existed. Once I knew the possibility, I knew I had to get this job."

It took her months of following up, calling her contact at Lego at least once every month, before she was given a job. Three months after graduating from architecture school, upon her return from an extended vaca-tion traveling around the United States, Lego called and offered her a job designing the large Lego model displays for places like F.A.O. Schwartz and the National Toy Fair in New York City. The Lego design department grew from three people to forty-eight in 1990. Francie manages five designers respon-sible for envisioning the models, and she has been featured in *The New Yorker,* on the Discovery Channel, and in a PBS children's series.

Francie's story is a good example of how it is possible to find work that really matches your interests. In order to do this, though, you sometimes have to allow yourself to dream BIG and to think beyond the immediate possibilities. Once you've found your vision, then it takes ingenuity, creativity, and perseverance to see your dreams come to fruition. Now you are going to do just that. Using the insights you gained from your personal inventory, you are going to design your possible success stories. Include everything that the perfect job entails. Where do you work? What is the work environment? Does your job include travel? What is an average day like? What is your compensation (does this include your quarterly bonus)? Describe your position in detail. The goal is to make it real. Try to taste it, hear it, feel it. Don't hold back. No holds barred. *Write it down.*

Dream Job/Stellar Achievement 1

_____

_____

_____

_____

Dream Job/Stellar Achievement 2

_____

_____

_____

_____

Dream Job/Stellar Achievement 3

_____

_____

_____

_____

Now it's time to take your head out of the clouds and focus on planning strategies that will make these dreams become reality.

the narrowing process

O nce you've analyzed the bigger picture, pick two or three areas of interest and begin developing career strategies for each. You can write them down below. (If you don't know what to choose yet, come back to this after you've had more time to think.)

_____

_____

_____

_____

_____

using what you know

T he key to choosing career options is a willingness to explore. You could convert the basics of the "dreamboat job" approach to fit any possible path: poet, advertising copywriter, stockbroker, farmer, cowboy, or corporate psychic. Remember, you're interested in these careers (all of them) because you think they would be fun. So have fun finding out about them!

And while you're out pioneering, continue to ask yourself questions that will help to refine your career goals:

1. How can I gather more information about those careers that interest me?

2. Whom do I know in this field? (If you don't know anyone, do some research.) What can they tell me about the pros and cons of the work? What is needed to succeed?

3. What else can I do each week and each month to prepare myself? How can I get more experience? (Remember: Experience leads to intelligent decisions.)

life goals

It is crucial to think about what kinds of goals you have for your life as a whole. Pam Zemper of Security Pacific advises people to think about what their goals are in four areas—social, material, professional, and personal growth. "Once you have an idea of what you want in each of these areas, it's easier to choose a career."

"Your job becomes your lifestyle," says Tony Ponturo, director of media services for Anheuser-Busch. "So you'd better like what you're doing."

Tony is right. Know what you want, even if you don't know how to get it right now. The path to a really interesting career is often circuitous.

After college, Tony identified the three areas he loved most—business, sports, and television. He moved to New York City and got a job as a page for NBC, hoping to get a foot in the door of NBC Sports. This approach didn't work. So he took an alternate route and went into advertising, working for three successive advertising agencies as a media buyer. His work on a Coca-Cola campaign earned him a shot at his firm's Budweiser account. Anheuser-Busch was so impressed with his work that they lured him away from the agency and created a position for him in their home office in St. Louis. Since Busch promotes heavily during sports telecasts, Tony finds himself working in all three of the areas he enjoys: business, sports, and television.

Larry Maslon acquired his job through a similarly circuitous route. Larry is the dramaturge for the prestigious Arena Stage in Washington, DC. His various responsibilities include helping to choose the season's repertoire, interpreting the plays, researching their historical background, and editing the theater's publications. But when he started out, Larry knew nothing of dramaturgy—he only knew his interests. A lover of stage directing and Renaissance literature, he majored in both in college. For his thesis in theater arts he directed Shakespeare's *The Tempest,* and then he wrote a paper on the play for his Renaissance literature thesis.

"Unbeknownst to me," says Larry, "by both critically examining and producing a play, I was doing a dramaturge's work." Later, intending to become a theater director, he enrolled in a master's program in theater arts at Stanford. He was disappointed that the program primarily focused on the academic side of theater, so he directed some plays on his own time.

"Again, unbeknownst to me, I was becoming exquisitely prepared to be a dramaturge," he says. He now possesses something that is extremely rare: a challenging, steady job in the theater. He strongly advocates that every student pursue what he or she loves. He says he has benefited from following his heart, from doing what he's done "in spite of myself."

Malcolm Forbes, the late publisher of *Forbes* magazine, was quoted in *The Achievement Factors* by B. Eugene Griessman: "I think the foremost quality—there's no success without it—is really loving what you do. If you love it, you will do it well."

"You've got to have fire in the gut," says Milton Pedraza, a Colgate (the company, not the college) recruiter and marketer. "You have to be committed to your job once you land it, but in college you must commit yourself to becoming well-educated and as well prepared as possible, even if you don't yet know what kind of work interests you." If you don't develop a burning passion to get things done in college, Milton says, it will be hard for you to motivate yourself on the job.

get going

Your senior year of college, though it may seem like a long way off, is just around the corner. The trick to not being caught off guard by its arrival is balance: balancing the long-term with current agendas for the month, the week, the day, the moment. For now (this moment), set some career goals. Don't worry about revising them. This will come later. Time is very forgiving to those who act, which is what you're doing right now by committing to a career direction, however tentative.

"As you begin to discover what you truly enjoy, try to picture yourself two, five, or ten years after college involved in that interest," advises Bob Kinstle, a computer consultant for a large New York bank. "Imagine what your typical day might look like; then reexamine your current activities to see if they are helping you achieve that dream," he says. "College is a time for growth and adventure. You are building the foundation and honing the skills that will determine your success and happiness in the years ahead. Find out what your school has to offer—academically, socially, culturally, athletically—and try to sample as much as possible."

turning your dreams into reality

S omeone once said, "If you aim at nothing, you'll hit it every time." For our purposes, think of your target as being your goals, dreams, and ambitions. Consequently, the arrows are your plans. Stock your quiver full of them—your plans—and you're bound to hit the bull's-eye eventually.

Former college professor Lynn Troyka suggests a planning strategy that a friend shared with her years ago. The formula goes like this: "Envision where you want to be, then establish steps toward that vision." Notice that this formula has two distinct parts: a projection phase (envisioning) and a planning phase (establishing steps toward that vision).

The Projection Phase

The projection phase usually comes first. It entails thinking and dreaming about what you want (i.e., your vision). This includes the soon-to-be realized fantasy of your acceptance speech in Stockholm when you humbly receive the long-deserved Nobel Prize (you are thirty-three before the committee finally comes to its stuffed-up senses and has the decency and vision to recognize you). Envisioning the goal is where projection comes in, and that's important. But it's not enough. Lots of people have a dream; few turn it into reality.

The Planning Phase

The second phase, planning, involves work that is more long-term. Once you've visualized the epic ending, you have to figure out how to get there. You do this by establishing the steps that lead you toward the goal. The "how" part of the formula requires creativity, tenacity, and—most difficult of all—discipline. Living your dream means maintaining your focus on a goal and refusing to allow distractions to divert you from the time and effort needed to accomplish it. This may sound simple, but for many people, aligning their dream with their life habits isn't simple at all. Turning your vision into a reality entails weathering hard times, sometimes over long periods. You will not magically become a CEO overnight, no matter how potent your powers of fantasy. Achieving your dream takes 1 percent inspiration and vision coupled with 99 percent perspiration and hard work.

Dr. Michael DeBakey, a pioneer in cardiovascular surgery, including artificial heart research, and the driving force behind the establishment of the Medical Center in Houston, Texas, believes that dedication, self-discipline, and a clear direction and purpose are the keys to human achievement. "Success is the result of focusing your energies and efforts in a specific direction and exploiting your skills and capabilities to the fullest," he says. He advises students to master whatever it is they are studying. "Apply yourself fully. Once you have devoted your efforts totally to one project, you will be able to transfer those skills and habits to every other project."

It is your task to map out the road to the corner office or mid-office cubicle or outdoor post—from college classes, internships, work experience, and appropriate role models. Remember to take it one step at a time. One hundred thousand planned steps will go by much more quickly than one hundred thousand unplanned steps.

Following is a list of broad goals a college student might realistically expect to accomplish in four years of college. Look at the list closely. See how these activities begin to build on each other? For example, a summer job will help you learn the basic skills of managing responsibility, a key qualification for securing an internship. (See Chapter 8 for a discussion of the importance of internships.) Internships are usually offered only to those students who can prove from their past job experience that they are trustworthy. That's the idea: one year's accomplishments (such as a favorable reference letter from your summer employer) increase the next year's options (e.g., getting an internship).

If this agenda doesn't fit your projections and plans, fine. Come up with one that does. As your career adviser, I only make suggestions. You make the decisions.

COLLEGE GOALS

Freshman Year Objectives

1. Assess your study skills and habits. Improve on them if they need work.
2. Get off to a good start academically.
3. Apply for a second-semester or summer part-time job.
4. Join at least one extracurricular activity.
5. Adjust to the responsibility of your new environment.
6. Have fun.

Sophomore Year Objectives

1. Apply for a summer internship (apply for more than one).
2. Begin planning a summer, semester, or junior year abroad.
3. Make at least one career contact.
4. Join one or two clubs or special interest groups.
5. Continue to make good grades and get the most out of your classes.
6. Cultivate mentors (see Chapter 8 if you are stumped on the meaning of the word *mentor*).
7. Visit the career center.
8. Have fun.

Junior Year Objectives

1. Spend the summer, semester, or entire year abroad.
2. Plan an internship between your junior and senior years.
3. Join another activity or honorary society.
4. Mail out preliminary job inquiry letters.
5. Become a leader of one of the organizations you belong to.

6. Prepare your resume.

7. Take some classes that don't pertain to your major but that will make you a well-qualified job applicant and a more interesting person.

8. Have fun.

Senior Year Objectives

1. Wage a full-fledged job search in early fall.

2. Make many business contacts: gather information.

3. Send out at least twenty-five cover letters with resumes.

4. Research the companies with whom you wish to interview.

5. Hold mock interviews to prepare for the real thing.

6. Land the job, negotiate your salary, and start taking home the paycheck.

7. Have fun.

Should you aim to do all these things? Probably not. Choose the activities that suit you best, and be proud of yourself for trying new things and having the vision to see and plan for the bigger picture. Don't forget the common thread that ties each year together —having fun!

As you make projections and devise a plan on behalf of your noble destiny, keep in mind the three key areas you'll need to develop: academic, extracurricular, and work experience. Strive for balance. Keep this triangle in focus—maybe it won't be equilateral, but just make sure it's got three sides.

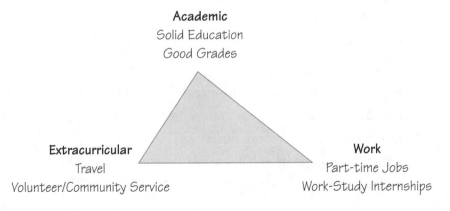

Academic
Solid Education
Good Grades

Extracurricular
Travel
Volunteer/Community Service

Work
Part-time Jobs
Work-Study Internships

In the spaces below, list the specific steps you think you'll have to take in order to get from where you are to where you want to be. The rest of this book will help you take the steps . . . one at a time.

Your Objectives

FRESHMAN YEAR

SOPHOMORE YEAR

JUNIOR YEAR

SENIOR YEAR

your first five steps

B elow are five steps designed to assure achievement wherever it is you want to go. Keep them handy for encouragement and as a gentle reminder.

1. Strike a Balance

"The most valuable experience I had in college was learning that it was a microcosm of life with opportunities to grow broadly in several areas," remembers David Glenn, who was a division manager at Chevron for thirty years. "Too often people focus on one area to the exclusion of others with the idea that they will develop after they finish college and get a job."

Kip Berry, assistant professor of veterinary medicine at North Carolina State University, spent most of his time in college doing academic work. "I believe this hurt me. In retrospect, I should have diversified my curriculum and educational experiences instead of focusing only on the hard-core academic work."

In college, you'll have to balance your academic, personal, and real-world experience. Make good grades, but realize that good grades alone are usually not enough. Even if you want to be an astrophysicist, you don't want to be a lonely astrophysicist. Therefore, you also need to make room in your life for the other essentials: extracurricular activities, sports, socializing, and work.

Denise Chamblee, a pediatric ophthalmologist, remembers her college years: "I worked hard academically, but I made a distinct pact with myself not to lose sight of social and extracurricular activities. I think that has helped me tremendously in keeping my sanity through the long road of medical training. It has been an even bigger help in relating well to patients."

2. Set Goals

Learn to set specific goals and have a plan by which to achieve them.

José Galvez not only balanced his schoolwork with a part-time job as a copy boy for his local paper, but he also set concrete goals for himself. After eight years at his hometown paper, José is now a photojournalist for the *Los Angeles Times*.

"Identify concrete goals," José advises. "Get as much out of the smaller places as you can—then run with it from there. Shoot for the stars."

3. Be Decisive

A wrong decision is better than no decision at all. If you spend a year as a pre-med student, loathe it, and then switch to French, you haven't wasted a year. You've learned something valuable—what you like and what you don't, or, to put it another way, what you'd be good at and what you'd be not so good at. And you've acted accordingly. Bravo for self-assertion.

Anthea Coster, a space physicist who tracks satellites at MIT, was struck by the words of one of her philosophy professors. "He said that there is probably more than one right choice. What is important is not necessarily the choice itself, but, once you make the choice, what you do with it. This has probably been one of the guiding principles of my life."

Sandra Day O'Connor, the Supreme Court justice, learned about decision-making early in her career as a trial judge. "I put all the time and effort in at the front end, trying to decide a case correctly in the first place and do the best I can. Then I don't look back and I don't agonize over it. I may have to live with the consequences, but I'm going to live with them without regrets, because I made the best decision I could at the time."

Learn to analyze your options and then make your move quickly. Don't dilly-dally in thermodynamics if neo-impressionism is what you love. Decisiveness goes a long way toward a glorious destiny.

In the words of Johann Wolfgang von Goethe, "Boldness has genius, power, and magic in it. Whatever you do or dream, begin it now."

4. Believe in Yourself

Know that you can succeed. The only difference between You and Them is that you've got the motivation to get the job done.

Jim Cochran developed self-confidence while attending the University of California–Davis. He had a part-time job for three years as a basketball referee for the intramural sports program. During his third year, he was the head student official.

"When making a call, it's all in the manner in which you carry yourself. If you blow the whistle and hesitate, wringing your hands and gnashing your teeth, people may pick up on your indecision. The fans and players will jump all over you, grabbing you by the collar and chanting 'Blood! Blood! Blood!'"

Gordon Bock, a Columbia graduate, was a UPI reporter when he heard that a *U.S. News & World Report* editor was coming to town. In a "Jobs" file, Gordon had kept a 1977 newsletter that quoted the editor as saying he would hire as many students from journalism schools as he could. Gordon sent a letter to the editor reminding him of this promise, adding, "I'm volunteering to help you in this lofty goal."

The editor hired Gordon. "I think he was impressed that I took that statement and threw it back at him, instead of begging for a job," Gordon says.

5. Go for It

Lauren Ward, a brand marketing manager with Pepsi in Purchase, New York, says getting a job as resident assistant her junior year was one of the most valuable "business lessons" she learned during college.

When Lauren applied for the RA job at the end of her sophomore year, she was refused an application because she had never lived in a dorm before. Since Lauren had transferred from another college during her sophomore year, it had been impossible for her to gain admission to the dorms, which had waiting lists. Still, the interviewing board would make no exception: there were too many people applying for the RA positions, and rules are rules.

Lauren was determined to get a fair shot. Believing in her own competence as an applicant, Lauren went up the hierarchy to the director of housing to ask for some rule-bending so that she could be considered with other applicants. She listed all of her qualifications, showed her keen interest and enthusiasm for the dorms and the women who lived there, and diplomatically presented her case. The director of housing bent the rules and allowed her to be interviewed.

Out of forty-four applicants, Lauren was the only one to score a perfect ten with each of the six interviewers. She was accepted as an RA.

The business lesson? As Lauren succinctly put it, "no" doesn't necessarily mean "no." People will always resist change—in school, in business, at home. Count on it. Action takers don't take "no" for an answer; they can't, if they want to get anything done. If you believe in what you're doing, whether it be yourself, your product, your ideas, or somebody else's, be prepared to utilize creative strategies to combat the stonewalling you'll find yourself up against time and time again.

Lauren, like Jim, believed in herself and convinced others of her abilities. If Lauren hadn't been 100 percent confident when she had her appointment with the director of housing, she would have been cooked. But once her foot was in the door and she had the interview, she had no problem convincing the panel of interviewers that she had potential.

Now it's your turn. Take the ball and start running.

take the plunge

4

Education has really only one basic factor . . . one must want it.

—G. E. WOODBURY

The direction in which education starts a man determines his future life.

—PLATO

While writing this book, I gave a few seminars in the New York area to high school seniors preparing for success in college. At the beginning of each seminar, I distributed a questionnaire to get the students thinking about what really scared, bothered, excited, thrilled, bored, or disgusted them when they thought about college. The opener was: What do you fear most about starting college? Here are some of the responses from the students in one seminar:

"I fear failing my freshman year."

"I fear the extra work that I will actually have to do."

"I fear loneliness, being stuck at a college that I hate, and failing out."

"I fear studying all day and night."

"I fear that college will be a letdown from what I've imagined."

"I fear not having a good time."

"I fear getting lost."

"I fear not making friends or finding my classes."

"I fear too much pressure and too much work."

"I fear not doing well academically."

"I fear not fitting in."

"I fear that I will become so socially active that I will not pay attention to my classes."

"I fear not being able to compete, work, and do well."

"I fear the responsibility."

"I fear I will not be able to work my way through school and support myself."

"I fear not finding a date."

"I fear I won't like my roommates. I'm afraid of leaving home and trying to meet new friends."

"I fear being on my own."

"I fear that I won't have a good time."

"I fear that I won't succeed."

"I fear the academic load."

"I fear not 'getting something' from my education."

"I fear that I will oversleep."

"I fear not doing well in class, having problems with roommates, and running out of money."

"I fear not being able to complete, understand, or do well on tests."

"I fear academic difficulties and no free time."

"I fear too much work and not enough discipline."

Notice any pattern? Almost everyone is nervous about starting college. They fear that they will be unable to keep up with the academic and personal challenges that college poses. That's understandable. It's a big transition from high school. But it's like the first day of school in first grade. It only seems like a big deal until the second day, after which you know what to expect.

The key is to convert your fears into positive actions that will help you conquer your academic weaknesses and master the skills needed for success in college. Once you've learned how to manage your time and develop your study skills, you will be up to the challenge.

"I never studied in high school," says Jon Jannes, a former high school basketball star who became an education major at Northern Illinois University. "It took me two years of college to learn to study effectively." Jon spent those first two years at Black Hawk Community College.

Unlike Jon, Matt Jacobson was a top student at Alleman Catholic High School. He was on the honor roll, captain of the football team, and class valedictorian.

"I didn't study much in high school—I just made sure I was ahead of everyone else," says Matt, now a pre-law freshman at Northwestern University. "But college was a lot different. I was so overwhelmed and excited about being away from home for the first time that I didn't study much my first semester. As a result, I didn't do very well. Since I'm on scholarship, I'll have to do better next semester." One of the challenges Matt faces is improving his grades while honoring his extracurricular commitments—as a fraternity pledge, a member of the pre-law association, and an assistant at the campus library.

Succeeding scholastically in college is very similar to succeeding in every other area of your life: first, make an honest self-appraisal of your strengths and weaknesses, then develop a game plan to achieve your goals.

selecting a major

Some college students know from Day One that they want to major in chemistry to become doctors, or major in business or a particular field of engineering. For these students, there is generally a set curriculum defined by the college with some latitude for elective courses.

However, if you're like many college freshmen, and you haven't decided on a major, you may want to stick to a broad, general curriculum for your first year until you can narrow down your true interests. (I didn't declare a major until the end of my sophomore year.)

As a freshman, you will be required to take the general courses that are required for any four-year degree. These courses are usually referred to as the *core curriculum*. For most universities, it takes approximately the first four semesters to complete your core. This places you at the end of your sophomore year—the time at which your major takes a front seat. The last two years of your undergraduate studies are geared specifically to your major; therefore, it is before you begin your junior year that you absolutely have to have decided on your major course of study. Don't fret if you don't know what you want to major in as a freshman—you've got plenty of time to decide. Your best bet is to find classes that are offered within the core (there are generally choices rather than a rigid list) that appeal to your tastes. From there, you may begin to get a feel for where your interests lie.

As a peer adviser, Julie Balovich speaks with many freshmen who simply aren't sure what they want to study and what career they want to pursue. "What you learn from not picking a major in your first year, and being open to new things, is that there is a lot more out there than you originally thought. Even if you do decide what you want to do, there are ways to experience more than just English or mechanical engineering. By making a point of taking at least one really random, non-required class every semester, I found out to my surprise that I was very interested in Evangelical Protestantism, the politics of developing nations, and the genre of autobiography. I also found out that I was not interested in deconstructionism or bureaucracy in government. I feel like my wide range of interests will give me more to offer law schools in the way of diversity when application time comes around. Instead of saying, 'I'm undecided,' I think we should say, 'I'm Discovering' or 'I'm Exploring.'"

Suzanne Babinsky believes it is important to choose the more challenging courses, even when they aren't required. "The harder classes kept me on my toes. They held my interest because I had to focus harder on the material. And when I decided after teaching high school science that I wanted to go to medical school, I had no problem getting in because I had taken the rigorous prerequisites."

Employers often urge students who are undecided on a major to gain a broad liberal arts or business education. "I believe that businesses should go back to basics in recruiting, should forget about the business schools, and recruit the best young liberal arts students we can find," says Felix Rohatyn, a senior partner at one of New York's largest investment firms.

Darren Walker, an investment banker in New York City, agrees. "Resist the temptation to specialize in anything. In the long run what will benefit you most are good writing skills, good reasoning skills, and people skills. My greatest disappointment was realizing that law was an unfulfilling profession for me. However, because of the wide breadth of my academic background and extracurricular activities, I was well positioned to move into a number of different professions."

Here's a recap:

1. Take at least one elective each semester you are in school.
2. Remember to say, *to others as well as to yourself,* "I'm exploring" instead of "I'm undecided."
3. At least in your first two years, resist specializing. Take a broad range of courses.

When Steven Harwood began his college career, there was a demand for professors. So he decided to get a doctorate in biochemistry and a job in academics. When he graduated, however, the job market was dry. He then decided to go on to medical school and eventually specialized in nuclear medicine.

He advises students to find out what the real job situation is. "Also take a wide variety of courses and get as much enrichment

WHEEL OF FORTUNE

MUSIC TEACHING MEDICINE FINE ARTS SOCIOLOGY PHYSICS BIOLOGY MATH CHEMISTRY RELIGION COMPUTER SCI ANTHROPOLOGY

experience as possible. Be flexible and be prepared to change. The job situation may be different by the time you finish four years later."

Arnold Popinsky, a potter and former art professor, remembers, "Concern over good performance and a safe curriculum were too dominant in my mind . . . it kept me from seeking adventure in my college experience." He advises students to take risks and to enroll in courses outside their majors.

Colleen Smith, a counselor who runs a program for women over fifty returning to school, has the following recommendation: "Study what you love. Don't think you have to have it all figured out in advance, because life takes amazing twists and turns."

Jesse Keller, a junior at Yale University, originally decided to major in computer science because he felt it would be broad enough to allow him to participate in whatever field he chose after college. But after several semesters, he realized the standard computer science curriculum was not meeting his needs.

"I arrived at the idea of an interdisciplinary major—'The Impact of Information Technology on Society.' With this trendy title, I approached the sociology department and suddenly had a new major. My course requirements are drawn from the sociology, computer science, and engineering departments. As a senior, I will write a thesis dealing with some aspect of the impact that all of our progress has had on our day-to-day lives. I am looking forward to doing the research—it's my own version of computer science."

Here are some examples of what your first two college semesters might look like:

THE FIRST-YEAR SCHEDULE: SOME IDEAS

Sample A

First Semester	Units	Second Semester	Units
Freshman Composition	3	Freshman Composition	3
Algebra (or Calculus)	3	American Government	3
Introduction to Psychology	3	Astronomy	4
French I	4	French II	4
Economics	3	Art History	3
Total	16	Total	17

Sample B

First Semester	Units	Second Semester	Units
Freshman Composition	3	Freshman Composition	3
Biology	4	Calculus	3
American History	3	Music Appreciation	3
Spanish I	4	Spanish II	4
Racquetball	1	Anthropology	3
Total	15	Total	16

Consult your school catalog or a counselor for more information on courses and majors.

General advice: Take fewer, not more, courses during your first semester. You'll have many adjustments to make, so it's best to be underextended, rather than overextended. If you take fifteen or sixteen units, you'll be in good shape. Also, work as little as possible during your first semester to give yourself time to get used to school.

A good scholastic start should be your first concern. The knowledge you gain in college—and the grades you earn to show for it—doesn't assure job success but it will make you more attractive to a prospective employer. Good students are organized and responsible; top marks show you're able to learn and willing to work and apply yourself. Aside from helping you get the job, a sound education will open all kinds of other doors for you. An educated mind is your most valuable asset.

MY TWO CENTS   *How Do I Apply It?*

Wilson Ngui, Colorado State University

I think my family has made me a successful learner. My parents don't have much education, so I feel I need to learn a lot in college in order to take care of them. My parents decided to move to the United States so I could get a better education. The United States was totally foreign for them and they didn't know any English. I am so proud of them because they were so brave to live in a country that they weren't familiar with. In addition to that, I love going to school and learning. I know the only way to succeed in the future is to get an education. Also, I have set my goals and I know what I want to be in the future. Because of my parents and my understanding of the relationship between education and future successes, I will try hard to do the best I can.

While studying in the U.S., I have taken on various activities, and by taking on these activities, I have been forced to learn how to organize my time accordingly. I used to not be active at all because I was very concentrated on my schoolwork. Because I also needed time to adjust to things like the school system and the culture in America, I had no time to participate in other activities. Not until my sophomore year in high school did I get involved with extracurricular activities. I joined some business clubs, played on a boys' volleyball team, and worked at a part-time job. At that time, juggling these activities was easy because they took little of my time and I could still keep up with my schoolwork.

Now, I am an officer of a student organization, an active member of some clubs, and I still play volleyball. In addition to that, the workload at school is heavier than I had before. In order to balance all my activities, I have to be very organized. I have to manage my time really well in order to do all those activities. I set up a timetable by shading out the time on the calendar that is required for class time, work time, and so on. By doing this, I can tell how much time that I have available to do other activities. I also carry a planner with me, so that I know what I have to do every day. As my college life goes along, my activities are getting more and more time consuming. I try very hard to do all the activities and try not to take away from my study time. Often, I choose to sacrifice my sleep time and study until late at night. Although it is not healthy to do so, it's worth it to participate in all those activities.

There are lots of resources I use to succeed in my learning, activities, and so on. I think the essential part is to ask questions! I ask the academic advisers, people at each department, teachers, family, and friends. They are all there to help you and to give you ideas what you can do in order to get things done. Tell them what issues you are having and ask them questions; it will help you and save you a lot of time.

improving your ability to learn

Frank Landy, an industrial organizational psychologist at Penn State, teaches introductory psychology on a regular basis. "My first class each semester is on study tips," says Landy. He discusses different methods of learning, taking notes, and preparing for various exams. "If students learn basic habits of discipline and time management early, they will do best over the long haul," says Landy.

"I plunge into the material at the beginning of the semester, so I expect students to know what they're doing," says Doug Finnemore, who teaches a calculus-based physics course for engineers at Iowa State. Finnemore expects students to hit the ground running once he starts class; but if they need help, he encourages them to seek him out, or to ask any of the teaching assistants who lead discussion sections. "The people who do well in my course come to class and work throughout the semester, while the ones who do poorly show up once in a while."

If you're not a great student, don't be overwhelmed by past failure. There are certain tips that work well for all kinds of people—those who are commonsense smart, those who have high IQs, and those who may be infinitely wise. Consider the skills that all good students have, regardless of their particular learning aptitude:

- Critical thinking
- Active learning
- Good study and test-taking habits

- Time management
- Priority setting
- Effective note taking

Learning to Think Critically

The first step to successful studying is being a good student. College is more challenging than high school. Rote memorization of facts won't cut it—you'll need to learn to think critically. "Learning to think is the most important thing you can learn in college," says Bobbie Katz, who attended McGill University in Canada. Bobbie, now a lawyer with Milbank, Tweed, Hadley, & McCloy, a Wall Street firm, wanted to be a gym teacher when he started college. The more he found out about his future profession, however, the less well suited to it he felt he was. Ultimately, he opted not to pursue physical education. But because he had a broad liberal arts education, he learned to make good use of his mind, disciplining himself to think in increasingly complex ways.

Become an Active Learner

Since one of the primary goals of college is to learn *how* to learn, you must become an *active learner*. How? Well, one way is to finish your assigned reading (or at least skim it) before you attend the lectures. That way, the professor's comments become a review for you—not an introduction.

But don't think you can do the reading and skip the class. That's what Jason Moore tried to do during his first semester at the University of Washington. Much to his dismay, he discovered that some of the material covered on exams came from lectures.

If discussion groups led by graduate teaching assistants supplement your professor's lectures, attend them. "Go to class, take notes, and reflect on what you've learned," recommends Gigi David, a curriculum coordinator for a private elementary school.

Develop Good Study Habits

Nimbleness of mind is nurtured by developing good study habits. Below are several basic learning principles endorsed by memory experts.

Resist the urge to cram. The brain operates best when you feed it information repeatedly, over a period of time, rather than all at once. Therefore, plan to study a certain amount of time every day. Before a test, reread your notes several times over the course of two weeks and you'll have better recall.

Take study breaks. Your brain can pay close attention to only one thing for so long. You begin learning with a high attention span, but after a while, it drops off. Research shows that jumping from one activity to another, however, increases your mind's ability to retain material. For instance, read for twenty minutes; then play an instrument, exercise, or call someone on the phone. Then come back to your studies. Of course, if a learning period is going well and you're at a good pace, don't make yourself stop. You may lose valuable momentum. But such instances are rare. It's much more common to have lost attention and not be aware of it.

Set up your ideal study environment. When you are studying, do you like it quiet, with few or no distractions, or does a little background music and having other people around actually help you concentrate? Discover your optimal learning environment, then create that atmosphere for yourself.

Pick your best time for learning. As a college student, you will probably be able to determine your class schedule. Use that flexibility to your advantage. "I work best late at night," says Karen McMillen. "So my best semesters were those where I had no taxing classes earlier than nine or ten a.m. I hit a slump right after lunch, so I found that giving myself two to three hours in the middle of the day worked well. I could focus better on my classes if they were scheduled during my 'peak brain function' times."

Jill Rudidich, a computer technical specialist, could tell in her first five minutes of studying if her time was being spent effectively or not. If it wasn't, she went running or accomplished something else on her "to do" list. "Don't sit around putting in hours if you're not absorbing," she says. "Make sure your study time is quality time."

Give your brain a regular workout. Memory experts say crossword puzzles are one of the best forms of brain work. Begin with simple ones, then progress to those that are more difficult. Here are a few other suggestions for developing your mental prowess. Pick one or two that you don't normally do; that way you'll be adding variety to your thinking processes. The goal of these exercises is to stimulate your brain to think in new ways.

- Build something—a birdhouse, a model airplane, etc.
- Repair something—fix a broken bicycle chain, the latch to your door, or, if you feel inclined, take a stab at your car's engine!
- Grow a garden—herbs are especially popular right now, and window boxes are suitable for dorm rooms and other cozy living quarters.
- Work on a cube puzzle or other kinds of "brain teasers."
- Practice visualization. Think of a personal challenge you face. Perhaps you need to talk with your roommate about a problem in your relationship, or maybe you need to take an important test. Picture the steps that will move you closer to the desired outcome. Play around mentally by imagining several approaches you could take to meet the challenge. Also, when learning something new, visualize the information in mental pictures. Think about how what you are learning connects to something you already know. Try new methods of note taking that incorporate visual images. For example, draw a diagram of the information you are covering in a lecture or during your study time.

Engage your auditory senses as well. For example, repeat what you are reading aloud; this study technique might help ingrain the material in your mind.

Manage Your Time

Time is money, so why not budget it? Even a billionaire's calendar has just twelve months. As a student, you have many different classes, and if you're going to pursue the extracurricular activities or part-time work that will help you become well-rounded, you're going to have to make a time budget and then stick to it. There's no other way. It doesn't have to be elaborate. Consider Benjamin Franklin's typical schedule:

5 a.m.	Wake up, wash, and dress. Plan the day; breakfast
8 a.m.	Work
12 noon	Lunch, read
2 p.m.	Work
6 p.m.	Relax; dine; review the day
10 p.m.	Sleep

It's simple enough, and yet this daily schedule served Benjamin Franklin well for over sixty years.

In his autobiography, Lee Iacocca, former CEO of Chrysler, writes, "The ability to concentrate and use your time wisely is everything if you want to succeed in business—or almost anywhere else for that matter." As an engineering major at Lehigh University, Iacocca had to balance his studies, his job at the school newspaper, and his other extracurricular activities. "You've got to know what's important and then give it all you've got," says Iacocca. "Anyone who wants to become a problem solver in business has to learn fairly early how to establish priorities."

Jim Collins, a recipient of the Distinguished Teaching Award at the Stanford University Graduate School of Business, has a practical approach to managing responsibility. He writes, "When you start with an honest and diligent effort to determine the truth of your situation, the right decisions become self-evident. It is impossible to make good decisions without infusing the entire process with an honest confrontation of the brutal facts." His direct approach to decision making seems logical and simple, but its implications in your everyday life may prove challenging. But, if you have the desire

How to Test Best

Know the structure of the exam. Do the easiest questions come first? If so, do all questions count the same, no matter what their level of difficulty? Will the questions be multiple choice, essay, or a combination of both? Find out ahead of time so you can study accordingly.

- *Be prepared.* Sharpen pencils and bring an extra pen. You might also want to bring a book or your Walkman, so you can relax before the test.

- *Get a good night's sleep.* If necessary, spend a week getting on a sleep schedule so you don't come in blurry-eyed.

- *Eat a healthy snack.* An empty stomach is a distraction.

- *Don't cram.* Instead, review relevant material several times over the course of a few days instead of just the night before.

- *Don't panic.* If a question seems hard for you, it probably is for everyone else taking the test, too. Skip that one and move on to the other questions, then come back to it.

Adapted from Kaplan & Newsweek "Tipsheet," 1999 edition.

to make your life easier and more productive, organization will slowly become part of your life, not an addition to it.

Why is writing down your schedule so important? For one thing, writing things down commits you to action. If you just keep your priorities in your head, you may or may not remember what you have to do. Second, writing down your schedule helps you to determine which things are most important. The "do or die" things you have to do each day take priority over things you should do if you can find time. Third, crossing things off your list at the end of each day gives you a sense of accomplishment. You realize that you are getting from one point to the next and that you are setting the agenda. Your schedule enables you to be in control. Following are some sample schedules from college freshmen.

Let's be realistic. You may not want your schedule to be this detailed. But you'll accomplish more by having a daily game plan.

SAMPLE SCHEDULE 1

Monday

6:30   Wake up, breakfast

7:15   Read history assignment

9:00   Calculus

10:00   Freshman Composition reading before class tomorrow

11:00   Astronomy

12:00   Lunch

1:00   Library time

1–2   Calculus homework

2–3   Finish rough draft of paper on Hemingway's
        A Farewell to Arms

3–4   Read Chapter 4 of Astronomy text; review and
        highlight class notes

4:00   Visit Julia Plant, composition instructor; review rough
        draft; make notes for revision

5:00   Golf class

6:30   Dinner

8:00   Revise composition paper; double-check calculus homework

9:30   Madeline's surprise birthday party in the dorm

10:30   Sleep

To do today:

1. Buy Madeline's birthday card
2. Invite Eric to coalition meeting
3. Finish History
4. Double-check calculus homework
5. Finish draft of paper

SAMPLE SCHEDULE 2

Monday

8:30	Wake up
9:30	Management Information Systems
10:30	Computer Center—run program
11:00	Begin reading The Odyssey
12:00	Introduction to the Humanities
1:00	Lunch
2:00	Accounting
3:00	Marketing Club meeting—bring advertising plans
4:00	Library time
4–5	Accounting homework
5–6	French lab work
6–7	Read at least to page 50 of The Odyssey
7:00	Dinner at Student Union with Cynthia and Alex
8–9	Write rough draft for composition assignment on Keats's Ode on a Grecian Urn
10:00	Watch the news, read the newspaper
11:00	Review French for tomorrow's test
11–12	Organize/write schedule for tomorrow

To do today:

1. Finish French assignment
2. Run program
3. Begin reading The Odyssey
4. Meet with Marketing Club
5. Double-check accounting homework

Set Priorities

Francis Bacon probably said it best: "To choose time is to save time." You won't waste time on things that don't matter if you identify your priorities. But before you can decide which task to tackle first each day, you have to set goals. These goals should encompass your daily life as well as the life you have planned for the future. A good way to start is to divide your life's goals into three categories: long-term (entire life), intermediate (the next 10 years), short-term (the next six months to a year), and daily. Include detailed goals that will satisfy spiritual, educational, health, social, and financial needs and desires. As your list becomes longer and more detailed it will be necessary to prioritize your goals. The following questions will help you prioritize tasks and stay focused on your daily journey toward long-term success:

1. Which task demands my immediate attention?
2. If I cannot complete this task today, what will be the consequences?
3. Does this task help me move toward my short-term, intermediate, and long-term goals?
4. If not, is there something I can do to change the task(s) into something more oriented toward my goals?

Throughout the day, keep asking yourself: "What is the best use of my time right now?" It will only be a matter of time before you notice that your world is more ordered and purposeful. Taking charge of your time will help you with one lifelong goal—that of achieving your personal best.

Take Effective Notes

Frank Landy, a professor at Penn State, once found the notebook of one of his students. "Since I had just given what I thought was a particularly clear, well-delivered lecture, I opened the book to see what kind of notes the student took. To my dismay and surprise, the student had written down only the anecdotes and stories that described the main points. The real meat of the lecture was scribbled in the margins as an afterthought."

Professors will often use stories or real-life applications to explain a concept or term. "The bones are the theory, while the flesh is the story," says Landy. To truly learn the subject matter, you must listen for and grasp both.

To take good notes you must go to class. Don't kid yourself. You need the material your professors give you in their lectures no matter how well you've read and retained the information in the texts.

Most professors will organize their lectures around several controlling points. Obviously, you can't write everything down, but the main ideas—which your professor may write on the board or summarize at the end of each lecture—are what you want to record on paper and commit to memory. Some students organize their lectures in outline form. Others write in more of a prose style, which they can highlight later on. Occasionally, students who are having a hard time grasping a concept will bring mini tape recorders to class to record the professor's lecture (with permission). They can then review the taped lecture later and organize their notes in a way that helps them understand. Find a style that's comfortable for you and stick to it.

Keep your notes organized and in one place. Date each set of notes so that you can easily match the lecture up with the corresponding text chapter. If necessary, go back and rewrite your notes after the lecture. Or sit down with your professor during his or her office hours and make sure you are grasping the information.

Review your notes. In the same way that you must continually review the summaries after every chapter, you must continually review your class notes. If you keep up with the material along the way, studying for exams will be a lot easier. You can't cram for life, so start your good planning habits now. You'll be prepared for the long haul.

achieving your personal best

I n the first half of this chapter, you learned about how to become a better student. Among other things, you now know how to set priorities and how to take effective notes. To achieve your personal best, however, you will also want to add a few additional skills. In the second part of this chapter, you will learn more about how to develop your potential.

Get to Know Your Professors

When John Diaz was a reporter for the *Denver Post,* he also served as part of a panel on a weekly discussion program on a PBS affiliate that dealt with issues central to the state of Colorado. During the summer, John taught a newswriting course at Colorado State University.

"I was amazed at how few students sought me out," he said. "The ones who went the extra nine yards to ask me outside of class how they could improve benefited the most from the course."

John was surprised that one of his students, a journalism major, said she didn't have time to read the newspaper.

"That's like an aspiring doctor who doesn't have time to be with sick people," John says. John was able to help this student organize her time so that she could read the paper every day, and he helped her brainstorm other career avenues to ensure that journalism was what she truly wanted to pursue. John was both a teacher and a mentor to her.

Few college students bother to get to know their professors. They don't take advantage of office hours unless they fail a test or miss a class. Remember that your college professors are an invaluable resource.

Margie Oemero, an honors student at the University of Texas, agrees. "A lot of students are intimidated by their professors. They worry that the professor will feel bothered if they seek him out. My experience is that it is worth it to build that mentoring relationship." During her sophomore year, Margie took an honors seminar on marriage taught by a prominent researcher. She enjoyed the material and took the time to get to know the professor. "Now I work for him, have taken graduate courses with him, will do my senior thesis with him, and may write an article with him. Deciding on a graduate school will be so much easier with the help of a professor who knows which departments and professors are reputable."

Colleen Smith felt extremely intimidated by one of the psychology professors in her graduate program. "I was sure he had evaluated all of my faults and decided that I was unfit for the profession," she says. "During a staff meeting, I was describing a new client that needed to be assigned to a counselor. As I spoke the professor started scowling—I felt like I would either start to cry or laugh hysterically any minute. So I made a joke about how he was scowling. Everyone laughed, including him. It turned out he was trying to figure out who would be the best counselor for the client. He was not thinking negatively about me. In fact, I soon found out he thought I was a talented counselor. That experience reminded me that teachers and employers are human—they are much easier to work with if we take them off the pedestals we put them on. This man has turned out to be of great assistance to me in my career, encouraging me and sending leads my way."

Diana Cuddeback, a hospice social worker, believes finding a mentor was one of the most important experiences of her college career. During her sophomore year at Sacramento State, she took the required abnormal psychology course. Over the course of the term she sought out her professor for questions and advice. The following year he offered her a position as teaching assistant for the course (she was still an undergraduate student). Through the experience of being a TA, she got firsthand training in leading discussion groups, grading papers, and supporting students, and her professor was also able to see how she handled the responsibility.

During Diana's senior year, this professor nominated her for the Most Outstanding Senior award, which she won. He encouraged her to attend graduate school. "He provided opportunities for me to grow and learn about myself. He also introduced me to other faculty members. His friendship and encouragement helped build my confidence and self-esteem. Under his guidance, I began to see myself as a professional, as someone who had natural abilities to develop."

Start to visit your professors' offices during the first few weeks of school. Go over your class notes with them to make sure you properly understand key concepts. Let them know that you are truly interested in learning their material. They will be impressed by your diligence and your willingness to go above and beyond what is expected. If you have a good rapport with a professor, he or she will probably give you the benefit of the doubt if your grade is on the border between an A and a B. If you are trying harder than anyone else to learn the material, chances are your professors will recognize and admire your tenacity.

What about the aloof professors who would rather spend time doing research than talking with undergrads? Well, you're going to meet them. So instead of giving up and assuming that all professors are like that, go to the ones who are willing to help. And remember: you are the consumer. You are paying for your education, and you deserve your professors' attention. Each semester you'll probably have at least one professor who becomes your favorite. Pursue the aloof ones, too. This will build your confidence, and it will prepare you for the aloof people you will need to build relationships with in your career.

Think of your professors as "senior advisers." They can ask you questions regarding your major, start the wheels in your head turning, inspire you to superior effort, and give you insights on how to learn, think more broadly, and achieve your goals. The best professors you have in college are similar to the best managers in the working world. Learning from them will go a long way toward discovering what being the best means—as a manager or as a teacher.

The cynic in you may say that this sounds like the behavior of a brownnoser. Resist the impulse to believe this. Many "brownnosers" who work hard and build successful relationships with peers and professors make the best grades, get the best recommendations, and go on to get top jobs.

Kevin Dellsperger, a cardiologist and professor of medicine at the University of Iowa, believes the mentoring relationship was one of the most valuable and enjoyable experiences of his college career.

The relationship with his mentor turned into a lifelong friendship and professional relationship.

During his freshman year at Tulane, Kevin heard a lecture given by David Wieting at a meeting of the Biomedical Engineering Society. The lecture was about prosthetic heart valves. "After his lecture, I was excited and told my friends and family about Dr. Wieting. I also thought I wanted to work with him during my time at Tulane. I actually made an appointment to talk with him about working in his lab. Unfortunately, at that time he had nothing available, but he put me in contact with another faculty member.

"During my junior year I took Dr. Wieting's physiology course and he rekindled my great interest in prosthetic heart valve work. This time he did have a position in his lab. Without a doubt, those last two years were the happiest of my undergraduate years. I must have seemed like a child of four or five, constantly asking him questions about heart valves and bioengineering principles.

"He may tell you otherwise, but I would not be where I am without his guidance. In our program, we were to do research as part of our curriculum. I remember during the summer of my junior year asking David for advice about prosthetic heart valves and complications. After two or three weeks I told him I wanted to design a new valve. He had a smile on his face and asked me what it should look like. I told him I didn't know. He told me to think about it and bring him a design. Well, several weeks later I had a brilliant idea. I took it in to David and the look on his face was one of shock. He went to a locked file cabinet, took out a book of his personal ideas and showed me a nearly identical thought. I believe it was at this time that our relationship changed from student–teacher to student–friend–teacher.

"The next year, working on the valve and in the lab with him was wonderful. I was having such great fun that in March or April I strongly considered delaying medical school for a year to get a master's degree. It was at this time that David was the best mentor I could have had. He told me emphatically that since I always wanted to go into medicine, I should not delay my training. He said that other research opportunities would come to my attention and that I could jump on the bandwagon.

"We kept in touch after I graduated. When he left Tulane he joined Mitral Medical (a heart valve company) and asked me to

come out during the summer to help set up the lab and do some testing. His job as my mentor was not over, as he directed the research
portion of my Ph.D. work. Now I believe that I can scientifically
contribute as an equal partner for the first time. While my emphasis
these days is not primarily heart valve prostheses, I am still active in
that area with collaborative efforts with David. He is like a big
brother to me. I value his advice and care deeply about him."

Master Your Communication Skills

"No higher-level job can be obtained without a good command of
the language," says Steven Harwood, chief of nuclear medicine at
the Veterans Administration Hospital in Bay Pines, Florida.
"Writing skills are the most important skills you can develop—especially for obtaining higher management–level jobs. You must be able
to clearly communicate your ideas to others."

Mick McCormick, a Nike sales director, believes written and
oral communication skills are essential for success in the workplace.
"I have seen qualified, gifted people passed over for top promotions
because they could not communicate their ideas effectively.
Corporations value verbal skills."

"Look for examples of great writers so that you can have the
best models for your own work," says Greg McCaslin, who has
taught students from kindergarten to college. "Read the newspaper,
ask your teachers to let you see the work of some of the best writers
in your class, and seek styles which vary from your own." Greg,
who taught for fifteen years and became director of the New York
Foundation for the Arts, says that with writing, as with learning
anything else, the determination to improve and a nondefensive
response to criticism will overcome any lack of aptitude.

Freshman composition may be one of the most important classes you take in college. Even if it's not required, try to take a writing
class your first semester. Learning to become a good writer means
learning to communicate, to refine and develop your thoughts—so
that what you mean to say, or what you think, is clear to others. If
you learn to be a good writer as a freshman, you will be successful
in your sophomore, junior, and senior-level courses, when you will
be required to write research papers and do special assignments.
Also, beyond the freshman level, essays become the norm.

> ## Tips for Becoming a Better Writer
>
> 1. Keep up your journal. You'll be able to look back over your entries to see if your thoughts are coherent. Do your sentences make sense? What style do you use?
>
> 2. Write letters. Instead of picking up the phone to call your friends or parents, try writing. Do your thoughts flow easily? If they don't at first, don't worry. And remember that you are going to improve with practice (as well as lower your phone bill!).
>
> 3. Read magazines and the newspaper. Analyze the writing of columnists and reporters. What is clear and crisp about their writing? How could you apply the same techniques?
>
> 4. Have a friend look at and comment on your writing. Your teacher is not the only resource for feedback. Meet with a friend or two outside of your composition class and do some peer editing. Analyze their writing and ask them to make constructive criticisms of your own work.
>
> 5. Write your thoughts down in lists that you can refine later. Jotting things down before you have to write—or think—them out will help you crystallize your original thoughts.

In the business world, good writing is essential. Throughout your career, you'll likely be writing memos, business letters to clients, reports, strategic and planning proposals, persuasive or informative speeches, and more. If you can communicate effectively on paper and orally, you'll have an advantage over those who know how to manipulate numbers, but know little about expressing themselves or their work.

"I try to make it fun," says David Plane, who teaches geography at a large state university. He helps his students understand their audience by asking them to write from the point of view of someone in the field. "I ask them to write on a topic and pretend that they are an urban planner. What questions would that person ask? How would they best explain and communicate their ideas to a reviewing committee or to their managers?" The following week he might ask them to write a paper from the manager's point of view, presenting the urban planner's proposal.

Becoming a good writer means becoming good at revising your thoughts and observations. Writing, like thinking, is a process. Working on several drafts means distilling your ideas. So, get comfortable with rewriting, crossing things out, and throwing away some of your initial thoughts. That's part of the fun of writing.

Among the many composition books available, I think *The Simon & Schuster Handbook for Writers* by Lynn Troyka stands out. It explains how to become a good, even a great writer. It also contains everything you need to know about the rules for writing. After your freshman year, you'll use it to write research papers for your higher-level courses.

Here's an excerpt from the book that should help clarify how you (and everybody else) can master the art of writing:

> Many people assume that a real writer can pick up a pen (or sit at a typewriter or a word processor) and magically write a finished product word by perfect word. Experienced writers know better. They know that writing is a process, a series of activities that start the moment they begin thinking about a subject and end when they complete a final draft. Experienced writers know, also, that good writing is rewriting. Their drafts are filled with additions, deletions, rearrangements, and rewordings.

So remember that good writing means practicing. And be patient with yourself. You're embarking on many new things at once.

Understanding Technology

In addition to mastering your communication skills, you will also need to keep up with computer technology and the ways it can help you during college and in your career. Computer technology touches every possible field and job.

Although technology has made life easier for many people, it's also the source of a lot of anxiety for others. More to the point,

Tips for Becoming a Better Speaker

1. Contribute to class discussion as often as possible. As you begin to share your ideas and ask questions, you will become more comfortable speaking in public and articulating your thoughts in front of groups of people.

2. Assume a leadership position in your extracurricular organizations. Whether you are the president or a committee leader, you will have many opportunities to practice communicating your ideas in a group.

3. When you have a formal presentation to prepare, practice your speech in front of a friend. Ask your friend to give you feedback. Did you enunciate your words clearly? Were your ideas interestingly presented? Did you speak too fast? Too slow? Too quietly?

4. Enroll in a public speaking or debate class where you can hone your speaking skills. Not only do communication classes teach you specific tips, they also give you plenty of chances to practice.

5. Find out if your college has a student chapter of Toastmasters, an organization that is specifically designed to help you become comfortable and skillful in public speaking.

some people are afraid of their computers. In a 1994 MCI-Gallup survey, almost half of the white-collar workers (people employed in office jobs) identified themselves as "cyberphobic."

In today's information age, however, avoiding computers is no longer an option. Since 1984, the number of jobs that require knowing how to use a computer has risen from 25 to 46 percent. More than 70 percent of management positions now demand computer literacy. Becoming computer competent is easier than you might think. Experts suggest taking these steps to overcome your fears:

1. *Don't be snowed by terminology.* When you shop for a computer, decide what you'd like to do with it and list those goals, advises Kris Jamsa in *Welcome to Personal Computers*. Then, if a

salesperson asks an obscure question—such as "How many megahertz do you want?"—respond: "I don't know. You tell me what I need to accomplish my goals, which are . . ." The salesperson should be able to answer in plain English.

2. *Dive right in.* You don't need to know the technical details of your computer any more than you need to understand the technology behind your microwave oven. "Don't get bogged down in a hefty computer manual," advises Joe Kraynak, author of *The Complete Idiot's Guide to PCs.* "Go ahead and flip the switch, click and move the mouse." For some people, the biggest obstacle to pressing that first key is the fear of hitting the wrong one. Don't worry about your mistakes. Your computer won't remember how many wrong keys you press—unless you ask it to. And don't worry about losing information. Most computer programs have a feature that can retrieve lost data or undo the previous command. According to Kris Jamsa, if you master just three specific tasks— saving and printing a document, sending and receiving e-mail, and browsing the World Wide Web—you'll be as computer proficient as most of the population.

3. *Ask for help.* Most schools require students to take computer courses. Many schools also have computer resource centers on campus complete with computers for students to use and staff to assist them. Tell someone within that circle that you need help getting started. A fellow classmate who navigates the computer easily might be glad to help you get started.

Overcoming your apprehension of computers may enrich your life in ways you'd never imagined. Computers today can be invaluable in helping you research topics and compose papers. They can also be useful in helping you balance your checkbook and keep track of your daily responsibilities. And with the explosion of online services, you have a wealth of information at your fingertips.

While terminology changes rapidly, here are a few buzzwords that you should know now:

- *The Internet* is a worldwide electronic superhighway that carries electronic mail and information services from a variety of sources. It connects all kinds of computers and computer systems, regardless of size or program. Many college professors now put their syllabi, lecture notes, and tests on the Internet. Some schools are hooking up each dorm room to a campus network, which in turn allows students access to the Internet.

- *Online services* such as America Online, Prodigy, and Netscape are available by subscription and provide a wide variety of information in an easy-to-use format. They operate through a modem hooked to your phone line. These services have an incredible array of information, available anytime you need it, on topics such as current events, investment opportunities, technology news, and advice on purchasing computers or other software. Online services also allow you to "talk" with other subscribers about issues that interest you. You can browse through the system and find bulletin boards that feature discussions on specific topics, or you can send e-mail to friends. The online service can also provide access to periodicals you might need for researching papers.

- *E-mail* is mail sent from one personal computer to another through an online service. A special issue of *Time* magazine, "Focus on Technology," describes one way e-mail is used at MIT: "A student who wants to talk about a particular problem at 2 a.m. doesn't have to wander the dormitory halls looking for slits of light under doorways. Instead, the student posts a message on Zephyr, MIT's instant-message system devoted to specific topics—many of them classroom-related—where similarly stumped students are likely to be discussing precisely that problem."

- A *CD-ROM drive* allows your computer to deliver complex and expanded programs contained on compact disks. If you loaded these kinds of programs onto your hard drive, your computer's memory would be crammed with information in no time at all. So you need to have the CD in the disk drive in order to run the program. Sarah Lyman Kravits, a writer in New York City, uses her CD-ROM to run programs such as Bookshelf and Encarta. "Bookshelf gives me instant access to a dictionary, thesaurus, quotation reference, condensed encyclopedia, atlas, chronology, and almanac. When I am using my word-processing program, the icons appear at the top of the screen, so whenever I need to look something up, I slide my mouse up there and click. That's all it takes. Then I have a whole library to browse through."

Technology is rapidly changing the ways companies function—how managers manage and how employees communicate with one another and their supervisors. Many businesspeople find it necessary to return to school periodically to update their skills in order to continue to be valuable to their companies. If you take advantage of the services computers provide now, and learn how to keep abreast of the changes and developments while you are in college, you'll have learned an invaluable skill for whatever career you choose.

asking for help

If you find out early that you're having problems reading, writing, or understanding class material, get help fast. There are plenty of people available to help you in these areas. You can hire a professional, or you can go to one of the tutors your campus may provide. If you need to take a semester off to refine your study skills, do it. It will be well worth your time and energy in the long run. Better to make mediocre grades for one semester than for four years.

Christina Bernstein felt "unmotivated" during her sophomore year in college. She was especially challenged by the language requirement, which calls for four semesters of a foreign language. After taking the first semester of her junior year off and living with a family in Bogota, Colombia, Chris was able to return to school speaking Spanish fluently. She not only finished up her language classes, she also had new enthusiasm for the rest of her studies.

To get you started focusing on your study skills, fill in the academic evaluation chart below:

ACADEMIC STRENGTHS   ACADEMIC WEAKNESSES

1. _____   1. _____

2. _____   2. _____

3. _____   3. _____

if at first you don't succeed . . .

You may fall short of some of the goals you set for your freshman year. Maybe you won't achieve a 3.0 average or become captain of the women's soccer team. Instead of dwelling on your defeats, think about ways to improve next year. Can you sharpen your study skills? Manage time better? Better apply yourself to your studies until you improve? Whatever your problem, see what can be done the summer before your sophomore year begins. You may want to spend part of the summer taking reading and writing courses so that you'll have better study skills as a sophomore. You may want to take a year off to attend a community college where you can refine your basic study skills. Whatever your reasons for not meeting your goals may be, analyze what happened and develop a strategy for remedying the situation.

Maybe you gave it your best shot and you've come to the conclusion that you're just not cut out for college. Okay, it's not the end of the world. It does mean, however, that you'll have a somewhat different path, which may lead you to something equally as rewarding as the college-grad path.

Jack Naughton never graduated from high school. He sold Fuller brushes and La-Z-Boy recliners until he had a brainstorm one day: a reclining chair that dentists could use to treat their patients more effectively. He patented the idea internationally and made his life's fortune from that one idea. The original chair, by the way, is now in the Smithsonian.

However, unless you have the unbridled ambition and fortitude to forgo a traditional education, you're better off staying in school. You may never be on the dean's list or make Phi Beta Kappa. That's okay. The most you can do is try, learn as much as you can, and go forward. Most people improve with time.

be on your own

BALANCING THE DEMANDS OF YOUR WORLD

Freedom is not worth having if it does not connote freedom to err.

—MAHATMA GANDHI

Responsibility educates. —WENDELL PHILLIPS

L eaving home to attend college was really my first experience of being on my own," remembers Ingrid Damiani. "All of a sudden, it was completely up to me to decide when and how much I studied, how late I stayed out, and how I spent my money."

The freedom you experience as a freshman can be thrilling. The responsibilities that come with it, however, can be overwhelming. "How you face decisions in college can determine whether your college experience is filled with challenges you master or a series of crises that drain you," says Ingrid's husband, Tim Damiani, a psychiatrist who has counseled college students. "Many of the personal habits you establish during your college years will follow you through your life."

residence-hall life versus life off campus

L iving in a residence hall is one way you can make the transition from your parents' home to being on your own easier. Residence halls are usually less expensive than living on your own; most provide meal plans so that you don't have to worry about grocery shopping and meal preparation during your first year. Residence halls also come with built-in support systems. In addition to being a source for many new friends, they offer the help and support of resident assistants.

Amir Abolfolthe, a biomedical engineer and product manager, believes that living in a residence hall during his first two years of college was an important part of his adjustment to college life. "Many of the people in the residence hall are new and have the same anxieties you do. The residence hall also helps you to keep a balance between your social and academic life. When you want to play, there are always people who are ready to go out. When you need to study, you can always find someone to go to the library with. And when you are having trouble with a tricky calculus problem or are feeling blocked on your term paper, there are always other students around who are taking the same classes to brainstorm with. In my residence hall we supported each other and looked out for each other. We were like a big family."

As a foreign student, Amir found that living in the residence hall helped him to form friendships with American students. "Many of my Iranian friends lived at home and stuck to themselves on campus. I felt fortunate to be able to interact comfortably with everyone."

juggling your finances

My brother Craig was the first person to sit down and talk with me about finances. Although I was making minimum wage, he explained how important it was to save at least 10 percent of what I made.

"If you get in the habit of saving now, you'll have a decent cushion of savings all your life. It is one of the most important disciplines you can impose on yourself," he said. "You never know what is going to happen to you. You may want to quit your job someday or you may lose your job. You could get sick. You could decide you want to take six months off and travel the world. If you have learned to save, you will have more options as you get older."

Craig helped me open my first investment account with Merrill Lynch, in a money market mutual fund. At the time, this was yielding about 9 percent, which was far better than a standard checking or savings rate. Now that the market conditions have changed, money markets are not as good as bonds or stocks. Several years ago, I made a switch from the money market fund we opened when I was in college to a more diversified investment plan, which is a much better deal for me at this point in my life. A good financial adviser can help you make the best decisions about investing and saving your money.

That initial sum of money has really grown over the past fourteen years since I began college. And what is more important is that I have been strict about saving. Craig was right. The more you learn to save, the more options you will have later when those inevitable unforeseen circumstances arise.

Tim and Ingrid Damiani handled their money very differently before they got married. Tim knew exactly where he spent his money and carefully budgeted his income. During college, he passed over some things he wanted, but he graduated with no debt and had saved enough to put a large down payment on a car he had been dreaming about. Ingrid spent money more impulsively. She didn't spend a lot at once, but she never knew just where her money was going. "I felt like I was living on the edge financially. I was never sure I'd have enough to cover all my bills."

During the year before they got married, Tim and Ingrid earned about the same amount of money. When they got married Tim deposited several thousand dollars he had saved into their joint savings account, and Ingrid contributed several thousand dollars of credit card debt.

"We quickly agreed on a budget. It was rough at first, but now that we've set and stayed on it, I love it," says Ingrid. "It's such a good feeling to have a plan for our money. When we spend money we enjoy it and do so without guilt or worry because we know it's in the budget. We can save for specific goals in the future. It is a more peaceful way to live."

When you are in control of what you spend, you can feel good about what you buy. Being confident that you've got enough to cover each bill allows you to feel secure and to pursue other interests without money worries hanging over your head. Further, if you budget you will be able to save money that can be used toward special worthwhile goals, such as traveling.

Establishing a Budget

Whether your parents, a scholarship, a loan, or your own hard work is paying for your education, you will be managing your own expenses. Money problems are stressful but avoidable. If you can get a handle on the money available to you and develop a plan of how you will spend that money, you will avoid wasting your valuable time.

The first step is to determine the amount of money you need to cover the essentials—rent or mortgage payments, utility bills (electricity, gas, phone, water), transportation, tuition and books, food and toiletries, insurance (car, health, renters), and clothes. After you have determined the amount that these basic needs will cost, you will know how much you have left over for saving and spending on entertainment (eating out, movies, concerts), gifts, and other fun purchases.

There are now computer software programs that help consumers establish budgets and track spending habits. Check with your local computer store for budgeting software.

Financial aid counselors also provide budget advising. Contact your school's financial aid office for information. There are also private financial counselors who can establish budgets, but they will charge a fee for this service. Examine your options and determine what will work best for you.

Learning to Budget

Sample College Student Monthly Budget

Income:

Parental support	$2,000.00
Student loan ($2,500/yr.)	283.00
Part-time job (20 hrs./wk.)	640.00
Total income	$2,923.00

Expenditures:

Tuition ($15,000/yr.) (9-month payment plan)	$1,600.00
Transportation (car payments, gas, insurance, repairs)	350.00
Phone	30.00
Utilities (electricity, water, gas)	30.00
Groceries and necessities	150.00
Rent	400.00
Taxes	160.00
Entertainment	50.00
Total expenditures	$2,770.00
Amount left over for savings	*$153.00*

YOUR PERSONAL BUDGET

Income:

Parental support	_____
Student loan	_____
Part-time job	_____
Total Income	_____

Expenditures:

Tuition	_____
Transportation (car payment, gas, insurance, repairs)	_____
Phone	_____
Utilities (elec., water, gas)	_____
Groceries and necessities	_____
Rent	_____
Taxes	_____
Entertainment	_____
Total Expenditures	_____
Amount left for savings	_____

Smart Ways to Use Credit Cards

Credit cards can be very helpful if you use them shrewdly. Many credit card companies make their cards easily available to college students. When choosing a card, pay attention to the annual fee and interest rates; they vary from card to card. Pick one with a low interest rate, and try to find one with no annual fee.

Using credit cards modestly and paying them off every month will help you establish a good credit history. Credit cards can also help you in an emergency and provide a clear statement of how you've spent your money. However, a word of caution: avoid paying your tuition on a credit card.

When Joe Wieting was in college he did not have enough money to pay for everything he needed. "When I was short of cash, I charged what I needed, reasoning that I would be able to pay off my debt quickly when I got my first job after graduation. I was always careful to pay the minimum amount due each month so that my credit history would be acceptable. What I didn't realize was how fast the interest charges would build up. By the time I graduated, I had a hefty debt that was not easy to pay off. Now I wish that I had taken out a bank loan—the lower interest rate would have made it much easier to pay off and I would have had the peace of mind of knowing I had enough money to cover my expenses." Be careful to keep track of how much you are spending on your credit cards. Some people make notes on their check register so they can make sure they aren't overspending.

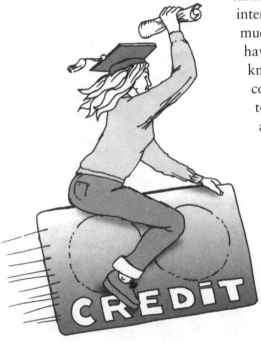

If you are spending more than you are able to pay off at the end of the month, you will be incurring further debt because the interest rates are always high. If you miss a payment or make a late payment, your credit rating will be lowered. Bad credit ratings can prevent you from securing a bank loan for a car or a new home, and prospective employers often check credit ratings to get a sense of how responsible the applicant is. The way you use a credit card says a great deal about whether or not you are responsible, so use it wisely. Leo Murphy, a financial specialist at the Chicago Board of Trade, offers the following guidelines:

- *Create a budget and stick to it.* Doing so will help you accomplish three objectives:
  1. To control your spending,
  2. Know where your money is going, and
  3. Meet your immediate needs (necessities) and future plans (priorities).
- *Avoid impulse buying.* If you see something you want, always ask yourself the question: "Do I really *need* this?" Also, don't buy anything on the spot. Instead, wait at least a day or two before making a purchase. The wait will help you determine whether you really need the item or not.
- *Prioritize your spending.* This guideline involves defining your life goals. Sometimes it's wise to spend money; your college education, for example, is an investment in yourself. Therefore, prioritize your spending on the basis of these three categories:
  1. Necessities—food, housing, medical care;
  2. Priorities—your hopes; things that show appreciable growth. Example: your education; and
  3. Luxuries—things you may want but don't need and that can hurt your present and future. Live in the present, but keep your eyes on the future.
- *Limit credit card spending.* Remember that advertisements will entice you to spend with slogans like "Buy now with no money down." See these ads for what they are: they want your money.

As Murphy says, "The lack of money doesn't prevent people from achieving their goals as much as mismanagement of it does." Therefore, begin to establish good financial habits now, and you'll have one of life's major responsibilities in check.

the dating game

College offers many opportunities to meet different kinds of people and to find out what kinds of people you enjoy being with. I'm not an expert on dating during college, since I had only one serious boyfriend in college, and that was in my senior year. Before I met him, I was frankly more interested in my studies and my friends than anything else. But I was clearly the exception. Most of my friends had boyfriends from the start of their freshman year.

Pam Zemper, an RA (resident assistant) who worked in a women's residence hall at the University of Texas, found that many freshmen are confused about how to handle relationships from high school. "These students are so excited about college. They want to meet new people and to enjoy all the new, interesting things college has to offer. But they also want to maintain the same level of closeness with their boyfriends from home. I always advised the girls on my floor to establish new ground rules with their boyfriends. If they talked every night on the phone in high school and their boyfriends want to continue this, it will hold the girls back from activities they want to try. They need to discuss their expectations about how often they will see and talk to each other. And if they are attending different schools, they probably need to talk about dating other people."

Jeanne Stark, who began dating someone seriously in the middle of her freshman year, remembers opportunities she let slip by because she was in a relationship. "He was an English major like me—he was poetic, charming, and distinctly unambitious. At the time I found him attractive and enjoyed his company. What I didn't realize was that my involvement with him was keeping me from pursuing other activities and friends I was genuinely interested in. After my sophomore year, he graduated and spent the next few months traveling around Europe. While he was gone, I became a reporter and eventually the copy editor for the school yearbook, and I began working on an honors tutorial with one of my English professors. All of a sudden, all of these doors and opportunities started to open up. What an eye-opener! I realized that I was wasting my time with someone who did not share my goals or values. A few years later I met the man I eventually married. He has shown me that the best partner is someone who shares your interests and dreams, challenges you, and cheers you on to greater successes."

This doesn't mean that it is wise to date a clone of yourself, or that college has to be the end of your high school romance. What it does mean is that it's important for you to take stock of yourself—to know what you want from your time in college and what your life goals are, and to spend time with people who support rather than distract you. Even if the person you are dating is the person of your dreams, you still need to make sure you are allowing time to get to know yourself.

Toward the end of college, many of my friends were engaged or starting to think seriously about marriage. Some of them seemed to be using marriage as an escape from the demands of academic work and graduation. Obviously, the decision to get married is personal and the right time for marriage is different for everyone. I'm a slowpoke. I just got back from my ten-year college reunion, and only five of us weren't married. I felt really out of it when people were passing around pictures of their kids. And yet, I'm not making one of the biggest decisions of my life unless it is for the right person. Why compromise?

Ingrid Damiani married her husband three years after she graduated from college. "Having time to truly be on my own, to earn my own living, and to feel like an adult in the working world has been invaluable to me in my marriage. That time on my own helped me to define my goals and to learn about myself. Looking back, I can see I grew a lot in those first few years after college. For me, that growing happened better while I was single. It was important for me to know I could succeed on my own terms before I made a commitment to someone else."

Rachelle Shaw is a pediatric dentist in Albuquerque, New Mexico, and the mother of three children. She says, "You can always get married and have children. You won't always have the opportunity to go to school. Following your dreams and achieving goals allows you to subsequently focus on your family or others, enriching all."

Dating Violence

Dating relationships should be fun, enriching experiences. Unfortunately, statistics reveal that sometimes they become the exact opposite. One of every five college females will experience some form of dating violence, and the Bureau of Justice Statistics report on intimate partner violence from 2000 shows that women ages 16 to 24 experience the highest per capita rates (20 per every 1000 women) of intimate violence. In addition, studies have shown that 67 percent of young women reporting rape were raped by dating partners. Even more alarming is the fact that every abusive relationship has the potential to end in murder. The same Bureau of Justice Statistics report shows that women ages 16 to 19 were killed by an intimate partner at the rate of 18 women per every 1000 murder victims, while 21 women per every 1000 murder victims ages 20 to 24 were killed by an intimate partner.

Anyone can end up in an abusive relationship, but you have to be strong to get out of it. Young men and women often become emotionally involved with their partner before they really know the person. They think they love their partner (and maybe they do), and because they are in love, they think they can and should tolerate anything their partners do, say, or prefer. Abusive relationships revolve around this kind of power and control.

Experts say the cycle of violence often begins with small things like name calling and then builds to an explosion that often results in verbal, physical, or sexual aggression. Being alert to the warning signs that trigger the cycle will make you less vulnerable to unhealthy dating patterns. Below are questions for you to think about and maybe talk over with your friends, student counselors, or parents.

Warning Signs of Dating Violence

The following is a list compiled from the National Domestic Violence Hotline and Rape Assistance and Awareness Program. If you answer yes to two or more of these questions, your partner is likely to be abusive.

- Has your relationship begun quickly and intensely, and you feel it is moving "too fast too soon"?

Dating Violence (continued)

- Does your partner verbally put you down or call you names that hurt your feelings?
- Does he or she ridicule you for being stupid or for characteristics that he or she thinks are "typical" of women or men?
- Does your partner have a quick temper?
- When your partner gets angry, are you afraid?
- Does your partner always blame other people when things go wrong?
- Does your partner abuse alcohol or drugs?
- Did your partner grow up in a violent family?
- Does your partner always expect you to follow his or her orders or advice?
- Has your partner ever bragged about intimidating or hurting other people?
- Is your partner jealous of you when you are with your friends?
- Does your partner act self-centered and ignore your opinion?
- Do you like yourself less than usual when you're with your partner?

When you enter a new relationship and aren't really sure if your date will be abusive or not, be sure to take some precautions. Below is a list of dating safety tips from the Domestic Violence Advocacy Program of Family Resource, Inc. Whenever you are unsure about the person you are dating, it is always better to be safe, so be sure to follow this advice.

- Double-date the first few dates with a trusted friend.
- Make exact plans, tell someone you trust these plans, then make sure your date knows you will be checking in with this person sometime during the date.
- Know that you will experience decreased ability under the effects of drugs and alcohol.
- If you leave a party with someone you don't know too well, make sure someone knows who you are leaving with and have that person call to see if you arrived home.

(continued)

Dating Violence (continued)

- Be assertive and straightforward.
- Trust your instincts if you feel uncomfortable and leave the situation as soon as possible.

If you are in an abusive relationship, take immediate steps to get out of it. If you think he or she might freak out and try to hurt you (a classic response of abusers when their partners try to leave them), break up in a public place and arrange for family or friends to take you home.

Also, be alert to your partner's response. If it is anything like "You're not going to leave me," be sure to tell someone (your parents or a roommate). The more people who know, the safer you are. For more information, call the National Domestic Violence Hotline at 1-800-799-7233 or reach them on the Web at www.ndvh.org. A trained counselor is there twenty-four hours a day. The hotline provides help, not only for the victim, but for the abuser as well. If you have a hearing disability, call the hotline at 1-800-787-3224 (TDD).

Healthy Dating Relationships

Just as unhealthy dating relationships are marked by certain characteristics, so are healthy ones. Healthy intimacy is based on cooperation and equality. Here are the characteristics of a mature, nonviolent relationship:

- *Negotiation and fairness.* Seeking mutually satisfying resolutions to conflict, which includes a willingness to accept change and to compromise.
- *Nonthreatening behavior.* Talking and acting so that you both feel safe and comfortable expressing yourselves and doing things.
- *Respect.* Listening to each other without being judgmental, being emotionally affirming and affirmed, understanding and valuing each other's opinions.
- *Independence and autonomy.* Recognizing each other's interdependence, yet accepting "separateness" as nonmarried persons. Fostering individual identity.

Dating Violence (continued)

- *Trust and support.* Supporting each other's life goals. Respecting each other's rights to have personal feelings, friends, activities, and opinions. Overcoming issues like envy and resentment.

Of all the demands you encounter in college, developing healthy dating relationships is one of the most critical. Every dating relationship is serious because it plays a part in defining who you are. How you relate to your dating partners, and how they to relate to you, are key to your well-being. Establishing equality in your dating relationships now will help ensure a lifetime of close, supportive relationships.

overcoming obstacles

College students face challenges of all kinds—in academic work, health, and finances, and in combating prejudice. Whatever you are facing, there is probably a resource on campus to support you. You may feel as if you are the only one who is struggling with a problem, but chances are you aren't, and there are people on campus who can help.

Academic Challenges

Most colleges have a learning resource center to give students support with study habits, time management, writing, test anxiety, and other such matters. In addition, many departments offer study groups or tutoring sessions to assist students with particular subjects. Your professors will often be able to send you in the right direction to find these support systems.

Emotional/Psychological Problems

Most universities have a counseling center available specifically for students. These centers usually provide for a certain number of counseling sessions at no cost and then offer another set of sessions

MY TWO CENTS   *How Do I Apply It?*

Jesse Walker, Hamilton College

After completing a semester at Hamilton College, I learned that no one can truly be prepared for everything college throws at you. I even devoted a significant portion of my summer preparing for college. Truthfully, learning to live on my own was probably the biggest transition I had to make. High school is much different. There are teachers who recognize daily whether or not you have done your work, and your parents are around to help you with laundry, the condition of your room, and budgeting. To others these problems may seem trivial, but they become much more difficult in college.

Most likely one of your first observations upon spending a week or two in college is that no one sleeps nearly as much as in high school. Before, school started at 7:00 or 8:00, so the absolute latest time to go to bed might be around midnight. But in college, 8:00 might not be your first class. Most morning classes start at 9:00, but most students will opt for later classes. Either way, most people fall into a routine where they stay up until 1:00 or 2:00 in the morning on a regular basis. Sometimes it's unavoidable, papers are due or tests must be taken. You will have a few of these nights in college no matter how well you plan out your work. However, try to get to bed by 11:00 or 12:00 a few times a week. You'll feel better, and the following day will be far more productive than roaming around campus like a zombie. If you have a lot of work, and you find yourself staying up late for a couple nights at a time, take a few power naps.

The next problem you may encounter after two or three weeks is that you and your roommate don't see eye to eye. He or she may keep you up at night, or cause other sorts of disorder in your life. My roommate, for example, would stay up until three in the morning. This would not have been so problematic if he had been quiet when going to sleep, but he liked to do push-ups in the room right before he went to bed! Thus, I urge you to explore living options in residential life if there is controversy between you and your roommate. I did, and I am much happier with my living situation. Think of it this way, schoolwork and other commitments are far bigger problems than your roommate, so why deal with him or her? Don't hesitate to move in with a more compatible roommate; it's less of a hassle than spending a whole semester with someone you can't stand.

Another potential mishap could be with your laundry. If you become too preoccupied with school, you may find a gigantic pile of dirty clothes in the corner of your room. Make a designated laundry time every week, a couple hours or so, so that you don't fall too far behind. Don't fall into the precarious situation of debating over which T-shirt is less dirty before you go to class. Your classmates will thank you.

My last tip is budgeting. It is imperative that you budget in college. Before you blow all your money ordering pizza at 11:00 every night, it's important to stick to a plan so that you don't have to call home to your parents for extra cash. If you have the time, check out the work-study program at your school. Most of the jobs are quite painless and only require you to work a few hours a week. College is a fun time where you can enjoy your personal freedom, but just make sure you do so wisely in order to enjoy college to the fullest.

at affordable rates (way below the rates you would pay for a private therapist). Counselors can often provide the support or the resources you need to get through your problem.

There are also many groups in the community that can provide support for specific problems such as bulimia or anorexia, being the child of an alcoholic, or suffering from alcoholism, and programs for people who have been abused. The counseling center at your school may offer these programs or be able to send you to the right place. If not, check one of the local churches—they often host support groups in their building, and they can usually provide the name and address of a support group near you.

Physical Disabilities

Cyrus Sarmadi, a junior at the University of California at Santa Barbara, is hearing impaired and a foreign student. Has he let these challenges slow him down? Not on your life. So far, he has co-founded and supervised a computer club at his college, and he was a gold medallist on the Men's National Deaf Water Polo Team at the World Games in 1993. He is also in the planning stages of starting a Persian club at his school.

"My advice is to take a deep breath and plunge. If you fall, get up and jump again."

Cyrus advises other students with challenges to "take advantage of all services that are available at the university, such as note taking and tutoring services, or any other campus assistance."

Look in your school directory for an office designed to help students with special needs and take advantage of the help offered to you as a student. These offices usually have people who can solve problems quickly (such as finding you a reader, getting a ramp installed, and so on).

alternative routes

Dick Christensen, a psychiatrist, remembers beginning college "in a very rigorous pre-med program which was heavy on the sciences and light on the arts and letters. Not realizing at the time that there was room for flexibility in the curriculum, I blindly accepted the overwhelming program as a given and proceeded to flunk one exam after the other. Desperate and panicked, I sought out an academic adviser. He allowed me to create my own curriculum, which not only was more manageable but eventually led to a dual major in biology and philosophy. I learned two lessons: each person has unique strengths and weaknesses, and there are always alternative routes to achieving the same goal."

roadblock? detours are allowed

If you have pursued every avenue for help and you still feel overwhelmed by a problem at college, you might consider taking some time off. Carla Summers, an archivist at the University of Florida, dropped out after her sophomore year and spent several semesters waiting tables. "Taking some time off was the best decision I could have made. Before I left, I was unmotivated, underdirected, and making poor grades. When I returned to school, I had a clear sense of wanting to be there and I was very focused. My grades reflected my new sense of direction."

Jesse Keller decided to take a year off between his junior and senior years at Yale. His detour was carefully planned to give him a variety of work experiences and to provide him with a refreshing break. For the first half of the year, he worked with a professor on a computer music software development project. "I found this to be a satisfying situation. I lived in New Haven and kept in touch with my Yale friends, but I worked full time (and was financially independent) in a job that was both interesting and resume-building." The second semester, Jesse worked at Microsoft as a software designer for a few months. Working at Microsoft gave him hands-on experience in his field. Finally, he spent six weeks traveling across the country before he went back to school. According to Jesse, the year off provided "work experience from two different perspectives in the same field and a chance to see a whole bunch of possibilities as I traveled. It also gave me time to renew my academic enthusiasm."

appreciating your diverse world

Unfortunately, equality is an ideal this country has not always honored. Now more than ever we need to make a commitment to create an environment where all people have the opportunity to use their skills and to succeed regardless of race, religion, gender, or disability.

"We must cooperate to compete in a global marketplace," says George Fraser, an author and founder of Success Source, a company that publishes networking guides for African Americans in various cities. "That means leveraging the collective resources of every single cultural group within our country."

A recent issue of *Time* magazine devoted to diversity in the United States noted, "Immigrants are arriving at the rate of more than one million a year, mostly from Asia and the vast Hispanic world. The impact of these immigrants is literally remaking America. Today more than 20 million Americans were born in another country."

American companies are responding to this diversity by making sure their workplaces reflect the diversity in society. A recent issue of *Fortune* magazine, which featured an article on workplace diversity,

noted that executives are starting to see positive results as they implement work-force diversity. "Says IBM chief Louis V. Gerstner, Jr.: 'Our marketplace is made up of all races, religions, and sexual orientations, and therefore it is vital to our success that our work force also be diverse.'" Companies are finding that when the work force is made up of people from different backgrounds, their teams are able to come up with more creative solutions.

Ted Smith, a video producer in Washington, DC, worked as a RA in an off-campus apartment complex at Virginia Commonwealth University. One of the university's policies was to pair RAs from different backgrounds to solve problems. Usually a white RA would be paired with an African American RA. "In addition to resolving residential disputes, we also prepared presentations about resolving racial conflicts. This job helped me to see some of the challenges of living in a diverse environment and showed me creative ways of resolving problems. I use these tools every day in the work I do."

Racist or prejudiced feelings, or disrespecting others because they differ from you, can only be damaging to you as an individual as well as those with whom you associate. These feelings can hinder you from advancing. If you learn to overcome your prejudices or feelings of discomfort with those who are different, you will be an asset to your future employer. In today's world, people value those who care about the advancement of others and who show through their actions an open mind toward people of all backgrounds.

Working with people whose backgrounds are different from yours takes practice and patience. College is an excellent opportunity for you to broaden your experience with other cultures. Through extracurricular activities, volunteering, and friendships, you can meet people who think and live differently from you. Many schools now require students to take courses that help them understand multicultural issues. The University of California at Berkeley, for example, requires students to take courses that focus on at least three ethnic groups (Asian, Latino, Native American, African American, or European).

In the words of George Fraser: "Every cultural group is like an instrument in a symphony orchestra. Each instrument brings a different tonality and character—together, the instruments make powerful music."

when there's resistance

I n his book *Out of the Madness,* Jerrold Ladd, an award-winning journalist, tells his story—how he fought to succeed against the odds of growing up in the projects in Dallas surrounded by drugs, violence, and poverty.

He faced many discouraging setbacks in his attempts to gain an education and find meaningful work. At the height of his despair, he asked, "Where was the black man's wisdom and guidance to lead us around snares and guide us through tribulation?"

Since he had no role models in his life to turn to, he found them in the pages of history. He spent hours in the library "reading about black heroes, philosophers, and thinkers. . . . My discovery of dead literary role models permanently cured my doubt and made me go back to the fundamental truth," he writes. "Knowing the great accomplishments of my people, when they existed in their own civilizations, started a chain reaction that would change the foundation of my mind."

He goes on to say, "I felt that my entire life had been like that of a man who had wings of strength and splendor. From childhood this man had watched his brethren sweep the heavens and glide gracefully in the sunshine. But because his wings were a different color, he had been fooled into believing that he could not fly. He knew his wings looked the same, were built the same, flapped the same. But he never had proof. So he had never tried. Then he discovered in a remote cave, a cave that had been kept well-hidden, pictures of men of his color flying in the clouds. And on this glorious day, in desperation, he jumped off a cliff, was swooped up in the wings of truth, flapped his damnedest, and found he could fly above them all."

Maybe you have not experienced prejudice and poverty to the extreme that Jerrold Ladd did, but his experience of finding role models can benefit anyone trying to overcome an obstacle. We gain inspiration and encouragement from the stories of those who have succeeded before us.

"There are no magic solutions," says author George Fraser. However, he too believes that education is critical in overcoming prejudice. His advice? "Read about people who have succeeded despite racism. Seek out mentors and role models and learn about yourself.

Through education and knowledge of self, it is possible to overcome the obstacle of racism. Find ways over, around, and through it. Racism is a reality that many people have to face, but it is not a reason to fail."

Many schools have ethnic student centers (an African American student center, a Hispanic student center, a Middle Eastern student center, etc.). These offices can provide support in many ways—they can help you obtain financial aid, they can intervene in problems you may be having with the administration or professors, and they can introduce you to students who may be facing similar challenges. Some of the centers also offer mentoring programs in which they pair you with a member of the community.

Women in traditionally male-dominated fields such as engineering or science often find an effective support system when they join women's organizations in their field. Rama Moorthy, an engineer in technical sales, says that joining the Society of Women Engineers put her in touch with other women who deal with the same kinds of pressures she does.

When Anthea Coster was a graduate student in space physics at Rice University, she found that women friends in her field were a great support. "We studied together—more as a team than as a group competing against each other."

Being on your own can be scary, lonely, exciting, exhilarating, and sometimes plain uneventful. Balance the highs and lows by getting the rest, relaxation, and rejuvenation you need in order to feel inspired so that you can appreciate what is great in your surroundings and within yourself.

6
stand up
and be counted

Is there any way of predicting the capacity to lead? The only way I know is to look at college records. If they were leaders during the ages of 18 to 22, the odds are that they will emerge as leaders in middle life.

—DAVID OGILVY

Y ou've got to make it happen," says John Garcia, who cites belonging to organizations as the best way not only to enjoy yourself but also to learn to relate to people. John, who was a civil engineering major, was hired by Sandia National Laboratories in Albuquerque, New Mexico. Sandia sent John to Purdue to get a master's degree in structural engineering.

"Engineers are typically great theoreticians and scientists," says John, "but most of them have a hard time getting their ideas across." To balance his college experience, John worked part-time, skied, hiked, and was active in the honorary engineering society Beta Pi.

Lynne Ewing buried herself in her books during her freshman year at Notre Dame. "That was the worst semester I ever had," says Lynne, whose grades were far below the goals she had set for herself. "The next semester, I joined the choir, the school newspaper, and a religious group. My grades went way up. So did my morale, the number of friends I could count on, and my interest level. I kept busy, managed my time, and no longer had a reason to feel sorry for myself for being from out of state and away from my friends and family."

Dawn Pakluda began college at the University of Texas at Austin. She wishes she had joined extracurricular activities. "I could have had a lot more fun and met many more people during college," says Dawn. "Since I only studied and worked, I feel I don't have the strong friendships and rich experiences that college should provide."

My own extracurricular college activities included joining a sorority and several honorary societies, doing volunteer work at a hospice for cancer patients, and participating in the International Students Club's English tutoring program for foreign students.

Although large group projects taught me leadership in a broad context, the one-on-one contacts I developed through my other activities helped me to "read" people in business. I learned to listen, to question, to analyze problems, and to motivate even the most unenthused people.

Join extracurricular activities to expand your world. You'll be more interesting, and you'll learn to work with people. By better understanding others, you'll better understand yourself.

To succeed in the workplace, you must be a "team player." Those who give beyond what's expected command the respect of their peers and supervisors. Chances are greater that they'll be promoted to positions where they manage and motivate others. Being valuable to an organization in college will teach you how to become valuable to a company.

Darren Walker, a New York investment banker, was president of several organizations in college. As a student board member for the University of Texas Student Union, he learned how different people competed to run the union. "When you work with successful people from diverse backgrounds, you have to learn to work toward consensus. I learned to be open to different people and different ideas. Through extracurricular activities, I learned a great deal about politics, group dynamics, and egos." Learning those skills now will give you an advantage when you start your first job.

Companies want to hire employees who will go above and beyond what is expected of them. If you balance work, school, and play, you'll be prepared to juggle your career and personal life. You'll learn to naturally think of new ideas and projects, and you'll learn to be the first person to volunteer for additional responsibility. The busiest people are often the ones who are most likely to take on new projects because they know how to manage their time.

What exactly does the college recruiter learn about you from your extracurricular activities?

- You are a self-starter.
- You've got your act together enough to balance classes with activities.
- You like people and get along with them; you can be a team player.
- You aren't a one-dimensional grind or some gnome buried in your books. You know there's a world beyond the classroom.
- You have sought out career-related experience.

Sometimes extracurricular activities can lead you straight into the business world. Bob Rogers, a pre-law student, says, "Working as the associate editor of the student newspaper prepares me for my long-term goals by teaching me to write, analyze political issues, and persuade readers. I have interviewed attorneys and criticized their arguments, studied how the battle for public opinion works, observed office politics within the paper, and seen the results of different management approaches."

During her freshman year in college, Jeannine DeLoche became a writer for Columbia University's *Course Guide,* a student publication that reviews most of the classes at the college. After writing more articles than the rest of the staff, she was promoted to the post of executive editor. When she needed extra money that year and decided to apply for a job, she interviewed for positions as an editorial assistant, banking on her *Course Guide* experiences. Her first interview was for the editorial page of *The Wall Street Journal.* Says Jeannine, "I remember the interviewer saying, 'You have real editing experience. That's unusual in someone your age.' He offered me the job right then!" Jeannine continued to work as an assistant to the editorial features editor of the *Journal* while at Columbia. She's considering staying there after graduation. "In addition to joining clubs just for fun, try to find extracurriculars which may match your career interests. That way, you can develop the necessary skills and see if you enjoy the work," Jeannine advises.

participating

Y ou may belong to the right organization, but unless you get involved, you won't have much to show for it. Joe Durrett, the chief executive officer of Broderbund Software in Novato, California, says that when he considers applicants for his company, he looks for their record of accomplishment. If the record of accomplishment is more about having been at certain places than having done something there, this tips him off that the applicant probably won't work out.

Julie Balovich, a college senior at a large university, found that she had to be responsible for seeking out ways to become involved. "The first thing I learned about student organizations is that the best way to get involved and have people recognize you is to do the grungy work. During my freshman year, I participated in several functions of the student association, and in every one I stayed after and helped clean up. Each time, without fail, upper-class persons would approach me and introduce themselves."

In addition to collegiate-affiliated organizations to join, keep your eyes and ears open for other groups that might intrigue you. Consult the campus counseling center for lists of activities. Read the school paper. Check bulletin boards. Then dive in. If you don't like your first choice, get out. Once you find a group you like, participate fully. Volunteer to chair projects. Accept responsibility. Run for office. And if you don't get accepted by Kappa Psi Whatever or you get cut from the snorkeling squad, don't be discouraged. Try something else!

developing friendships

One of the greatest aspects of joining any organization is that you meet interesting people, some of who will become your close friends. Campus organizations will also introduce you to other students who are focused on their goals. Gregory Sapire, a law school graduate, recalls, "Working in student government put me in

MY TWO CENTS   *How Do I Apply It?*

Rui Lu, Johns Hopkins University

I moved to the United States in 1991 from Jiangsu, China (near Shanghai). My family likes to discuss many things ranging from history and politics to the arts. Often, we read books or watch movies and discuss their merits. For example, last summer, my Dad and I read *Clashes of Civilization*, and we analyzed it from different perspectives. My parents always have stressed the importance of being well-rounded and culturally sensitive. I've discovered that extracurricular activities can help me achieve both of these qualities.

Aside from my schoolwork, I am actively involved in organizations both at Johns Hopkins University (JHU) and also back home in New Jersey. At Hopkins, I am co-crisis director for the NATO committee of the JHU Model United Nations Conference (JHUMUNC). This club allows me to explore my interest in world affairs through organizing an event that offers a chance for high school students to obtain hands-on experience in this mock conference.

I am also the treasurer of Project Prevent, a student organization which provides free medical services to the underprivileged in Baltimore. Even though I am an economics major, and also the only non pre-med participant of this group, I have a strong interest in health care. Many times, students from poor social economic backgrounds are not able to receive the adequate care needed for them to develop properly. As a result, they suffer from health problems, which can inhibit their ability to function in school and ultimately lead a better life. I am committed to this club because I believe that everyone, regardless of their income level, should have a chance at a healthy life.

In addition to Hopkins, I am still actively involved in my local weekend Chinese school in New Jersey. Since coming to the States, I have attended weekend Chinese schools that local Chinese parents have helped organize. One of my most memorable experiences happened during one of the Chinese New Year festivals when I met Sang Lan, the famous gymnast who broke her back in a competition two years ago and became paralyzed. Even though she is in a wheelchair, she has so much passion for life. She still is an inspiration to me. Extracurricular activities help you meet so many wonderful people.

In addition to the activities listed above, I've also volunteered at the Chinese school as a language teacher and student newsletter editor. Three years ago, I was also an assistant camp counselor at the Year 2000 Root-Seeking Summer Camp in Beijing, China. Furthermore, I organized a pen-pal program between students in my Chinese school and those in China. I work with these students to allow them to retain their native cultural heritage while in the U.S. This way, instead of forgetting their Chinese heritage, these students find a way to straddle both cultural worlds—and so have I.

contact with a number of other ambitious students who challenged me to achieve my best. Through their experiences, they suggested opportunities—study abroad, summer enrichment programs, research positions—that I found interesting. If you hang out with people going places, you'll find yourself going places too." Another student advises, "Try to make friends with other students who are striving for excellence. They will inspire you to achieve more." That's excellent advice. Unless you're a social recluse, developing friendships in college will be central to your happiness.

becoming a leader

A leader is one who, among other things, motivates, teaches, trains, and organizes others. Those skills will help you in almost any career—whether you want to flip Whoppers at Burger King or become President of the United States. If you develop leadership skills in college, these will keep the door of management open for you. You may never want to manage anybody, but it's nice to be prepared enough to have the option.

Being a leader doesn't mean you have to run the country. But wherever you wind up, you will spend most of your time dealing with a small circle of people. Be a leader for them.

Bob Rogers tended to stay away from leadership positions until his black belt in tae kwon do thrust him into a leadership position.

Because he had achieved so much in this discipline, he was automatically seen as a leader. He didn't feel comfortable immediately, but his skill allowed him to offer strong leadership to the group. He felt that the experience gave him a chance to "see different leadership and teaching approaches and to hone leadership skills."

How do you become a leader? Well, if you haven't done it before, start small. Volunteer to head a committee. Then put as much energy into it as your studies allow. The most important part of your activity is gaining the goodwill of those you work with. As your confidence increases, accept more responsibility. Run for office. If you win, great—accept that as a sign that your peers respect you. If you lose, don't be discouraged. As Winston Churchill said, "Success is the ability to go from one failure to another with no loss of enthusiasm."

WHAT MAKES A GOOD PARTICIPANT?

- Contributes ideas
- Organizes events
- Volunteers to help
- Follows through on commitments

WHAT MAKES A GOOD LEADER?

- Has a vision of where the organization can go
- Makes decisions
- Motivates others
- Sets goals
- Plans and organizes
- Listens carefully
- Inspires people
- Delegates responsibility
- Shares credit
- Isn't arrogant
- Acts diplomatically
- Recognizes others' achievements and contributions

Don't worry if you've never led before. Give it a try and see how it feels. You may hate it, but you might love it. Either way, it pays to know. Student activities often have resources such as workshops and seminars to help you develop leadership skills.

doing volunteer work

There are many good reasons to volunteer. Volunteering offers the chance to develop both leadership and team-building skills. Also, you'll typically interact with a diverse group of volunteers, which will enrich your life perspective and enhance creativity.

Gretchen Van Fossan, national program manager for the Points of Light Foundation, says, "Service is an incredibly valuable experience both in and out of college, particularly if you're willing to step out of your own familiar and comfortable environment in order to participate with others in community work. Helping people in situations that are different from the ones you've grown up in and working in a group with diverse perspectives are invaluable in building a real and balanced view of the world around you."

Increasingly, schools are making community service part of the core curriculum. For example, at the University of Maryland School of Law, the entire clinical program is centered on volunteer work. In order to graduate, students must integrate two hundred hours of community service into their regular coursework. To meet that requirement, some law students have helped local high school students reclaim abandoned properties in the depressed Baltimore neighborhood of Park Heights. "One group is white and one is African American," says Daniel P.

Henson III, commissioner of housing and community development, "but there's a great camaraderie between them." Next, UM is opening a law office in one of the formerly abandoned buildings to take on everything from landlord–tenant disputes to misdemeanors.

Several companies encourage community service as part of their company philosophies. For example, take IBM, which has implemented numerous community service programs to help its employees balance the demands of their jobs and their personal and family lives. One such program, Community Service Assignments, allows IBM employees to continue earning their salaries while working for nonprofit organizations.

CSA helps selected nonprofit tax-exempt community service organizations in times of need, and at the same time supports IBM employees with special talents in the efforts to help such organizations.

Volunteer work can also be great for relieving stress because it takes you out of yourself. Your history final will seem less catastrophic after you've worked an afternoon in a children's hospital ward, or played basketball with a fatherless child, or analyzed a famous painting with a group of high school students.

Your participation in service projects also says something very positive about you: your future employer will know that you care about people. Therefore, on the job, the chances are greater that you'll treat others with sensitivity and respect. When you face unexpected snags, for instance, you'll be less likely to take out your frustrations on those around you.

If you've been a volunteer or feel that volunteering is an important part of your "life philosophy," your future employer will have reason to believe that you are a good hire—conscientious, ethical, and concerned about the well-being of others, not just your own advancement. Employers want to hire people who will be role models for others; they want people who care about others above and beyond the rudiments of the professional relationship. Good citizenship is good business.

organizations

So where do you begin? There are literally hundreds of clubs on and off campus. Here are several ways to find out more about campus activities:

- Student activities office
- School newspaper
- Campus fliers
- Orientation week activities
- Friends and siblings

Start brainstorming about what you might like to join. Then gather information and join up. Start small if you're not used to groups. Try one and then another a few months later. Here are a few suggestions:

CAMPUS ORGANIZATIONS

Alumni Association
Amnesty International campus
   representative
Association for African Americans
Chess club
Crisis intervention center
Residence hall association
Greeks (fraternities and
   sororities)
Honorary service societies
International student club
Intramural sports and
   recreation
Karate club
Marketing club

Political groups
Pre-law Society
Red Cross campus
   representative
Religious groups
Sailing club
Ski club
Student bar association
Student government
Student media
Student newspaper
Student Union
Women's groups
Yearbook

VOLUNTEER ORGANIZATIONS

Campus hospital

Childhood abuse center

Drug addiction clinics

Home for the mentally retarded

March of Dimes

Mental health services

Nursing homes

Planned Parenthood

Political campaigns

Hospice program

Hospital care

Humane Society

League of Women Voters

Public Library

Red Cross

Ronald McDonald House

Sierra Club

World Wildlife Federation

ACADEMIC AND PROFESSIONAL HONORARY SOCIETIES

Phi Beta Kappa

Tau Beta Pi

Phi Kappa Phi

Blue Key National Honor Society

Mortar Board

Golden Key National Honor

Society

Who's Who Among American

College Students

setting limits

To what extent should you participate? This varies according to who you are. For example, if you're a skilled opera singer or lead the nation in a competitive sport, you may have to focus entirely on that to be the best. Take Steve Kendall, for instance. Steve's college grades were average, but Steve was captain of his college tennis team. Although his rigorous training and travel left him little spare time, his athletic and academic record prompted the college recruiter for Procter & Gamble to seek Steve out for an interview during his senior year.

"Because I was successful in a competitive sport, Procter & Gamble believed I would apply the same principles of diligence, effort, teamwork, and competition to my future career," says Steve. P&G's faith was well placed: Steve worked for them for several years before accepting another position as sales and marketing director of Nabisco.

So, what if your forehand is unimpressive? Does that mean that extracurricular activities are off limits? Of course not.

Leigh Talmage, for example, didn't focus on any one activity, as Steve did. She spread herself out and joined several organizations. Leigh, now trader for a foreign bank, was president of her sorority, qualified to be a member of scholastic honor societies each year, and spent two semesters in London. "Get activities under your belt," advises Leigh. "That's what counts the most at interview time." Leigh is one of five women out of 250 people in the world who trade international debt. Leigh is considering another career, working for a nonprofit organization. "All of the activities and leadership positions I held in college have given me solid, transferable management skills," she says. "Because of these skills, I feel comfortable moving from one industry to another."

"It's problems with people, not problems in engineering, which constitute the real power struggles," says Steven Fisher, a senior engineer for Westinghouse in San Francisco. "If you swallow your ego and learn from others in your small group, you'll pick up the commonsense aspects of the job, which the technical training you receive in college doesn't provide."

Steven, who graduated from Stanford with a degree in mechanical engineering, cites extracurricular activities as the best way to learn about people and how to get things done: "That's how you prepare yourself to be successful in the long term with a company. You must realize how people work, what motivates them, and what the company can do to help them be most happy and most productive."

If you're shy and you're not used to being around people, it may be enough to join one organization and participate in it so that you become comfortable with the members and perhaps run for office. Stretch yourself, but take things in steps, not quantum leaps.

what if you don't get accepted into organization X?

Does that mean you've failed? Of course not. You only fail if you don't try. It sounds trite, but it's true. I didn't get a lot of the things I applied for in college, but I didn't let it stop me. My freshman year, I didn't make it into the freshman honorary society.

I was disappointed. But before I said, "To hell with it," I stopped to think about *why* I didn't make it in. Had I blown the interview? Was I not well-rounded enough? Were my grades not good enough? Most of the answers to these questions were yes, and the other people who made it were better qualified than I was. I worked on the areas that needed improvement and, at the end of the year, I applied for the sophomore honorary society. I got in.

I was seriously disappointed when I applied for the Rotary scholarship and didn't even make the first cut. I had invested a lot of time and energy into filling out the lengthy application, getting all my professors to write me letters of recommendation, and fully researching the three countries where I wanted to study. They wanted an "ambassador of goodwill," which I thought I could be! But there were others who were more qualified: I had to accept that.

And there were plusses that came from that disappointment. I learned how much I truly loved studying other cultures. I swore to make travel a major life priority. I also met fascinating people who were also applying for the scholarship: one of them, a unique person who spoke fluent Chinese, Spanish, and French, became my true love for the next two years. (He didn't make the first cut either.)

When you get a job after college, you may be initially passed over for a promotion you want. Chances are you were not as well qualified as the person who got the job. Find out specifically what you can do to ensure that you get the next opening, and *take action.*

How you deal with defeat says a lot about your overall

character. If you learn in college how to handle defeat graciously, you'll be well prepared for the working world, where you'll need to transform tough situations into new challenges and opportunities.

So don't let defeats defeat you. Look at the situation in a broader context. Extract the positive things you learned and go on to the next challenge. Don't let the temporary setbacks take any wind out of your sails.

dealing with your supporters (and detractors)

Anytime you join a group of people and you assert your opinions about what you think the organization should or shouldn't do, you will have some people who agree with you and others who won't. Sometimes, especially if you are leading an organization, you will have to stick your neck out for what you believe in while communicating to others your vision of what the group can do.

Be cool. If people always agreed with you, you would be among a dull group. The best ideas and the best teamwork come from stimulating discussions that allow all points of view to be considered. When people disagree with you—and sometimes during college and in the real world they will strongly disagree with you—keep a positive attitude and remain confident. Acknowledge their opposing viewpoints and thank them for their suggestions. Remaining mature and controlled will help you put the situation into perspective and allow you to reaffirm your position. Remember, leaders are sometimes unpopular in some camps. That's okay. It's helpful to get used to this feeling in college—to let your skin get thicker—so that you will be more resilient when you deal with people of varying maturity levels once you start working.

Part of being both a leader and a participant is learning how to draw out the best suggestions and ideas from others. Often, discussing your thoughts with your colleagues helps you to crystallize an already good idea of your own. Recognize that sometimes it's good to change your mind, to concede someone else's points or plans. This is all part of developing your judgment.

the real world

I don't like work—no one does—but I like what is in work—the chance to find yourself. Your own reality—not for others— what no other person can ever know.

—JOSEPH CONRAD, HEART OF DARKNESS

The summer after his freshman year at the University of Wisconsin, Jeff Colquhoun worked at the Kellogg factory near his parents' home in Michigan. Occupation? Well, what does one do at a cereal factory? Eat and run?

Guess again. Jeff frosted flakes. And when finished with his frosting duties, he stuffed coupons by hand into boxes the machines had missed. His was a manual counteroffensive to mechanical incompetence. It was an incredibly boring job. But for Jeff it was by no means a waste of time. Besides earning money to help pay tuition, Jeff learned several things that helped clarify his career direction.

1. The Kellogg experience opened Jeff's eyes to people whose backgrounds differed from his. There were many people there who hadn't had

125

Jeff's advantages, whom he might never have encountered in his "ordinary" college experience or in a more typical summer internship for the up-and-coming college student. The job helped Jeff appreciate his education. He developed real respect for people from all walks of life who worked hard for a living, regardless of job title.

2. He did not let the boring aspects of the job interfere with his work or his attitude. For the purpose of sanity, he stretched his mind and imagination. He went through the letters of the Greek alphabet forward and backward. He marveled at the mind of the engineer who designed the machine. (He thanked God for him, in fact.)

3. Jeff learned that when you're not in an ideal situation (we seldom are), you've got to expand your mind and envision a broader context. Idle is bust.

Thirteen years later, Jeff is a doctor of ophthalmology in New York City. He went through years of studying and rigorous on-the-job training in emergency settings and operating rooms. What he learned at the Kellogg factory that summer in college—to see even the most difficult or mundane tasks in a broader context—helped him in his pursuit of medicine.

Joy Wake, a marketing planner at Hallmark in Kansas City, Missouri, had several part-time jobs during college. As the youngest of nine children, Joy supported herself 100 percent through college. She had several work–study jobs and one summer internship in Washington, DC. And she saved enough money to travel one semester through Europe.

"Hallmark hired me because I had worked hard to put myself through college," Joy says. "They believed in me because I had a successful track record. They knew I could overcome obstacles. They also recognized that I had done different things to make myself stand out."

Instead of attending school during the day and working at night, Chris Barnett did the opposite. He got an entry-level job paying $185 a week selling space in the yellow pages. He took three classes at night per semester. Although it took Chris two additional years to graduate from college after transferring from the University of Southern California to Columbia, he feels the trade-off—financial and experiential—was worth it.

Chris is graduating this spring. He has been promoted three times within the last two years and is now supervising eleven people. It's true that Chris hasn't had time to join extracurricular activities or participate in intramural sports, but he has, at age twenty-four, earned a living, put himself through school, and maintained a 3.2 grade point average at an Ivy League college. He's learned firsthand about leadership through direct professional experience.

Gaining work experience in college is one of the best ways to prepare for your future. First, you learn to support yourself, partially or entirely, which tells your future employer that you have a sense of commitment, responsibility, and financial savvy. Second—and most important—you acquire skills and techniques that will prepare you to work with others.

what work is best for you?

Almost any job you have during college will benefit you in ways far greater than the financial. Obviously, some jobs are better than others. Before you take the first job you apply for, spend some time learning about yourself and the kinds of jobs available on and off campus.

Phoebe Finn applied to several expensive acting schools in New York and London while studying drama at the University of Maryland. To support herself and save money, she drove the campus shuttle bus at night. Not glamorous for someone aspiring to be Meryl Streep, but the job served its purpose. It allowed her to save money and attend the London School of Dramatics. Phoebe's London experience helped her land her first big job in the Folger Shakespeare Library's production of *Macbeth*.

Of course, if you've got your sights set on a highly competitive field, it may be worth it to take the extra steps necessary to get a job providing experience that will help you later on.

"Broadcasting is fiercely competitive," says Nancy Kilroy. To prepare herself during college at Yale, Nancy worked at National

MY TWO CENTS *How Do I Apply It?*

Angela Cryan, Central Michigan University

After I graduated from high school someone asked a question I had been dreading. "What are you going to do now?" I was fortunate enough to have the answer. I would go to college, of course. Then someone asked, "What will you major in?" That was the worst question because I had no idea. It took me three years of my college career to decide on a major. (Mostly because the university required that I do so before my senior year.)

I chose my major on two factors. First, I liked my current part-time job and I received friendly feedback from my co-workers. Second, one nagging friend said that I would excel with a major in communications, and from what I knew, she was right.

I'd been working for the human resource department on campus since my freshmen year. I worked in the training and development office along with the employee relations office. I was fortunate enough to love my job and what I did. My title was clerical aide, but I managed to do more than just filing paperwork for my bosses. I was given work related to marketing and publications developed within my department. Even though I was only making minimum wage, I embraced the responsibility because I knew the experience would help me in the future.

I also was able to attend many of the training meetings presented by my department. I realized through this job that it was not necessarily answering phones that I enjoyed, but more the interaction with the staff on campus. I was trained in customer service and had a lot of fun with my co-workers at the office. They were able to increase my responsibilities over the years and allow me to grow at a pace much faster than normal student employees. They also were considerate of my class schedule and gave extra time off to study if needed. During an interview with my boss about my major, she suggested human resources. Although I considered this option, I did not like many aspects of a business education. I enjoyed the personal side of working. This led me through the career services department and an exploration into interpersonal and public communication (IPC).

This major was perfect because I got to talk about talking. As my mother said, there were times when you weren't able to get me to stop talking. This major also was more focused on the humanistic side of business. With the organizational concentration, I was able to learn common business practices and how they affect a work environment. As my friend had told me several times, it was important for me to consider communications because I was naturally good at communicating. I am now in my final year of school with an organizational concentration in communications and a human development minor. I am planning on starting a career within the training domain of a company allowing me to follow in my boss's footsteps and become a trainer.

Public Radio, where she learned how to interview people, how to be persistent, and how to pull together information for a five-minute broadcast. "Experience is everything in broadcasting," says Nancy. "You'd better learn early on that most people have already worked at least two jobs in the profession by the time they graduate."

What to Consider

As discussed in Chapter 3, there are three basic areas of work: working with people, information, or objects. You might enjoy each of these areas, but if you're like most people, one appeals to you more than the other two.

Richard Bolles, the author of *What Color Is Your Parachute?*, identifies several characteristics that can help you analyze what area best suits you. How do you answer the following questions?

PEOPLE-RELATED SKILLS
Taking Instruction

- Do you like to take instruction and then carry out a plan?
- Do you enjoy executing and providing support services?

Serving

- Do you like helping, teaching, waiting on, or serving others?

Sensing, Feeling

- Are you intuitive with respect to the needs of others?
- Are you generally responsive, empathic, warm, and able to understand the position of others?

Communicating

- Are you a good listener? Do you question others?
- Do you enjoy writing, giving speeches, and giving instructions to others?

Persuading

- Do you like to influence, inspire, and recruit others?
- Do you like publicizing and promoting causes, people, or things?

Performing, Amusing

- Do you like to entertain others?
- Do you like to dramatize your point of view or your own experiences as a means of teaching others?

Managing, Supervising

- Do you like to plan, oversee, and develop programs with people?
- Do you like to encourage and critically evaluate others, using your expertise to help them to improve?

Negotiating, Decision-Making

- Do you like to discuss, confer, and resolve difficult issues?
- Are you skilled in conflict management?
- Do you appreciate and consider opposing points of view?

Founding, Leading

- Are you able to work with little or no supervision?
- Do you have maverick qualities? That is, do you like to forge your own, possibly better path?
- Can you enlist the enthusiasm and support of others?
- Do you delegate authority? Do you trust others to execute a job?

Advising, Consulting

- Do you enjoy helping others resolve a physical, emotional, or spiritual problem?
- Do you enjoy being an expert, reading, and keeping up with what is happening in one field?
- Do you make effective use of contacts? Do you give others insight and perspective on their problems?

Holistic Counseling

- Do you like to facilitate the growth of others by helping them to identify solutions to their problems?

Training

- Do you like to teach others through lecture, demonstration, or practice?

INFORMATION-RELATED SKILLS

Observing

- Do you like to study the behavior of people, information, or things?

Comparing

- Do you enjoy analyzing two or more different things?

Copying, Storing, and Retrieving

- Do you like keeping records, storing data, memorizing, filing, or reviewing information?

Computing

- Do you enjoy working with numbers, taking inventory, solving statistical problems, using a computer, budgeting, projecting, or processing data?

Researching

- Do you like uncovering hard-to-find facts and information?

Analyzing

- Do you like to break things down, taking information apart and examining it?

Organizing

- Does giving structure and order to things turn you on? Do you always have a place for everything? Do you typically classify material?

Evaluating

- Are you a diagnoser or inspector? Do you like to assess, decide, appraise, and summarize information or situations?

Visualizing

- Are you able to perceive patterns and images? Do you picture things you want to do before you do them? Do you enjoy painting, drawing, or designing?

Improving, Adapting

- Do you like to take what others have developed and expand upon it? Are you good at improvising, improving, and arranging?

Creating, Synthesizing

- Do you like to pull together seemingly unrelated things? Do you like to develop new concepts, approaches, and interpretations?

Designing

- Do you like to create models, sculpture, or other things?

Planning, Developing

- Do you like to oversee and carry out a plan? Do you prioritize and develop strategies?

Expediting

- Do you naturally tend to speed up a task by organizing your objectives ahead of time? Do you have a sense of urgency or immediacy?

Achieving

- Do you enjoy accomplishing tasks or specific goals? Do you like to increase productivity and create results?

OBJECT-RELATED SKILLS

Manipulating

- Do you enjoy working with your hands? Do you like using your body to move objects?

Working with the Earth and Nature

- Do you like nurturing, weeding, harvesting?

Feeding, Emptying (Machines)

- Do you like placing, stacking, dumping, and removing things from machines?

Monitoring (Machines)

- Do you like monitoring and adjusting machines, pushing buttons, flipping switches, adjusting controls?

Using Tools

- Do you enjoy using hand tools?

Operating Equipment or Machines

- Do you like to have specialized knowledge about equipment or machines?

Operating Vehicles

- Do you like to drive, pilot, or steer vehicles?

Precision Working

- Do you like jobs such as keypunching, drilling, sandblasting, making miniatures, or performing other specialized tasks with your hands?

Setting Up

- Do you like to construct or set up displays, machinery, or equipment?

Repairing

- Do you like to restore, repair, or do preventive maintenance?

As a freshman, you may not be able to complete this questionnaire. But as a junior or senior, you'll have many more experiences under your belt. For now, just get a general idea of your strongest suit.

Below is a list of job possibilities.

COMMON JOBS FOR COLLEGE STUDENTS

Campus

People	Information	Objects
Resident assistant	Word processor	Library aide
Campus guide	Administrative assistant	Lab technician
Health aide	Secretarial aide	Mechanic
Study tutor	Writer (yearbook or	Maintenance assistant
Lecturer	campus newspaper)	Groundskeeper
		Researcher

Community

People	Information	Objects
Waiter/waitress	Legal assistant	Short-order cook
Sales clerk	Secretary	Gas-station attendant
Host/hostess	Word processor	Technician
Bartender		Gardener/yard worker

where to find work

Many colleges have job placement centers right on campus. Often campus jobs are listed there, and professors may also list job vacancies there (babysitting, housework, construction, house-sitting). You'll find a wide range of jobs and hours. Getting a job through a placement center can also put you in contact with professors who may introduce you to fields you might not be exposed to through your major.

The Co-Op Experience

Another way to get "real-world" experience is to enroll in a cooperative program. These programs are sponsored by a wide range of corporations and are designed to give students work experience while they are taking classes. You can find out more about these programs through the college placement center.

Mick McCormick, a director of sales for Nike, worked in a co-op program during college. He studied electrical engineering and finance and worked for IBM as a hardware and software programmer. In addition to providing him with a stable income during college, co-op experience helped him to realize that he did not want to work with computers all day. At the same time, it gave him invaluable computer experience.

"I have the technical knowledge to do word processing, PowerPoint presentations, and other computer applications I use in my present work. I also learned a lot about my working style. I needed a career where there were no barriers to getting a job done. I don't thrive when there is strong managerial control over my work."

If Waiting on Tables Is Not for You . . .

If you decide to forgo a traditional part-time job, such as waiting on tables, for a more educational, experience-earning job, such as working for a legal clerk, you'll have to demonstrate to your potential employer that you are worth hiring despite your limited experience. If you can convince the person interviewing you that you are a quick learner, extremely reliable, motivated above and beyond what is expected, and truly interested in pursuing a career in that area, chances are you'll get the job despite your youth and inexperience. Remember that the people interviewing you were once in your place. A determined and inquisitive mind and the capacity to work hard and achieve enabled them to be where they are today. If your potential employer believes you have the same qualities that contributed to his success, it is in his best interest to hire you. After all, you will be graduating in a few years, and you could be an attractive employee. Ask for the chance to prove what you can do. Both you and the employer could have a lot to gain.

If you don't get the experience-earning job you sought, don't despair. Follow up your interviews with a thank-you letter and reconfirm your interest in the company. If you try again six months or a year later, the company may be in a better position to take you on as an apprentice. If you know that the experience gained on the job would be more valuable than the wages you would earn and you can afford it, volunteer for the first six months. It might pay off in the long run.

The experience that a "real-life" job will provide could make the difference when you are competing for the job you most want during your last semester of college. If you have solid job experience, you will probably get hired even if the other candidate has superior grades and a more impressive background. You learned firsthand about the job and, consequently, you have much more to offer than someone without such experience.

Whatever the part-time job you hold—be it gas-station attendant, hotel clerk, or real estate apprentice—you'll learn to juggle work, school, and other activities while sustaining your motivation and sense of self-reliance. You'll have the best-rounded education upon graduation; you'll gain satisfaction from knowing that you are self-reliant, independent, and responsible for your own accomplishments; and you'll gather important data to help you make career decisions in your junior and senior years.

a final note

J enny Harris has been out of college for three years, and she is a producer for business news at CNN. She believes the key to her success (in addition to good grades) was her commitment to part-time work and internships. "I tried to get exposed to as many different industries as possible to get a firsthand look at how that industry worked. After working as a paralegal in a law firm for several summers, I realized that maybe I didn't want to be a lawyer. I had to sit back and rethink my plans."

Jenny worked on a committee at Cornell University that brought speakers to campus. While on the committee she did a variety of jobs—advertising and promotion, budgeting, setting up for the speaker. She enjoyed the work, but she didn't feel that she would enjoy doing it as a career. After reflecting and talking with other professionals, she decided that broadcasting might be a career she would enjoy.

In order to see what broadcasting was like, she worked for the student-run radio station at Cornell. That work allowed her to experience reporting, broadcasting, writing, and news meetings—all of the facets of putting together a broadcast. She liked it, so she applied for an internship with the prestigious MacNeil/Lehrer news program in Washington, DC. During her internship there, the Gulf War broke out.

"I got to be in the newsroom and experience the excitement. After this internship, I was convinced that this was the field I wanted to pursue. When I graduated, I worked for CNN as an intern for four months without pay before I was hired as a production assistant.

"All of my jobs and internships provided me with a perspective. I knew something was missing when I was working for the law firm; I wasn't happy or comfortable in the work environment. I never would have discovered what I really liked without getting the firsthand work experience that I did."

intern we trust

GETTING THE INTERNSHIP

What we learn to do, we learn by doing. —THOMAS JEFFERSON

I think the most valuable thing a college student can do while in college is to intern in his or her field of interest," says Stephanie Ward, who was the director of casework for Big Brothers/Big Sisters in Dallas. Internships help you learn if the profession you're considering is what you really want for a career. If you do, the internship gives you credibility in the job market and a leg up on those with no experience.

"I was responsible for hiring caseworkers," explains Stephanie. "What type of internship, how they performed while at their internship, and references from their internship carried more weight in my hiring decision than grades. If a decision came down to

139

two applicants and one had more experience in the field than the other and could verbalize what he or she had learned and discovered about him- or herself, then this would be the applicant I would hire."

Even if the only thing you discover from your internship is that you don't like the work, you're still ahead. You will have invested only your summer, not your life. Sometimes students really enjoy the coursework in a particular field, but when they actually have the opportunity to do the job, they find they don't like it. That happened to Jill Ruvidich, who had wanted to be an accountant since high school. "I really enjoyed studying accounting; however, an internship between my junior and senior years proved I found the real stuff extremely boring."

Rod Garcia, admissions recruiter for the MBA program at the University of Chicago, says that internships are very useful for people who don't yet know what they want to do. "Internships give students an idea of what's out there. The experience that even an unpaid internship provides is just as valuable as, if not more valuable than, some of your key college courses."

Rama Moorthy, an engineering sales specialist, loved her engineering courses in college. She did well in her classes and received several job offers. "When it came down to it, none of the actual jobs interested me. I decided to get an MBA and apply my engineering degree in a way I would enjoy. During graduate school, I make sure to intern in several different areas so I could see what it was like doing the work I was studying. This time, when I graduated I had a much better idea of what I wanted to do."

Brigitt Berry, a quality development consultant, had several different internships in college. One of the most valuable came about through a representative she met at the college's career fair. "Different professionals had come to the college to talk about their fields of expertise. I sat down with a human resources representative and spoke with him at length about the profession—what it included and what it would take to enter the field. I was really impressed with him and what he had to say. When I look back on that conversation, I have to smile, because I asked him all sorts of questions that were of interest to me, but I never really bothered to ask him what he did with the company or if he liked his profession. I spent no time making it a two-way conversation.

"Two days later, I went to the college career center to get his address and found out he was the vice president of personnel for a Fortune 500 company. I wrote and asked if I could spend a month with his company in New York. He was impressed with my quick request and flew me to New York six months later.

"During my experience with his organization, I learned that I was not at all interested in the communications department, but that I *was* interested in the training and development department."

In addition to giving you a ground-level view of the profession, internships can also open the door for full-time employment when you graduate. So keep in mind that the organization you intern for will be checking you out, too. Rita Rather is a management information systems senior at the University of Illinois. An honor student with a strong personality, she so impressed management at the Cellular Telephone Company in Chicago during her internship last summer that they offered her a full-time job upon her graduation in the spring.

internships during school

J im Cochran, an economics major from Los Alamos, New Mexico, had three internships during college. From each one he learned something different.

During his sophomore year, Jim had an unpaid internship working twelve hours a week with a commercial real estate company, Kimmel Property Management. This was Jim's first exposure to business, and it enabled him to build confidence and to establish valuable contacts. Four years later, when Jim began his first job out of college, he talked with the president of Kimmel to ask advice on his future career. Today, Jim is still in contact with several people from his first internship.

The second internship was in a law firm where Jim worked ten hours a week during the school year. Jim learned here that he did not want to become a lawyer. He still did not know what he really wanted to do, but at least he was learning what he did *not* want to do.

During his senior year, Jim worked ten hours a week for Merrill Lynch. He wanted to explore finance and investing and to continue making contacts. He enjoyed the job at Merrill Lynch, but didn't feel passionate enough about it to make it a career. He opted not to pursue a career in investing and got his first job with a real estate consulting firm.

When you know what you want to do, it can be valuable to let one internship lead to another in the same field of interest. This shows future employers that you are not only interested in them, you are *very* interested in them. Gordon Bock, a former reporter with both *U.S. News & World Report* and *Time*, was the youngest news director ever at Columbia University's radio station during his sophomore year. One day, the nationally syndicated Campus Radio Voice called for an intern. Gordon said, "I'm interested." He was hired, and over the next two years he was heard over the air at 460 colleges nationwide, interviewing celebrities and newsmakers. That internship led to the most prestigious one of all: becoming the first undergraduate in the history of the school to teach communications at Columbia's Graduate School of Journalism.

The result: when Gordon graduated, he moved immediately to a reporting job with AP Dow Jones in New York, writing radio copy. Three months later, he was hired by UPI New York at a third-year pay scale (based largely on his college jobs), and four years after that, he was hired by *U.S. News & World Report*. At the age of twenty-six, when many reporters are moving from one-town to three-town beats, Gordon was given a job covering eight states and half of Pennsylvania at a major national magazine.

Landing good internships, Gordon says, can be very important. And once you have them, he says, make the most of them. "Be gung-ho about whatever you do."

Summer Internships

"Summer activity is a great indicator of future job success," says Dee Milligan, first vice president and director of insurance marketing for Kemper Financial Company in Chicago, who interviews and hires many graduates straight from college. "I want to see that the applicant has taken initiative. I'm not interested in someone who has just messed around and not thought about using his or her summers wisely."

Dee says that working during the summer in a standard corporate environment gives students the opportunity to learn about the workplace—by diving in and experiencing it for themselves. It's the kind of education you can't get in the classroom.

Brenda White is from Ainsworth, Iowa, a town of five hundred people. She attended Augustana, a small Lutheran college in Illinois. During her junior year, Brenda applied for a nonpaying summer internship with the United Nations. She was selected as one of twenty college students in the country to come to New York.

Although the internship was nonpaying, Brenda talked to several people at the financial aid office at Augustana to see if she could get funding. And she did.

The most valuable part of Brenda's experience? She became "street smart." She learned to survive—and thrive—in a big city. After that summer in New York, Brenda felt herself a match for any environment.

Jeff Cantany is an economics major who hopes to work for a nonprofit agency in international development. To qualify, he needs to go into the Peace Corps, and they require construction skills. So what did he do the summer after his freshman year? He worked for a builder in New Mexico. He earned a good salary, learned a trade, and was introduced to a culture very different from that of his native New York.

Winter Internships

Many companies and firms have programs for students during the winter semester break. During his senior year at Columbia, Tim Dalton had a full-time four-week internship in January with the

Lawyers Committee for Human Rights in New York City. Tim worked with other volunteers on LCHR reports about human rights violations and refugee issues.

"I learned about issues not covered in the newspapers," says Tim. "Although I wasn't paid, the internship was invaluable because I gained insight into the nonprofit organizations which rely heavily on volunteers. I provided them with much-needed labor, but most of all, I enjoyed the work."

internships after graduation

Think about internships after college, too. Kim Caldwell already had a B.A. in art history when she began her six-month internship at the Metropolitan Museum of Art in New York City. Kim was able to work in several administrative areas of the museum and visit other museums in the city. She got the job through Aniso, a monthly job posting put out by the American Association of Museums.

"Becoming involved in a professional organization kept me abreast of openings in the museum field as well as informing me of the latest trends in museum policies," Kim said.

no pay? okay

Internship work seldom provides a paycheck. Particularly in some industries, unpaid internships are the norm. Your reward is the experience. This means, quite obviously, that you may have to work a part-time job to help pay for your living expenses.

I was a summer intern in Washington, DC, between my sophomore and junior years. I worked without pay for Common Cause, a grassroots lobbying organization. I attended Senate and House hearings and reported on the Clean Air Act and the daily debate on the constitutional amendment to balance the budget.

On the less glamorous side, this internship didn't pay the bills. Therefore, I worked as a waitress at an Italian restaurant atop an apartment building overlooking the Washington monuments. Because the restaurant was expensive, I made good money in tips, so I only had to work three nights a week.

I remember working on the Fourth of July and feeling glum because all my friends were down on the Mall watching the fireworks and listening to the Beach Boys concert. However, I was lucky to be in Washington. I was also lucky to have a part-time job that enabled me to have my nonpaying, though thoroughly rewarding summer internship.

meeting mentors

Lisa Heinlein, a special education teacher, learned a great deal about how to be an excellent teacher from watching other great teachers. "Allow yourself to be taught," Lisa says. "Don't be afraid to try things and make mistakes—that's how you learn."

Lenny Feder, now a senior at Columbia, had his first internship during his sophomore year. He worked for three weeks at American Marketing. Though he had held a lot of different jobs, this was his first experience in the corporate world. His boss, who happened to have belonged to the same fraternity as Lenny when he attended college, served as a mentor. He let Lenny sit in on meetings, allowed him to help plan projects from day one, and even gave him advice on what type of suit to wear. "My mentor gave me a sense of what skills I'd need in the business world. But I couldn't just copy him. I learned those skills by myself—with my mentor serving as a guide."

Through your internships, you'll meet people who can be your teachers. Choose two or three people whom you respect to be your mentors. Pick their brains to find answers to the following questions:

- How could I do my job better?
- What could I do at school to prepare myself for the industry?
- How did you become interested in this industry?
- What are your toughest challenges?
- What part of the job do you like the most?
- What will be the toughest challenge facing the industry over the next five years?
- Where is the growth potential?
- If you were interviewing me today, would I get the job? If not, why?

- What qualities do you look for in a qualified applicant?

Getting answers to these questions will help you learn about the profession and about yourself. You'll gain insight, and your employers will gain respect for your initiative.

developing a professional self-image

O ne of the transitions you will have to make when you start your first job after college is the change from seeing yourself as a student to seeing yourself as a legitimate professional. Internships can give you the opportunity to develop your professional self-image.

Carla Schnurr spent a summer on a fellowship in science and mass communications. The fellowship, which was sponsored by the American Association for the Advancement of Science, placed fifteen students in reporting positions in radio, newspapers, television, and magazines around the country.

Carla joined the science desk at the *Atlanta Journal-Constitution,* where she was assigned stories with other science reporters. She learned by doing. The editor would give her a story and it was her job to research it, conduct the pertinent interviews, and write it. The editor and the other reporters coached her as she worked through each phase of the job.

"I gained confidence by being thrown into new situations where I was expected to perform as a professional rather than as a student. The internship helped me to develop my 'reporter's persona,' to be comfortable talking with all kinds of people as an adult. I remember being very nervous on my first interview with the new director of the American Cancer Society. As we began talking, however, I became interested in the person and the work he did. From then on I lost my feelings of shyness around people in prominent positions. My interviewing skills really grew with that newfound confidence."

The people Carla worked with became mentors and role models. "They have become real friends in the workplace. Through their experience, I got to see alternative routes to my goals which I might not have thought of on my own."

how to get the internship

et's hope that I've convinced you that an internship is worth pursuing. Now what? First, know that you *will* get a job as an intern. Banish all doubts—they aren't going to help you. Believe you are going to succeed.

Second, realize that securing an internship is very much like interviewing for your "real" job at the end of your senior year. In fact, the whole process of writing your resume, interviewing, and landing the internship is *exactly the preparation you'll need* for your full-fledged job search upon graduation. Now for the practical steps.

What to Do

1. Get a copy of one of the current summer internship directories for college students, or make an appointment at your school's career office. I also recommend Betsy Bauer's *Getting Work Experience*. (See Appendix B also.)

2. From the college directory and/or other resources, make a list of the internship positions that interest you. Select at least twenty.

3. Review your list carefully, thinking about which skills a potential employer might look for in an applicant.

4. Take stock of your qualifications. Look at the skills listed below and ask yourself two questions: (1) Which of these skills can I offer my potential employer? and (2) What other skills not listed here can I contribute to the internship positions? In the column on the right, add your own words to describe your strengths and give examples of something you've done that illustrates your know-how. For instance, if you've served as the head of a school club, describe how this experience helped you develop leadership abilities. The more specific you are, the better prepared you'll be for your job search.

SKILL:

My strengths in this area and an example of what I've done that demonstrates this ability:

Organizing

_____

_____

Working with others

_____

_____

Developing ideas

_____

_____

Writing/researching

_____

_____

Prioritizing time

_____

_____

Observing

_____

_____

Repairing things

_____

_____

Founding/leading

_____

_____

Paying attention to detail

_____

_____

Following instructions

_____

_____

Speaking in public

_____

_____

Other

_____

_____

Where to Go

Geography may play a part in which internship you choose. For instance, if you're interested in banking, New York, Chicago, Los Angeles, and San Francisco would be great cities to work in for a summer. If you're interested in computers, you could work in almost any large metropolitan area, although California's Silicon Valley might be the best. Maybe you don't know which career interests you yet. No problem. Half your classmates don't know either, but they're probably not taking steps to find out. Pat yourself on the back. Okay, that's enough. Now back to work . . .

If you can afford it, seek contrast. If you're from a small town, apply for a spot in a big city. The more diversity you experience, the more versatile you'll be. Working in a new city conveys maturity, confidence, and determination to your future employers. I waited tables on the weekends so I could afford to intern for a summer in New York. I'm from Arizona, so living in Manhattan for three months was an educational experience in itself!

When to Apply

Begin early. If you want to get an internship between your sophomore and junior years, ideally you should have your resume, cover letter, and target companies ready during the summer after your freshman year. Also, since you may not get a response from any of your top five picks, plan to send letters to at least fifteen other companies. From the twenty letters you send, expect to receive at least two offers.

Whom to Contact

Once you have considered internship possibilities based on your skills and your career interests, it's time to narrow your scope by choosing the five internships you'd like to contact first.

1. Desired career: _____

   Name/address/phone number of organization:

   _____

   _____

   Contact person: _____

2. Desired career: _____

Name/address/phone number of organization:

_____

_____

Contact person: _____

3. Desired career: _____

Name/address/phone number of organization:

_____

_____

Contact person: _____

4. Desired career: _____

Name/address/phone number of organization:

_____

_____

Contact person: _____

5. Desired career: _____

Name/address/phone number of organization:

_____

_____

Contact person: _____

How to Apply

Now that you know which organizations you want to contact, here's what to send:

- A *resume* briefly stating your objectives as an intern, your education, your work experience, and your extracurricular activities. Be prepared to provide three references, and notify these people that they may be contacted by your prospective employers. (See the sample resume on page 152.)

- A *one-page cover letter* explaining your interests, abilities, and reasons for choosing this organization. This letter, like your resume, should be flawlessly written and typed; see the example on page 153. Have a couple of your friends or your composition professor read it for clarity and accuracy. Make sure you're sending the letter to the right person. Don't rely on the information in your internship directory. It's a changing world, so call the company to verify the address and the contact person.

- A *letter of recommendation* from a professor or employer (not one of your three references). The right recommendation can make a big difference because it can help separate you from the pack. When you approach someone to write a letter, let him or her know why you are asking for a letter. For example, it is helpful for a teacher to know that you have chosen her because you are proud of the research project you did in her class, and not simply because she gave you a good grade. (See the sample letter of recommendation on page 154.) Be sure to thank the professor or employer for the letter.

About two weeks after you've mailed your cover letter, resume, and letter of recommendation, call the person to whom you wrote. Make sure he or she received your letter, and ask when a decision will be made. Reiterate your interest in the company, but also let the person know that you have other summer job options.

Is an interview required? If so, read Chapter 12.

don't give up

I f no organization in your field of interest is listed, find one on your own! In Appendix B, you'll find a directory of many businesses in the United States currently offering summer internships for college students. Although this is an excellent reference list, don't depend on it completely. Some of the most rewarding internships will

Sample Resume

Mary Ann Van Camp

6680 North Anywhere Avenue   mvancamp@aol.com   Duluth, MN 55806

EDUCATION

College sophomore
English Major, Business Minor
University of Georgia, Athens, GA

OBJECTIVE

Summer Internship in Marketing or Sales

EMPLOYMENT
April 2004 to present

Administrative assistant, Adler & Adler Public Relations Agency. Responsibilities include working with clients and partners, answering mail, and routine paperwork.

March 2003 to April 2004

Hostess, Spaghetti Company Restaurant

ACTIVITIES

Resident Assistant, Coronado Dorm, University of Georgia. Responsibilities include organizing dorm functions, helping students adjust to college, and providing support during difficult times.

Member, International Students Club; Spurs; Sophomore Student Honorary Society. Participated in philanthropy program.

HIGH SCHOOL HIGHLIGHTS

President, Thespian Society. Organized actors' league, performed for charities, worked with professional actors in the community.

Graduated with a 3.2 GPA. Mainstream High junior-year representative to Girls' State.

References available upon request.

Sample Cover Letter

Mary Ann Van Camp

6680 North Anywhere Avenue   Duluth, MN 55806

Mr. Ryan Rinaldi   September 30, 2004
Pillsbury Company
Pillsbury Center
Minneapolis, MN 55402

Dear Mr. Rinaldi:

I am a sophomore majoring in English and minoring in business at the University of Georgia. My goal is to work for Pillsbury this summer as an intern in either sales or marketing.

Attached is a copy of my resume and a letter of recommendation from one of my professors. As you can see from my resume, I am committed to achievement, both in and out of the classroom. An internship with Pillsbury would provide me with an unparalleled "real-world" experience. Because I am a dedicated, energetic, and inquisitive worker, I would be a benefit to Pillsbury as an intern.

I will be calling before October 15 to inquire further about internship opportunities. In the meantime, if you have any questions, don't hesitate to call me at 313-888-1017.

I look forward to speaking with you soon. Thank you for your consideration.

Sincerely,

Mary Ann Van Camp

mvancamp@aol.com

Sample Letter of Recommendation

September 25, 2004

To Whom It May Concern:

I met Mary Ann Van Camp the first semester of her freshman year. Mary Ann was enrolled in my Western Civilization course, and she immediately impressed me as a top-notch student. She came to see me during office hours, asked questions about class lectures and writing assignments, and followed up after tests to ensure that she had learned all the pertinent information. Seldom do college students today take the extra time—especially in a survey course—to get to know their professors and to seek their help outside of class.

Although Mary Ann received a B for the course, her efforts deserved an A for the amount of time she devoted to a class normally taken by sophomores. The first semester of college is a tough adjustment period for any student, but those who persevere and learn the materials, not just to get a good grade but for the sake of learning, are truly distinguished. I know Mary Ann will get more than most out of college because she tries harder.

I highly recommend Mary Ann for a summer internship at your company. Her delightful personality, coupled with her intellect and desire to learn, will be an asset to any company or organization.

Please feel free to contact me.

Sincerely,

Robert Timmons

Dr. Robert Timmons
Department of History
University of Georgia
Athens, GA 00010

be those you research and find yourself. Use this list to land your first summer internship, but for the following summer, go for the challenge of landing the job no one else could find. Sell yourself to the organization that may not have an established internship program.

Rama Moorthy suggests that one way to learn about a company and to get your foot in the door for an internship is to try to meet some of the recruiters who come to campus to interview graduating seniors. "Ask them if you can meet with them briefly in between their interviews," he says, "then use the opportunity to find out what kinds of internships they offer or if they would be open to creating an internship position."

If you can convince an employer to "make a position" for you, you'll be successful at selling your ideas and getting support after you graduate. The more you develop these "maverick" qualities, the more fearless you'll become. To be effective, you must believe in yourself. If you learn early to convince others to believe in you, you'll be several steps ahead of the game.

once you begin your internship

Some internships are better organized than others. Jonathan Bober, a curator and art professor at the University of Texas, says that internships are valuable only if they are extremely well organized. Otherwise, you may spend your time running errands rather than learning about the field. Keep in mind that you will often need to be the initiator to make your internship as valuable as possible. It's up to you to formulate some goals—what you want to learn about this career.

Pam Zemper knew she was good at understanding how an organization ticks—seeing the broad patterns. When she began her internship at an ad agency in Austin, Texas, her goal was to learn every department of advertising. She chose this particular agency because she would gain experience in television, radio, print, and

MY TWO CENTS *How Do I Apply It?*

Jordan Austin, University of Colorado, Boulder

I'm sure you've heard the saying, "It's not what you know, it's who you know." Well, it's true and not for the reasons you might think. One year after graduation, I began to look for an internship. I knew if I wanted a chance at a well-paying job, I needed experience. But to justify taking an unpaid position when my wife was still student teaching for free, I would have to look at my *volunteer-intern* time as an investment for my future. So, I made the decision to follow my dreams and make the very best of my experience.

I applied for an internship at one of the best TV stations in the country. I got it. I arranged with my employer to work part-time and I threw myself into learning. I decided to give it everything I had. No good job for a good company is ever going to be given on recommendation alone. You have to earn it.

It was a bit intimidating at first, but I quickly adjusted. If you take initiative, it's amazing what kind of respect you get. If those around you know you'll work hard, they'll help you succeed. Ask questions and ask some more questions. Make yourself a valuable member of the company's team. Volunteer to work extra hours. Above all, take some chances and don't be afraid to make some mistakes. They'll forgive you. After all, you're an intern.

At the end of my internship, I was serving, more or less, as an associate producer. I had real jobs and had even been hired (and paid) to do some work for the station as a freelancer. I had the experience to move forward. More than that, I had the people around me who had seen me work, who liked my work and could vouch for the quality of my work.

After I had finished my internship, I applied for almost 20 TV jobs. When I was granted an interview, the people I had worked with called on my behalf. They called of their own free will to express their satisfaction with my work. The people I knew got me the job. They proved to my new employer that my resume wasn't just something that looked nice. They proved what a resume couldn't prove: that I'm a good worker and will give my all to the task at hand.

So today, I'm doing something that seemed so crazy and far-fetched a year ago. I'm a TV news reporter. There are not many industries where

> who you know can be as important as it is in this business. But the power
> of personal recommendation goes a long way in every business. So maybe
> it's fair to say, "It's not just what you know, it's who you know that can
> prove it."

public relations. "The agency I interned for had agreed to give me a
chance to work in each division. But when I got there, I realized it
was up to me to seek out extra projects in those areas."

Pam formed a mentoring relationship with an account executive who gave her background reading in many areas of the
business. "This material was written by an advertising agency and
gave me a working knowledge of the process and the vocabulary. I
was able to apply this information during my internship and talk
comfortably with the other executives." After graduation, the agency offered her a job.

When Things Go Wrong

What happens when you make your first mistakes on the job? Well,
if you're not making mistakes, you're probably not trying hard
enough. Mistakes are the process by which we learn. One of the main
purposes of an internship is to learn some lessons that will make you
better prepared once you start your "real" job after college.

Jim Burke, the CEO at Johnson & Johnson, has a favorite story
about his former boss. General Robert Wood Johnson discovered
that Burke had failed miserably at one of his really innovative
ideas—a children's chest rub. Johnson asked him, "Are you the person who cost us all that money?" Burke nodded. "I'd like to
congratulate you," the general said. "If you are making mistakes,
that means you are making decisions and taking risks. And we won't
grow unless you take risks."

If you mess up on the job, admit it, correct the mistake, discuss it,
and above all, learn from it. The greatest fool is one who will not admit
his or her own mistakes and get help from others when necessary.

When things aren't going as you expected, it's time to figure out
why. Were your expectations realistic? Internships will involve some
drudgery; it's not going to be exciting every minute you're there.

However, if you're not learning and experiencing what you had hoped for at least part of the time, there are steps you can take to remedy the situation.

- First, set up a time to meet with your supervisor. Tell him or her what you see as the problem and what you think the possible solutions are.
- Second, discuss what you believe the goals and objectives should be. Then ask your supervisor for feedback.
- Third, clarify with your supervisor what he or she wants you to accomplish, and together establish some specific goals for the remainder of your internship.

Evaluating Your Performance

Some organizations have formal evaluations. If yours doesn't, be forthright in asking for an honest appraisal of your work at the conclusion of your internship. Remember, you'll be able to improve only if you can take constructive criticism from those with more experience.

The following is a list of categories in which an employee is typically evaluated. Use the chart to grade yourself in each of these categories. If you believe you're doing an *excellent* job, put an *E* next to that item; if a *satisfactory* job, put an *S;* if a *poor* job, write a *P.* Then go over the list with your manager. Ask for specific tips on how you can improve on your weak areas.

PERFORMANCE REVIEW

__ Quality of work	__ Planning and	__ Communication
__ Quantity of work	organizing	__ Working with
__ Problem solving	__ Delegating	others
__ Decision-making	__ Self-control	__ Business savvy

OTHER CHARACTERISTICS

__ Creativity	__ Adaptability	__ Attitude
__ Initiative	__ Persuasiveness	__ Maturity
__ Teamwork	__ Leadership	__ Foresight
__ Judgment	__ Self-confidence	

OVERALL EVALUATION

- Your strengths: _____

  _____

- Areas that need improvement: _____

  _____

- Supervisor's comments: _____

  _____

where do you go from here?

I f you love your internship and decide that another summer at the same company would be valuable for your professional development, set things up for the following year. Many companies have an interest in cultivating students for two summers in a row so they can make them a job offer upon graduation. Just make sure to secure greater responsibilities for the next summer. This way you'll continue to develop your skills as well as make new contacts.

Then again, you may wish to keep your options open and work for another organization the following summer—in the same industry or a completely different one.

Adam Edwards, a senior at the University of Michigan, is completing his third internship at Microsoft. He feels his interning experience has benefited him in many ways. "The most tangible benefit of the internships is that by doing well at them, I give Microsoft the incentive to hire me when I graduate—these days it's comforting to have a job lined up after graduation." Adam has also gained valuable knowledge about his field. "I learned a computer language at Microsoft that is taught at my school—I learned it before I took the class, so I had an advantage over people who were learning it for the first time. I've gained enough knowledge about how software is developed that I could potentially develop commercial software using methodologies and technical skills I learned on the job at Microsoft."

windows on the world

The world is a book and those who stay at home read only one page.

—ST. AUGUSTINE

The use of traveling is to regulate the imagination by reality and, instead of thinking how things may be, to see them as they are.

—SAMUEL JOHNSON

People travel for a variety of reasons: study, work, leisure, and to volunteer. Regardless of the motivation, experiencing the world offers immense personal and professional rewards. For one thing, travel can be a deeply enriching experience. By venturing out of your safe, familiar environment, you gain insights about humanity and also about yourself. Your understanding of other cultures expands, and so does your self-awareness—important elements in developing a healthy view of the world.

Globalization has become the buzzword of the twenty-first century job market. Travel is now a practical asset for today's career seeker. Janice

161

Bellace, deputy dean at the University of Pennsylvania's Wharton School of Business, said in an interview for the Kaplan Staff/*Newsweek* "Tipsheet," 1999 edition: "Twenty years ago you could still go to work for a large American company and have limited exposure to businesses outside of the United States. That's not true today. You can't be in a major firm or investment bank without being part of the international market."

Even if you're not planning a career in business, job recruiters in other fields also look favorably on students who have traveled outside the United States. A summer or a semester abroad tells a potential employer that you possess attractive character traits such as the desire to learn and the courage to explore, key attributes for the kind of innovative thinking today's industries long for. Immersing yourself in another culture also develops the universally prized skill of *adaptability*. Your ability to adjust quickly to any situation, group of people, or environment will serve you in any occupation, particularly in today's multinational work environment.

Marty D'Luzansky taught English in France while on a Fulbright teaching assistantship after he graduated from college with a major in French. He ended up working as a trade consultant with the New Zealand Trade Development Board. "I can't stress enough how important it is to take a year between undergraduate school and whatever it is you think you want to do," he said. "My overseas experience has provided me with the cross-cultural skills essential to help me effectively advise New Zealanders on the best way to succeed with their products or services in the U.S. market. The ability to see the United States from a foreign perspective is critical to my work."

the world as your classroom

Hong Kong. Buenos Aires. Cairo. London. Paris. Milan. Faraway cities like these can be your first exposure to other people, cultures, and languages. World travel can even jump-start a career that you'll love. Diane Roberts is a case in point. As she traveled through Europe, Diane became enamored of the historic churches, and, more specifically, with the restoration necessary to keep them intact. Diane's curiosity led her on a search for studios where stained-glass restoration was done; the artists there told her that the churches and buildings in the United States were just then becoming old enough to need restoration, and they recommended that she pursue a career in restoration at home. Today, Diane Roberts restores antique stained-glass windows at Cummings Studios in North Adams, Massachusetts. "I wouldn't be working on American windows today if I hadn't spent that time in Europe," she says.

Spending time in another country can also help you clarify your career goals. Susan Finnemore studied for one semester at York College in England. On weekends she traveled with friends around Great Britain. In the youth hostels where she stayed, she noticed advertisements for "work camps." (Important tip: There are many jobs abroad. Some can be found on the bulletin boards of youth hostels, train stations, and schools.) One "camp" where she worked was on a Welsh estate, where she received wages and lodgings. The camp paid for food, and Susan cooked the meals.

Susan's parents are both professors, and Susan had always planned to go straight from undergraduate school to a master's program in history. Travel gave her the perspective to reconsider her options. "If I can travel through Europe," Susan thought to herself, "I can do anything." Instead of going to graduate school, Susan decided to pursue a career in publishing. She is now the psychology editor of college textbooks at Prentice Hall, where she's found her niche.

Your travel experience, however, doesn't have to be as structured as the examples cited to be worthwhile. Bill and Jonathan Aikens spent three months cycling about Europe with little on their minds except taking in the scenery. Yet they learned valuable lessons along the way. Between the two of them, they spoke five languages. Besides English, Bill spoke Spanish and French; Jonathan spoke German; both learned Italian en route! Travel can, therefore, provide another very specific, very tangible skill: speaking a foreign language.

In some fields, the more exotic the language, the more marketable the skill. UPI Beijing correspondent Mark Delvecchio skipped several rungs on the journalism ladder in this way. Reporters can work ten years to win coveted overseas positions—and some can wait an entire lifetime for such jobs, to no avail. Mark, however, rose out of a reporting job for a small Connecticut weekly to his job in China in just a little over four years.

An energetic reporter, Mark made rapid progress on the basis of hard work, becoming city editor of a daily after only three years in the business. However, when a job opened up on UPI's foreign desk in Washington, DC, Mark says it was his college year abroad in China, plus his University of Connecticut master's degree in Chinese history, that made the difference. "Few American reporters speak Chinese," he says. A few months after arriving in Washington, Mark was sent to Beijing. He was twenty-eight years old.

learning about yourself

Travel teaches you about other places and other people, but most important, it teaches you about yourself. For example, I spent the fall semester of my junior year in Segovia, Spain, a town of forty thousand people sixty-five miles northwest of Madrid. I lived with a delightful Spanish family and attended a local Spanish college, where I received university credit. I partied—in Spanish—with friends from the town while the other Americans partied (in English) with each other.

MY TWO CENTS   *How Do I Apply It?*

Mike Schloss, Regis University

Currently, I am a senior double majoring in sociology and peace and justice. During my sophomore year, through my activities, the people I have met, and the classes that I have had, I decided that my next step would be to study abroad. At that point, I had not decided where I would go, but I knew that I must begin the process of discerning what program would be a good fit.

Shortly after I decided to go abroad, my supervisor introduced me to the Casa de la Solidaridad program offered at Santa Clara University. At first, I was apprehensive because I did not know much Spanish. However, everything else about the program seemed perfect for me. I wanted a program that would include a community environment, supervision, spiritual opportunities, and a classroom experience. After I received the basic information, I questioned the people involved with the Casa program. I asked if not speaking Spanish would affect my experience and if I would be able to apply. Everyone encouraged me, so I applied.

I spent four months in El Salvador studying in a cultural immersion program. I was placed with a family of fourteen. A friend and I spent two days a week with the abundant Quintenilla family. We were able to form strong bonds with the family and the community. We also had the opportunity to work in a local public school teaching English.

There were ten American students and an accomplished professor in my class. We had one professor from Honduras, one from the U.S., and three from El Salvador. The professors were able to integrate our cultural experiences with our classroom lessons. The class that helped me the most was a weekly three-hour, one-on-one Spanish lesson.

If you are thinking about studying abroad, start planning early. Let your family, friends, and advisers know so that they can help you with your planning. Research the country before you go because most people don't. Be academically prepared and, if possible, study the native language. It will be a great asset, but don't be afraid if you don't feel comfortable speaking it.

On weekends I took the train into Madrid and explored other nearby towns. Once, my Spanish friend Ma Paz took me outside Segovia to visit her family's village: population, twenty-five. It was out of a storybook. The only public building was a small church where a friar came to perform mass each Sunday.

Ma Paz's father, a farmer, lived with her mother in a small house next to the barn overflowing with cows. Her grandparents' house was only a ten-minute walk away, along a path bordered by gorgeous, rolling Spanish hills. Her grandparents showed us where they made wine from grapes that they pressed themselves. They were intensely curious about my life back in the United States, asking many questions about my family, my hometown, and my university. We talked long into the night.

I felt lucky to meet these generous people. When I reminisce about my semester abroad, it's not the Prado, the Alahambra, or the 800-year-old castles that leap to mind first, but my experiences with people such as Ma and her family, who taught me much more than just how to be fluent in Spanish.

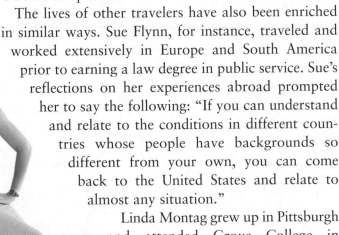

The lives of other travelers have also been enriched in similar ways. Sue Flynn, for instance, traveled and worked extensively in Europe and South America prior to earning a law degree in public service. Sue's reflections on her experiences abroad prompted her to say the following: "If you can understand and relate to the conditions in different countries whose people have backgrounds so different from your own, you can come back to the United States and relate to almost any situation."

Linda Montag grew up in Pittsburgh and attended Grove College in Pennsylvania. Although her school offered study abroad programs, Linda knew she could distinguish herself by getting work experience in a foreign country. So, with the encouragement of one of her German professors, she secured a work–study program in Germany for one summer and one semester in the field of insurance.

"My time abroad helped me develop self-confidence more than anything else I did in college," says Linda, who is now an assistant vice president of a German commercial bank headquartered in Frankfurt. "It was the first opportunity I had to truly assert myself and depend on myself completely to do everything—from finding my way around to learning my job to becoming proficient in a foreign language."

where do you want to go?

M aybe you'd like to visit France because you studied French in school. Maybe you'd like to visit Ireland because your ancestors were Irish. You've also thought about Canada or Mexico because they're closer and more convenient to visit. Below, make a list of five countries that interest you and, more important, tell *why* they interest you.

1. _____, because: _____

2. _____, because: _____

3. _____, because: _____

4. _____, because: _____

5. _____, because: _____

If no particular country stands out in your mind as the place you really want to go, take your travel wish list and do some information gathering:

- Talk to professors.
- Talk to friends who've traveled.
- Read whatever you can about the countries that interest you.

By now you should be passionate about visiting at least a couple of those countries on your wish list. Choose the one that best fits your interest in language, culture, and education. Remember, you've got a lifetime to visit the other cultures on your list. Your first extended visit to a foreign country will forever change the way you see yourself and the world. *Vive l'experience!*

How to Get There

Foreign travel is costly. Unless you win a scholarship such as the Rotary, Fulbright, or Rhodes, you'll have to come up with the money for your trip yourself.

Here are some low-cost options:

1. *You can take a year off from college to work, then travel.* Work hard to save money for the entire first semester and then travel for six months—or as long as your money lasts. You can travel by train with a backpack and stay in inexpensive youth hostels. It's safer, but not essential, to travel with a companion.

Advantages: You can plan for and take your trip without any outside interruptions. You can fully immerse yourself in travel: six months is a good chunk of time in which to see several different countries or to concentrate on only one.

Disadvantages: You'll be one year behind your classmates in school. However, this is actually an advantage, because you'll graduate with one more full year of experience over other applicants. Don't let peer pressure stop you.

2. *You can work in London or Paris as an au pair or nanny, taking care of children in the homes of affluent families.* In exchange for your services, which also may involve light housework, you receive free room and board and sometimes a small salary.

Advantages: This is a cheap way to learn about other cultures. It affords far more experience than, say, living in a college dorm. Usually you have weekends free to explore the city and surrounding countryside.

Disadvantages: Frequently you do not have the time to venture beyond your central city unless you are traveling with the family. The job itself can be quite demanding.

3. *After you graduate from college, you can become a Peace Corps volunteer.* This requires a two-year commitment in one of sixty developing nations, working in such areas as nutrition, agriculture, education, or hygiene. Contact your local Peace Corps office for more information or call 1-800-424-8580. If two years abroad is too long for you, shorter assignments are also available. The Young Men's Christian Association (YMCA) and Amigo de las Americas offer summer volunteer programs that might better meet your objectives.

Advantages: If you don't know a foreign language, the Peace Corps will teach you. You would work with a team of other volunteers in small towns and villages. You would learn a great deal about developing countries and the people who live there. This is probably one of the most eye-opening experiences you can have abroad. Its rewards are not in dollars, but in experience. Also, being a Peace Corps volunteer tells potential employers that you are both tenacious and hard-working.

Disadvantages: Peace Corps assignments are typically rigorous, and a two-year commitment is a significant amount of time. So consider the costs before you make the commitment.

4. *You can contact the Council on International Educational Exchange (CIEE).* The Council on International Educational Exchange is a nonprofit member organization of nearly two hundred universities, colleges, and youth service agencies. It runs service projects in Denmark, Poland, Portugal, Canada, Turkey, Spain, and other countries. These two-to-four-week programs involve voluntary community service—such as renovation of historical sites, forestry, or social work—in exchange for room and board. There are also long-term service projects, including semester-long programs on Israeli kibbutzim.

Advantages: There's no better way to learn about yourself than through helping others—the personal satisfaction and confidence gained through volunteer work is more than worth your time and effort.

Disadvantages: Again, unless you choose to volunteer during the summer, you'll lose out on time in school. Your time will probably be very structured on these trips, too. Also, conditions can often be quite rustic.

5. *You can study abroad—for a summer, a semester, or a full year.* Nearly all colleges sponsor programs abroad for credit, and most of these programs are open to students from other schools. In addition to joining a program sponsored by an American universi-

ty, you can enroll directly in a foreign university in a program designed for foreign students. There are programs in virtually every country—if you really want to study in Finland or Bora Bora, or both, you probably can.

Almost every college campus features summer- and semester-abroad programs for credit. Check with your foreign language, art history, or humanities departments for details, or perhaps your school has a separate study abroad office.

Advantages: This is a great way to learn the language and the culture while earning college credit. Living with a family abroad can be one of the most delightful ways to experience a country in depth. Also, you can usually apply for financial aid.

Disadvantages: Cost. Often these programs are very expensive, including airfare and spending money as well as tuition and room and board. Fortunately, most colleges encourage students to apply their financial aid packages toward study abroad. Another disadvantage is that the host family the placement service thought was just right for you may turn out to be less than all you'd hoped for. This is rare, however; most programs thoroughly screen the families to ensure that they provide a nice home, good food, and a pleasant atmosphere for their guests.

6. *You can contact Semester at Sea.* This program offers students college credit while they travel by ship to several designated countries. Check your study-abroad office for details.

Advantages: Students are able to see many different countries by ship, a thrilling means of travel by anybody's standard. You can also earn up to sixteen units of college credit.

Disadvantages: This is an extremely costly program. Since you are on a ship most of your time, you won't put down roots in a particular country. Also, because most students are American, you are essentially transporting America by cruise ship to wild and exotic places. "The best way to waste a summer or a semester abroad is to hang out with other Americans," says Susan Finnemore. Some of the adventure is definitely undercut. Finally, instead of traveling yourself, you are in a group—all the time.

7. *You can enlist in the armed services.* You're trained in a marketable skill, and you get to travel around the world. Other armed

services besides the Army have ROTC programs, consult your local recruiter or on-campus ROTC office.

Advantages: When you get out, you'll be able to continue your education with a healthy subsidy from Uncle Sam, or enter the job market, whichever you prefer. You might also want to consider ROTC. With this program, your undergraduate tuition at a host institution is partially paid for (usually the program pays 80 percent) and you have the advantage of not worrying about what you're going to be doing once you graduate.

Disadvantages: You have little choice in where you want to be stationed, and the time commitment is relatively lengthy—usually three to four years.

8. *You can apply for a travel scholarship.* You just might qualify for a grant or scholarship to study abroad. It is relatively easy to get scholarship money for study in non-Western countries. For example, Max Ward, a senior in Asian studies, spent a semester studying in China. His trip to China was funded by the University of Texas and the Institute of Asian Studies in Chicago.

Advantages. According to Max Ward, his experience "provided a chance for me to see a completely different way of life from my own." It moved him so much that he planned to go back to China after graduation to work. (He is now working part-time for a legal aid service, where he has had the opportunity to work with Chinese businesspeople.)

Disadvantages: Depending on your school, competition for travel scholarships can be fierce. Your knowledge of a foreign language, however, narrows the competition for scholarships. In the spring of her first year at Columbia's School of International Affairs, Elizabeth Thompson decided she wanted to go to Egypt to brush up on her Arabic. (She had learned some Arabic while abroad in the past.) Elizabeth, a native of Detroit,

who attended both Harvard as an undergraduate and Columbia's graduate school on full scholarship, could not afford to go on her own. When she asked an academic adviser if there were any scholarships that would send her to Egypt, he pulled an application for a grant out of the drawer. "In Middle Eastern Affairs departments," he explained, "there are sometimes more grants than students."
Elizabeth spent that summer in Egypt. Since then she has taught in Syria for a year and has been admitted to Ph.D. programs in Middle Eastern studies, both at Columbia and Berkeley.

Additional Search Strategies

Here are some other sources of information about traveling abroad:

1. *The Internet and the World Wide Web.* Get online and click on a search engine; then type in the words *study abroad* or *foreign travel* and see what you can find. If you know which country you want to visit, type in that country's name; many countries have websites. Also check out "chat rooms" and "bulletin boards" where you can get tips from other travelers.

2. *Travel agencies.* Look in the yellow pages under "Travel Agencies," then call and ask about student programs. Travel agencies also have information on which U.S. cities sponsor international events. They often offer package deals that can make travel a bargain. Your on-campus travel agency is a great place to shop for bargains. Students are often eligible for travel discounts for airlines and hotels. Agencies may also offer reduced rates on airfares, tours, and other travel items. You can also get an International Student Card, which allows you to visit museums and other attractions worldwide at reduced rates.

3. *International education offices.* Many campuses also have an international education office set up to help you. They have information on programs in places as diverse as the Orient, South America, and Russia. Vince Perez, for instance, had always been interested in international relations. As a sophomore, he applied for a job with AIESEC, an international student-run foundation for students interested in economics and management, through the international education office on his campus. Although Vince was from the Philippines, he got a paid job—$1,000 a month—in New

Jersey with an American firm. Through an exchange program with Rider College, AIESEC arranged for Vince to live with an American family. Vince enjoyed the program so much that he became president of the AIESEC for the Philippines. He attended seminars in Australia, Singapore, Belgium, and Washington, DC. Vince's sister joined the same organization and landed a job in Denmark, where she now lives and works. "AIESEC was my big breakthrough," says Vince, who is now director of an international trading firm, Lazard Freres and Company in London.

travel essentials

*C*heck with your doctor to determine whether you will need to be immunized before leaving the United States. Some immunizations must be completed *weeks* before you leave, so plan ahead.

For any type of foreign travel, you'll need a passport. These are available from courts and post offices throughout the country, as well as from designated passport agencies in most major cities. You'll also need a visa for travel to some countries. For visa information, you can contact the country's embassy or write to the Office of Passport Services in Washington, DC, for visa requirements.

it's never too late

*I*f you can't afford the time or cost of travel during college, don't worry. Cathy Stanley and Kim Corley waited until they graduated before they went abroad. For two months they traveled carrying backpacks and Eurorail passes. They explored England, Spain, Germany, Switzerland, Italy, and Greece. When they returned, Cathy began her job as a sales representative in the sales division of Procter & Gamble and Kim began her career with IBM.

Howard Sklar graduated from UCLA with a degree in French history, but he didn't think his education was complete. "I had spent four years cramming my head full of names, dates, literature, and facts—but to tell you the truth, I hadn't the slightest idea of what French culture is in real life. I'd never seen it. I'd never lived it." Howard decided to experience French culture firsthand from the seat of his bicycle. For three weeks he took in the French countryside as he pedaled his way from Paris to Pouilly. Near the end of his trip he finally realized what fascinated him about France. It wasn't the language or the history or the great works of art and literature. Rather, to his surprise, Howard found the heart and soul of France in its wine. Today Howard works as a wine importer in California.

Rich Matteson didn't travel during college either. Instead, he worked for one year as a restaurant manager after graduation before joining Up With People, the performance organization dedicated to promoting international understanding. After traveling to Belgium, Denmark, and Finland, Rich decided to become a full-time staff member with Up With People. He travels all over the world and stays with host families while organizing tours and performing with the cast. So don't be discouraged if you can't see the world right now. An opportunity to travel may open sometime in the near future. If it does, be sure to go for it.

travel opportunities in the United States

Although our focus up to this point has been on foreign travel, travel doesn't have to be international to be valuable. After her sophomore year at Brown University, Melissa Halverstadt spent twelve months hiking, kayaking, and mountain climbing in the wilderness education program at Prescott College in Arizona. She learned to lead, cooperate, conserve, and plan—survival skills in their truest sense.

So, if you can't venture outside of the United States yet you want to experience the world, never fear. There are plenty of activities and programs you can join right on your own campus and in your community that will "bring the world to you."

Where to Get the Facts

ON CAMPUS

1. *Contact the International Students' Organization.* Almost every campus has an ISO group where students from around the world join Americans in an exchange of culture, ideas, and good times (often centered around delectable cuisine). If there

is no such organization on your campus, begin one yourself. Each week, someone from a different country gives a speech or slide presentation, followed by refreshments and the opportunity to meet everyone. Also, there are dinners or banquets where a group of people will provide the regional cuisine, and perhaps demonstrate a traditional art or form of dress.

2. *Visit the campus residence for international students.* You could apply for a job as a clerk at the desk or as a food server. Or drop by sometime when you can introduce yourself to several students. Give them your phone number and tell them you would like to get together for lunch or dinner. Remember, they want to learn just as much about America as you want to learn about their culture.

3. *Volunteer to be an English tutor.* This is a great way to learn intimately about the culture of a foreign country through fellow students who will become your friends. Also, you can derive a lot of personal satisfaction from knowing that you are helping to open your culture and country up to someone else.

IN THE COMMUNITY

1. *Work in an ethnic restaurant or in a business run entirely by people from another country.* Expose yourself to a different set of customs and values. Ask questions about their home country. How is it different from the United States? How do they perceive Americans? What have they learned from Americans? What has been the biggest cultural barrier?

2. *Read the newspapers to find out about cultural events.* Frequently there are specific cultural festivals that feature music, dance, and foods from foreign lands. If you have time, get involved in a steering committee to plan such an event. Chances are you'll meet fascinating people from the community who will keep you posted on similar events.

3. *Contact AmeriCorps.* AmeriCorps is like the Peace Corps, except that the assignments take place here in the United States. You work for little or no pay in places like American Indian reservations, inner cities, or remote rural communities. Like the Peace Corps, AmeriCorps involves hard work and commitment.

other horizons

There are many ways to appreciate and enrich your travel experience before, during, and after your trip. Brushing up on the language, reading about the history of the country, and learning about the people before you go can make you feel more at home right from the start.

Let's say you've chosen to visit France. Before your trip, you may want to listen to some French-language tapes and practice the most commonly used phrases. (It helps if you've studied the language in school, but it's not essential.) What are other considerations?

- **Art.** Every region of the world has its own unique art forms. You may want to research the region you intend to visit.

- **Literature.** Read works by native authors as an entertaining way to learn about the country you are visiting.

- **History.** Invest in a paperback on the country's history so that the sights you see will have greater significance for you.

- **Music.** Listen to local radio stations during your trip. This will help you understand the language and expose you to the country's music.

- **Philosophy.** Who were the philosophers that influenced cultural development? How has their thinking affected everyday life?

- **Politics and Economics.** Think about the way the country is governed. How does it differ from the United States? What are the pluses and minuses? What is the economic system?

- **Business.** What is the local commerce? What are the major industries? Is the country rich in natural resources, human resources, agriculture, or technological advances? What American companies thrive in the country?

No matter where you plan to go, from Peru to Japan, getting a sense of the country beforehand will help you feel better upon arrival. You can learn and adapt on the road by carrying a guidebook as a useful reference and road map.

This is only a partial list. Don't stop here! Make foreign or domestic travel a goal. Your travel adventure may just be the most important experience of your college years.

networking

The need to be opportunistic, to think on your feet, again underscores the importance of tuning in to people—of hearing not only what they say, but the larger and underlying meaning as well.

—MARK MCCORMACK, IN *WHAT THEY DON'T TEACH YOU AT HARVARD BUSINESS SCHOOL*

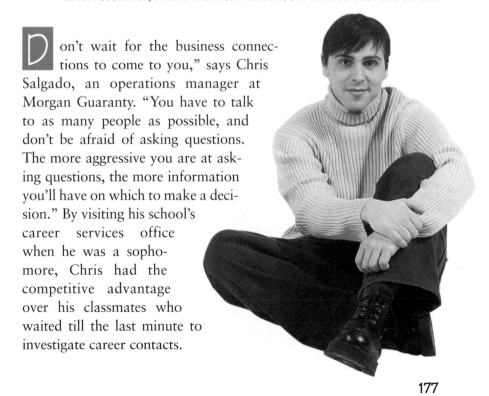

D on't wait for the business connections to come to you," says Chris Salgado, an operations manager at Morgan Guaranty. "You have to talk to as many people as possible, and don't be afraid of asking questions. The more aggressive you are at asking questions, the more information you'll have on which to make a decision." By visiting his school's career services office when he was a sophomore, Chris had the competitive advantage over his classmates who waited till the last minute to investigate career contacts.

177

Networking involves all the activities that result in contacts. Therefore, at the core of networking is a commitment to develop good relationships. Meeting people; making your career needs known to friends and relatives; keeping in touch and on good terms with past and present classmates, professors, employers, co-workers, relatives, friends, and virtually everyone you know—all are important elements of mapping out an effective career strategy. Learning to network effectively can mean the difference between landing a job or receiving a form letter that reads, "Thank you for your time, but . . ."

Your career network represents the connections you already have with the people you know, as well as those you want to establish. Therefore, Nancy Forsyth, a business graduate from the University of New Hampshire, advises, "Be gutsy. You can't expect people to help you out if you don't do something for yourself." Nancy built strong relationships with her professors and the counselors at the career services office. "Your mentors in college have the best connections, and they care about helping you assess what you should do," says Nancy, who became an editor for Boston publisher Allyn and Bacon. "But students must make the initial effort to seek these people out."

Although he had been a highly qualified student, the editor of his college magazine, and voted "Most Likely to Succeed in Journalism," David Herndon found that getting his first good job was not just a matter of talent and hard work. It also involved "circumstance and opportunity."

"You've got to be around to get around," says David, a *Newsday* features editor. After graduating from Columbia's Graduate School of Journalism, David had to spend three years doing odd jobs (including compiling sections for an encyclopedia, which was "like writing high school book reports") before he finally got his break. Ironically, it came from a former fellow student who had landed a job with *Sport* magazine and asked

David to write a few articles. David did, and was then recommended for a job as sports editor at *The Village Voice*. He got the job, and over the next five years, he made up for lost time, moving from sports editor to managing editor (at age twenty-nine), to features editor for *Newsday*.

In his book *Achievement Factors: Candid Interviews with Some of the Most Successful People of Our Time*, B. Eugene Griessman writes, "Opportunities are usually for the moment, and as they pass by, there is often only a brief moment to grab them." Therefore, keep in mind that contacts are everywhere, in the classroom and out, in the office and out.

the career search

Why not use your career search as a launching pad for networking skills? Basically, for career search purposes, networking means making contact with people who can

- Tell you about a specific job.
- Put you in touch with someone important at a company that interests you.
- Keep you in mind for a job that will open up in the future.
- Coach you in your career pursuit.
- Provide you with inside information.
- Introduce you to someone who can give you valuable information.
- Hire you.

Why is networking—or making career or business contacts—so important? For one thing, you always need people contacts, whether you're looking for a job or not. (Your GPA will not be your best friend.) Second, you need people to tell you firsthand how to make the transition from super college student to super job applicant. Meeting people who can help you in this transition will be more helpful than reading ten books on how to get the job of your dreams.

In fields like finance, connections can be everything. John Carrigan, thirty years old, has his own seat on the Chicago Board of Trade. He says his first contact in the field was made through a friend from high school. His three summer internships, and the contacts he made, were a foot in the door for his first post-college job trading futures for Paine Webber.

Where to Begin

First, take inventory of your summer internships and part-time jobs. Did the work interest you? What do you most value from your college classes and activities? What was most enjoyable?

Use these answers as clues to finding the jobs that interest you most. Then talk to people who have those jobs now. This advice should sound familiar, since you've already been "networking" with your professors, friends, and employers since your freshman year.

If possible, ask your networking contacts if you can observe them on the job. You want to get an accurate picture of a typical workday. Would you like to be alone or with people? Would you be closely supervised or independent? What environment would you work in? Would you travel?

George Fraser, author of the networking book *Success Runs in Our Race,* remembers one of his first jobs working in a department store stockroom. "I worked hard and looked constantly for opportunities to be promoted, and in doing so, I learned a basic principle of networking: Start wherever the door of opportunity opens, be it in the mail room or the back room. I see so many young people who want to start in the front office, if not higher. It doesn't work that way. Everything good that happened to me during this period was a result of people telling other people good things about my attitude. I learned the importance of developing good relationships with my co-workers. If you work hard and well with other people, you don't always need to job-hunt. Often, the jobs come hunting for you."

Cultivating Contacts Now and in the Future

Much of your success in work will depend on the relationships you have with other people. If you learn early to pick people's brains, to perceive what makes them successful, and to incorporate their qualities of success, you will be far ahead of your contemporaries. Know that you have much to learn from your mentors and your "role models" in business, but you have equally as much to learn from all your other work associates.

Networking doesn't mean just making yourself visible to those in the position to give you a promotion, though that is important. It also means cultivating relationships with all the people behind the scenes, the people who actually get things done—the receptionist, mail clerk, messenger, office manager, janitor—people whose jobs mostly go unrecognized by the corporate hierarchy. It involves a willingness to learn anything from anyone who works with you, in *any* capacity.

"You never know where you will run into someone again," says Nancy Wingate. "You may not think much of the receptionist or the intern or classmate next to you, but they may be sitting across a desk interviewing you down the line. It pays to treat everyone you work with with respect and consideration."

Robert Girardot, a chemical engineer at CSX Corporation, agrees. "You never know who's going to be your boss one day," he says. He remembers when an unpopular guy became the boss. "I'm not saying you should be phony . . . but do not participate in office gossip. Be a booster. If you don't have something good to say about a co-worker, boss, or company, don't say anything." Do you remember the Golden Rule you learned way back in kindergarten? Well, it still applies, even in your professional life. Not only is following the Golden Rule the right thing to do, your career will also function better in the long run. Therefore, maintain high ethical standards.

Business Week columnist Paul Nadler says he always sends postcards to the office's photocopying personnel. He depends heavily on quick and efficient photocopies, especially at deadline time.

Building relationships with all different kinds of people will help you if you ever want to be in management. As a manager, you are a leader, organizing and inspiring and working with others to achieve professional and personal goals. How do you learn the principles of good management?

"Not by reading about great leaders whose experience is so foreign it makes it impossible to identify with them," observes Andrew S. Grove, former CEO of Intel Corporation, in a *Fortune* magazine article. Grove does not endorse wilderness excursions, climbing down poles, or whitewater rafting as the secret to management success. Good leadership and good management is learned, according to Grove, "the same way each of us has learned the important, unteachable roles in our lives, be they that of husband or wife, father or mother: by studying the behavior of people who have made a success of it and modeling ourselves after them."

Networking means learning from others. It also means being a teacher to others when you have the knowledge, experience, and expertise to give someone else guidance.

John and Elizabeth were hired right out of journalism school by a major financial news weekly. Each held entry-level editorial positions. John was eager to learn, inquisitive, and helpful to co-workers in his training seminar. When Ann, a new co-worker, was having a hard time figuring out the computer system, John took the time to sit down and help her figure it out. He wasn't much more experienced with it than she was, but he figured he'd learn by helping. When they couldn't resolve a glitch, John was the one who went to the seminar instructor and asked for help. Not only was the instructor happy to help John

and Ann figure out the problem, he also became interested in the sample article they were working on. And he was impressed with John's editorial eye. This gave John the opportunity to get to know a senior editor in an informal situation, sincerely and without any grandstanding.

Elizabeth used a different approach. During the instructor's seminar, she constantly interrupted the other trainees, interjecting her opinion based on her vast experience working at her father's newspaper in a midsize, midwestern city. Once, when Ann asked Elizabeth to share her experience about working for her father's newspaper, Elizabeth refused. Instead, she looked briefly at Ann with a bored expression and said that she'd love to if she had the time, but right now she was "consumed" with a special feature proposal for the magazine.

At promotion time, Elizabeth was still laboring on her uncommissioned special feature while John was promoted to assistant managing editor, with responsibility for developing a financial news column for college graduates. The senior editors believed John would be a better long-term choice because he was a superior teacher, listener, communicator, and motivator. In short, John was a role model. Elizabeth's poor attitude closed the doors of opportunity.

How Have You Networked?

Have you networked during your summer internship or part-time job? Even if you have only waited on tables, think of how your success depended on your co-workers. Seriously.

An excellent waiter who is liked and respected by his co-workers is far more effective—and therefore more profitable—than the average waiter. Why? Because if the host or hostess likes him, he'll get his tables turned (cleared off and set) faster than the others. If the cook likes him, he'll get occasional special orders for his "preferred" customers. If the manager realizes how valuable his work and his good disposition are, he or she will make special arrangements—like letting him work as much or as little as he wants to accommodate his school schedule—just to keep him. Finally, the customer—the ultimate recipient of this entire team process—stands a greater chance of being pleased with the service. Therefore, this waiter will probably get a better tip—one of his goals in the first place.

Good human relations will help you in any job. Although some people have a natural knack for dealing with people, others have a hard time. If you are in the latter category, take heart. There are resources that can help you understand how you can better relate to people and how you can help other people feel comfortable relating to you. The classic self-help book on this subject is *How to Win Friends and Influence People* by Dale Carnegie. In it he outlines six basic principles for successful interaction. (There's so much common sense here it's easy to take this formula for granted. Don't.)

1. Become genuinely interested in other people.
2. Smile.
3. Remember that a person's name is to that person the sweetest and most important sound in any language.
4. Be a good listener. Encourage others to talk about themselves.
5. Talk in terms of other people's interests, not your own.
6. Make the other person feel important, and do it sincerely.

Networking is a relatively new word for, among other things, effective human relations. Wholesome, old-fashioned characteristics like good manners, sincerity, a positive attitude, and a generous spirit never go out of style. Together they formulate the essence of a winning career strategy.

finding a mentor

If you haven't already, find yourself a mentor. In short, a mentor is a teacher, a coach, a guide, a guru—somebody you have a rapport with and a respect for in your chosen career field. A mentor is less a model and more of a teacher. (Whitey Herzog, for example, was a mediocre baseball player but became one of the game's most successful managers.)

So how will you meet your mentor? Will he or she appear to you magically? Probably not. You must take the initiative. Seeking out a mentor will help you to define yourself and your chosen career path, so choose carefully. Asking yourself two smart questions will help you get started on your quest:

1. *Which professors most inspire you?* Talk to them after class. Ask them for special assignments.
2. *Whom do you know that works in your field of interest?* Perhaps your mentor will be a manager at an office where you get a part-time job or a summer internship. Set up an appointment to talk with that person about your career goals, and ask him or her for input or suggestions.

To be effective at networking, that is, cultivating good professional relations, you must first examine your own character and personality. Think about those people you most admire (professors, movie stars, politicians, characters from literature, and so on). Think about the people who've had the greatest and most positive influence on you. What distinguishes them from the rest of the herd? Why do they appeal to you? Why do they stand out? Learn how to ask questions of the people you work with who have more experience and more knowledge than you do. Take notes. Watch them in action. Analyze what they do. Study the people who are excelling in their fields; obviously they are doing something right.

One other thing: It's important that your mentor be someone you can get to know. If you want to be a playwright, Shakespeare might be an ideal, but he's dead; Arthur Miller might be a model, but he lives in New York City. Why not cultivate a relationship with the drama professor at your local college?

Thomas Easton, New York bureau chief of the *Baltimore Sun*, found his career shaped dramatically by a mentor. In college he was reluctant to specialize in any one area. He was interested in everything from film to history to political science. When he graduated, he had a vague idea that his broad range of interests might make him suitable for journalism, but he wasn't sure.

Then, during a job interview for a chain of Connecticut weekly newspapers, he met editor John Peterson, who had won awards as an investigative reporter. The two hit it off right away. Peterson's great curiosity and energy matched Easton's. "I asked him once if he wanted me to go out for coffee," Easton says, laughing. "And he said, 'No, I didn't hire you to get coffee. I hired you to get stories. Get out there.'"

Because of his mentor, Easton made an extraordinary career jump. After two years on the weekly, he worked for a daily for six months, went to business school, and ended up on one of the best papers in the country. Easton says the *Sun* weighed two things heavily: his business degree and a stellar recommendation from Peterson.

MY TWO CENTS *How Do I Apply It?*

Leilani Nussman, University of Portland

I have always wanted to be a doctor. At least that is what all my friends thought, but now we see that is no longer true. During the last few years of high school, I discovered a love for science, and decided, therefore, that I had to go to medical school. However, my last two years at school have significantly changed this outlook. After taking physiology and microbiology as preparation for medical school, I decided to try something a little different. I decided to take ecology (mainly because it was offered at a good time). About six weeks into the class, I fell in love. I was also taking immunology at the time, and came to see that I liked macrobiology so much more than cellular.

While taking ecology, I realized I have always loved nature and been interested in conservation. I began working with a professor to find a field research program for the summer. I didn't know what type of research I wanted to do, other than knowing I wanted to work in the field, not the lab. I finally was offered a position at Fordham University. I worked with my adviser there to figure out what type of research I wanted to do. After trying a couple of different projects, I visited Falkner Island in Connecticut and decided that I really liked the seabird colony. I worked in conjunction with the U.S. Fish and Wildlife Service and U.S. Geological Survey on a meta-population study of the tern colony. From this internship, I got much more than a pretty good salary. I developed contacts with the two government agencies that will hopefully land me a job for this summer in Alaska, again working in a seabird colony. By doing quite a bit of scud work over the weeks on the East Coast, I earned the respect and trust for my supervisors to allow me to conduct my own research project on the island. That research project has given me the opportunity to attend conferences, where just this last weekend, I met a professor from another university who does research with terns. Hopefully, the reference from USFWS will prove productive in getting jobs in the future.

Another opportunity I have had for networking is my current internship at the Oregon Zoo. I wanted to work with birds at the zoo, but the current opening they had was for someone to help raise butterflies for release into the wild. I decided I should take the opportunity and see where it led me. Thanks to my research experience, I was able to set up a more scientific design for determining the best conditions for raising the butterflies and earned the respect of the zookeeper there. While other interns were complaining about having to do things like taking out the trash, I just did it, and pretty soon, I was the one feeding the caterpillars while the other girls were washing dishes. The keeper I work with is currently trying to find a spot for me with the birds, and convincing the other keepers that they should find me a position, since I am "such a great worker." When this internship is over, I will be completely qualified to apply for a job as a zookeeper, and although it is not something I want to do, the experience and references will go far for finding me a career.

I think the most important thing I have learned in my different internships is that everyone has to start at the bottom. If you go into a job thinking that you are too good to do the little things, no one will ever let you do the important stuff. In biological lab work, there are lots of dumb little things that have to be done (like taking out the trash and washing the dishes), and no one is too important to have to do them. If you can show your supervisor that you are willing to do pretty much anything, and understand that your place as an intern is at the bottom, you will not stay at the bottom for long. Careers are not handed to you on a silver platter, but opportunities can be. However, the opportunity may not at first appear so silver lined. We often miss the silver lining because we are looking for gold, but everyone has to start somewhere.

The Mentor Dynamic

Within your career-strategy network, there will be people whom you admire more than others because of the quality of their work. Mentoring relationships naturally tend to form around your shared interest or passion within a particular field. Therefore, your boss might be a potential mentor, but it could just as easily be someone in a different department with whom you've worked on a specific project. Many fields and industries even require a mentoring relationship. In these situations, senior members are matched with newcomers for the purpose of advancing the work.

If someone takes a special interest in you because you have been an apprentice—taking on extra assignments, staying late to help on a special project, and so on—he or she is more likely to give you advice that is not commonly available to others at your level. For instance, you may learn how to best prepare yourself for a promotion. Or you may receive detailed advice on how to do your present job more efficiently. Therefore, seek out ways you can work with or for the people you want to model your professional life after. Then learn as much as you can from them.

I also recommend that you look to a number of different people for guidance, not just one person. The world has become so specialized that a single individual cannot possibly keep up with all there is to know in a given field. For example, at last count, there were at least three different types of eye surgeons, who operate on three different areas of the human eye. Therefore, plan to draw information and support from several people, according to their area of expertise.

In order to actually learn from other people, you must demonstrate an inquiring mind. Ask questions, and be willing to disclose what you do not know. Be open to feedback. Ditch any attitude of arrogance; it won't get you anywhere. I'm not saying that you shouldn't be confident—you have to believe in yourself—but have the wisdom to know what you can learn from others.

What does a successful mentor–protégé relationship look like in the working world? The answer: a two-way street. Harvard Business School graduate Linda Hill, the author of *Becoming a Manager: Mastery of a New Identity,* writes that good mentoring relationships are always mutually beneficial. "The mentor offers advice and opportunity; the protégé delivers results," explains Hill. In other words, the mentor's input yields fruit. You are improving, or you are growing in your understanding of a concept, as a direct result of the mentor's influence in your professional life. This tangible evidence of personal growth and development is gratifying not only to you, but to your mentor as well.

who are my contact people?

Throughout college, you've pushed yourself to branch out, experience things, meet people, and ask questions. Beginning with your junior year, narrow your focus to the career you think you want to pursue.

Here are some good people to contact:

- Company representatives who have registered with your career services office
- Company recruiters listed in the publication *Job Choices* (this is revised and updated yearly)
- Members of your school's alumni association who are in fields you want to pursue
- Professionals in your hometown
- Professors at your university
- Your parents' friends; your siblings or their friends
- Authors of books you've read in your field of interest
- People who have given speeches in your career area

Of course, this is only a partial listing, but it should at least get you started. Keep a checklist of important people you want to meet in order to gather information. Try to meet and speak with one key person a week during your junior and senior years. Keep notes on your conversations so you can make comparisons and analyze the advice you're given.

Getting Connected

Networking, for the purpose of mapping out a career strategy, entails six simple yet critical steps. First, you will need to make contact with people who already work in your field of interest. Therefore, make a list of anyone and everyone who is even remotely related to your selected career or job. If you can't think of at least five people to contact, you're not thinking hard enough.

Second, create a list of questions to ask the contact person. The goal of the questioning process is to determine whether the career path you are on is truly the right one for you. Here are a few questions to get you started:

- What are the pros and cons of working in the industry?
- Of working in that company?
- Of the company's philosophy?
- What does and doesn't appeal to the company?

- What has he or she enjoyed the most? disliked the most?

Remember, finding the answers to these questions will help you assess whether the field and the job are right for you.

Third, with each contact you make, take notes on the responses you get to your questions. Some contacts may even offer to call potential employers on your behalf. Be sure to ask each contact person with whom else you can speak in order to gather more information.

Fourth, while you have the contact on the phone, make the most of the opportunity. For instance, if the conversation went well, plan to ask permission to use the contact as a future reference. Be prepared, however, for a "no" response, and try not to take it personally. The individual may not feel familiar enough with you to give an honest reference.

The previous step leads naturally to the fifth one: Prepare yourself for unexpected outcomes. For example, your contact person may invite you for an interview, so have a calendar nearby so that you can set a date. Likewise, poise yourself for rejection. You may have caught the contact person at a bad time. If you sense that, ask if there is a better time for you to call.

Finally, regardless of what happens, always thank the contact person for his or her time. Then follow up with a brief note of appreciation.

Accessing Key People

Within every company or industry, there are key people. These key people are given job titles such as "chief executive officer," "executive director," "president," or "dean." Although the titles may vary, the power usually doesn't. These are the decision-makers of that institution; therefore, they are the people you need to gain access to.

Making contact with them, however, can be tricky. To contact the key person, you must first make a good impression on the person in the other power seat: the *administrative assistant.* Treat the assistant with as much respect—or more—as the other people you intend to contact. Tell him or her why you would like to see the key person. Explain why you are interested in the company, and talk about your experiences and abilities. Also, ask for information on the company so that you can study it before your meeting with the key person.

The administrative assistant is the eyes and ears for the person you need to speak with. He or she is skilled at knowing exactly what his or her boss values and looks for, so this individual is the first in the chain of people to win over.

If the administrative assistant does not grant you an appointment with the executive director, be gracious. Thank the person for taking the time to talk with you. Later, send follow-up letters to the administrative assistant as well as to the key person, restating your interest. Often the initial "no" is a smoke-screen. Your diplomatic, consistent follow-up may secure the appointment, so don't give up.

Face-to-Face with Key People

Mapping out a career strategy eventually translates into meeting the administrative assistant and other key people for the first time. Although one of your objectives for this initial encounter is to research the company or industry, your primary goal is to make a favorable impression on the people you meet. Doing so may lead to future employment at that establishment, or at the very least *open the door* to some great contacts. That's why some people refer to this stage of career strategy as "getting your foot in the door."

When meeting someone for the first time, you will want to present a professional, courteous, and direct demeanor. Therefore, right at the start, clearly state your interests and your reasons for wanting to interview this person. (This is especially crucial with a professional whom you have not met previously.) Be poised and well dressed, and don't smoke right before the meeting. You'll probably have only two to three minutes to set up the lunch appointment or half-hour meeting, so make the most of the opportunity by being prepared. Consider the sample dialogues below.

FIRST INTERVIEW

You: Hello, Ms. Marshall. Thank you for taking time to see me today.

Key Person: My pleasure. What can I do for you?

You: As your assistant probably told you, I'm one year away from graduating from State A&M with a degree in architectural design. Since your firm has designed some of the most outstanding buildings in this state, I wanted to express my interest in working with you someday. I wondered, specifically, if I might be able to set up a luncheon appointment with you or one of your junior associates so that I could learn firsthand about the qualities you seek in graduates you hire as first-year associates.

KP: I admire your foresight. Unfortunately, I'm swamped right now and would not be able to take two hours to meet with you. However, there is one exemplary employee who has worked with us for two years and who graduated from your school. His name is Jordan Simon, and he may be available to give you some advice.

You: I would appreciate speaking with him. Thank you very much for your time. I hope we are able to see each other in the next year.

KP: You're welcome. My assistant will be happy to give you Jordan's phone number. He manages our other office. Tell him I sent you. Good luck.

PHONE CONTACT WITH JORDAN SIMON

You: Mr. Simon, I am a junior at State A&M and will graduate next year with a degree in architectural design. Cynthia Marshall recommended that I speak with you about how I might best prepare to work for your firm someday. May I take you to lunch sometime next week so we can talk further?

JS: I exercise at lunch every day, but I'd be happy to meet you for breakfast if you tell me why it would be worth my time.

You: Gladly. I have a 3.6 GPA and two summers of experience working for your competitors. I am a hard
worker and a team player, and I have a very creative
mind. I'd like to speak with you in person and pick
your brains and find out how you think, plan, and
organize your time.

JS: (interrupting) That's a good start. Where and when
would you like to get together?

Before the actual appointment, make a list of good questions to
ask. You shouldn't be doing all the talking. Instead, you should be
listening and asking what else you can do to prepare for success. Be
confident, but don't be cocky. You may end up with an apprentice-
ship, which can get you in the door at graduation time.

narrowing your choices

Once you've completed several phone contacts and meetings,
you enter the narrowing phase of your career pursuit. On the
basis of all the information you've gathered over the past three
years, narrow your choices down to two or three career domains.
For example, if you have strong people skills and you want to be in
management someday, sales may be the place to start. If you're
strong in information skills, you may want to begin in an entry-level
position in market research.

If you're strong in the area of objects, you may want to begin as
an apprentice with a craftsperson or a professional in your technical
area of interest.

Once you've narrowed down your career search to a few companies within a particular industry, make a list of the employees
you'd like to set up an appointment with. (Again, one way to gain
access to these people is through their administrative assistants.)
You may not be able to talk to all of them, but writing down their
names will help you figure out whose advice may have the greatest
impact. They are the ones you will want to make every effort to contact first.

Therefore, to maximize the utility of your employee list, consider these questions: Who do you think is the happiest in his or her
job? Why? Is it the company, or is it that person's approach to the

Network Map: Chart It Out!

SYLVIA ROBINSON
Alumna; VP, Interstate Bank

CHARLES DEAN
President, Hometown Bank

MARY ROLATTA
Ex-employee

AL RUBEN
VP, Finance

JOHN SLOAN
Now has own business

MARK CORTEZ
Financial Planner, Merrill Lynch

ANNE GIBB
Teller

Career Network Map

Field: _____

Job: _____

Contact people:

1. Entry-level

   a. _____

   b. _____

   c. _____

2. Upper-level

   a. _____

   b. _____

   c. _____

3. Former employees

   a. _____

   b. _____

   c. _____

4. Alumni who are now in the field

   a. _____

   b. _____

   c. _____

Impressions of the industry:

Pros

_____

_____

_____

Cons

_____

_____

_____

job—or maybe a combination of both? Questioning as many people as possible, in a very diplomatic way, will give you volumes of information with which to make a good decision.

There you have it. As you can see, networking involves far more than just meeting people and gathering information for your own purposes. Keep in mind that it's a two-way street. Sure, you will gain a lot from others, but not unless you're prepared to contribute to them as well. If you can't help someone directly, at least be prepared to thank them in earnest for their support. In turn, when you can, determine to help others who are less experienced than you. Take pleasure in knowing that you're being a mentor or role model to them, just as others have been to you.

11

paperwork

Thought is the soul of act. —ROBERT BROWNING

Brevity is the soul of wit. —WILLIAM SHAKESPEARE

People vary in their reactions to writing resumes. Some students, for example, are excited about it. They look forward to the challenge of condensing several years of their life onto one sheet of paper. On the other end of the spectrum are those who approach the task as if they were waiting in the dentist's office for a root canal. Writing a resume isn't their idea of a good time.

How about you? Are you ready to promote yourself on paper? Whatever your degree of anticipation, writing a resume is an absolutely essential component of a successful job search. In this chapter, we will help you craft an effective one as painlessly as possible. We will also assist you with two other aspects of paperwork, namely, the cover letter and the job application.

197

the job search

ccording to William Potter, vice president of A Better Resume Service in Chicago, the key to a successful job search is:

- To know yourself
- To know your market
- To know how to market yourself effectively

By now you're well on your way to developing knowledge in two of these areas. From Chapter 2, "Discover Who You Are," you learned more about Potter's first recommendation, *to know yourself.* In Chapter 3, you tackled Potter's second recommendation, *to know your market,* by investigating the majors and jobs that interest you. Congratulations—you have covered a lot of ground!

Now you're ready to pick up Potter's third job search recommendation: *marketing yourself,* which is where resume writing comes in. Effective resumes will open doors to interviews. Therefore, to market yourself effectively, you'll need to craft a resume that emphasizes your unique skills and qualities.

planning your dream resume

Your career direction will find its shape, and its name, in increments. In other words, everything you study and explore now will contribute to the resume you send out during your senior year. Your resume will include the whole shebang—academic achievements, extracurricular activities, and work experience.

What do you want your resume to look like? Thinking about the answer to this question now will help you achieve the resume of your dreams. Consequently, the resume of your dreams will help you land the job of your dreams. So begin planning now!

Many students resist writing their resumes for as long as they possibly can, usually until the second semester of their senior year. While procrastination is understandable, it won't help you in finding a job. Wait until the second semester of your senior year and you may find yourself distributing political tracts at the local mall—for the opposition party—at minimum wage. So why tempt fate when it is so easily outfoxed? Start thinking now about how you'd like your resume to look. Can't picture it? I have a suggestion: write it out.

MY DREAM RESUME

(By the second semester of my senior year)

My grade point average is _____

My major and minor are _____

My career goal is _____

My academic honors include _____

_____

_____

My extracurricular activities include _____

_____

_____

I had a summer internship doing _____

at _____

I traveled to _____

I worked part-time as _____

My references are:

1. _____

2. _____

3. _____

Okay, now you know what you want to accomplish for your future. The first step toward getting there is to focus on the here and now. What does your current resume look like? Do you have a current resume? If not, now is definitely the time to begin thinking about it. Why? Because you want to land that internship, don't you? What about the part-time job? Regardless of the type of position you seek, a resume will always reflect favorably on you. It allows your prospective employer to see what you have accomplished thus far—your experience, skills and abilities, and any special training are there at a glance.

MY TWO CENTS *How Do I Apply It?*

Kati Pope, University of Denver

Why is paperwork important? How do you come across well on paper? Why does it all matter so much? Hiring mangers will tell you that the resume is the first impression that anyone will have of you. And they will only look at it, on average, for a few seconds. So, it has to make a solid impression so that people will want to keep reading. A resume is an organized illustration of yourself. Resumes allow an individual to expose his or her life experiences through listing jobs, skills, strengths, achievements, and interests. The resume is essentially a documented form of the self that represents you as the most ideal candidate for the job or internship you desire. By writing a good resume you are designing a primary advocate for your success in a future job. How much time you invest in your resume is reflected in the quality of the content. Is it too long? Is it relevant? Is it stimulating?

A resume should be organized, clear, and concise, and should contain the most relevant information regarding a person's job skills and experiences. Direct information relating to the desired job and the individual's capabilities will provide the candidate with a stronger resume. For example I have applied for zookeeping jobs and have included information regarding my animal experiences in zoos as well as some business experiences I have had because both were relevant to my desired occupation. This was effective for me because my resume was able to demonstrate that I have animal experience as well as business skills, which are also significant for obtaining a zoo keeping position.

Cover letters are another component of the resume. A cover letter should be no longer than a small paragraph and should immediately state what job you are interested in having. The cover letter is designed to describe specifically what position you are interested in obtaining with the potential employer. It tells the employer, briefly, why you are applying for the job or internship, why you are the best person for the job, and why you will be an excellent contributor to the job.

A thank-you letter is often sent after the conclusion of an interview. The thank-you letter should be brief and should be written in appreciative terms. For example, a thank-you letter can include something like, "I enjoyed meeting you and look forward to hearing from you again!", or "Thank you for your time and consideration." Thank-you letters are important because they not only remind the employer who you are, but they also make a positive impression.

So, how do you compile your current resume? You can begin by taking a look at what you possess that might be attractive to a prospective employer. Don't be afraid to toot your own horn—as long as it's all true and not exaggerated, of course! Completing the sentences below will help you begin to craft the resume of your dreams.

My objective is _____

I am currently studying _____

I graduated from high school in _____

Academic recognitions that I received in high school included _____

_____

My past work experience includes _____

_____

_____

I have special training in _____

_____

_____

I am especially good at _____

_____

_____

My other abilities include _____

_____

_____

Classes I have had that are relevant to the position I seek are _____

_____

My references are

1. _____

2. _____

3. _____

first impressions

E xperts emphasize that your resume gives potential employers their first impression of you. A good resume can help you get your foot inside an interviewer's door. For that reason, your resume may be the most important element of your job search. In addition to making a good first impression, your resume also serves as a springboard for a prospective employer's questions. And later it's a reminder on file of who you are.

A survey involving the top 100 U.S. companies by Robert Half, author of *How to Get a Better Job in This Crazy World,* revealed the four leading reasons that resumes are disregarded: 36 percent of all resumes contain distortions or lies; 19 percent have spelling errors; 12 percent fail to provide sufficient detail; and 10 percent give irrelevant information. Your career planning and placement center probably offers assistance in eliminating mistakes like these, so be sure to make an appointment with them. For now, here are the basic ingredients of an effective resume, in the order that they should appear:

1. *The heading.* A resume should begin with your name, address, telephone number, and e-mail address (if you have one) so an employer will know how to reach you, should he or she be interested.

2. *The job objective.* Next on your resume comes the job objective, which should be stated in one sentence. Including a job objective on your resume, however, isn't always necessary, nor is it always the best approach. "By stating a job objective," writes Robert Half, "you potentially rule yourself out of being considered for other jobs in that same company, jobs that do not match precisely with the objective you've stated."

One solution to the job objective dilemma is to drop the job objective altogether. Another option, however, is to write separate, "specialized" resumes, each prepared with basic honesty but beefing up those qualities you want to accentuate. For example, let's say your education and background have made you suitable for positions in marketing, selling, and advertising. Obviously, any of those areas might provide permanent employment for you, but one resume that attempts to cover all those bases may lack the necessary focus. Therefore, three specialized resumes should be created. One will emphasize the marketing aspect of your experience. The second will focus on your sales background and your accomplishments in selling. The third will have your advertising experience at the forefront. When you're invited for a marketing job interview, you will give the interviewer the version of the resume that highlights that aspect of your education and experience.

Since you can't, however, be all things to all people all of the time, Half recommends that you prepare a "general" resume so that "the disparate major focuses of your experience are given equal weight."

3. *The body.* The body, which is the largest portion of your resume, consists of four parts: (1) education; (2) job history; (3) activities; and (4) achievements. List these items in reverse chronological order, beginning with the most recent. Include any skills relevant to the type of employment sought, such as the ability to speak a foreign language, or secretarial or computer skills.

the cover letter

To get your resume noticed, you'll need an ace cover letter. A what? A personalized letter that accompanies your resume. You might think the best cover letter would contain a curling arrow and a boldface message reading "Resume Below," followed by a full line of exclamation points:

!!!!!!!!!!!!!!!!!!!!!!!!!!!!!!!!!!!

That might not be such a bad idea, but unfortunately this is not the kind of cover letter most employers have come to expect. The cover letter is not the domain of the abstract-expressionist avant-garde existentialist career hunter. Not as of this writing, anyway.

Basically, a cover letter lets you do two things: herald your resume and secure the interview. By taking your highlights and personalizing them, a good cover letter convinces the reader to pay attention to your resume. Therefore, take just as much care in preparing it as you do your resume. To make your cover letter visually appealing, print it on personalized stationery or at least good quality paper. Then briefly state your most compelling qualifications and request an interview. Also, be sure to mention the reason why you'd like to work for the company.

In short, the goals of your cover letter are:

1. To express interest in the company and a specific position.
2. To engage the reader's interest so he or she is compelled to read your resume.
3. To mention a specific date when you will contact the employer, if he or she doesn't contact you.

Of equal importance, the cover letter provides you with the opportunity to discuss the company to which you're applying. Mention something specifically appealing to you about the prospective employer. This lets the "personal approach" work in two directions—yours and theirs. And it makes things much more interesting.

In respect to cover letters, *Newsday* features editor David Herndon gives another important job search tip: Give the cover letter some zing. Don't dwell on the reasons why it would be a good experience for you to work for the prospective employer; rather, always stay focused on how you can help the company. "Tell [the prospective employer] why it would be a good experience for him to work with you." Then follow up with a phone call two weeks later.

Thank-you notes following interviews are neither necessary nor expected. All the more reason why it's so important to send them. They need not be elaborate. Just say thanks.

the job application

L ike your other work papers, the job application should be neat and well thought out. If you can, fill out the application at home. But before writing on the actual application, write your responses first on scratch paper. That way you can refine your thoughts before committing them to paper.

On the pages that follow is a fairly comprehensive sample job application. Fill it out for practice. Then look at your responses later and see what you think. Are you crisp and to the point? Are your examples convincing? Would *you* be interested in interviewing *you* based on your application?

Some sample cover letters, resumes, and thank-you letters follow. Remember, resumes and other paperwork are simply marketing tools. On average, job recruiters will spend only about thirty seconds looking at your resume; therefore, you want to give the very best impression.

The way you dress, speak, and follow up are also tools of self-promotion. Again, you may see a key person only briefly, but you want to make a lasting, winning impression. If you follow the advice in this chapter, you will.

Job Application

Please print in ink. Attach separate sheets if necessary.

Name: First, Middle, Last	Social Security No.
Home Address: Street, City, State, ZIP	Home Phone
How long at present address?	Are you in the U.S. on a temporary visa?

In emergency, notify (Name/Address/Phone)

List any friends or relatives working with the company, by name and relationship.

Have you ever worked for us or one of our subsidiaries?

Have you ever applied for work here before? If so, when?

Do you own or have access to a car?

Has your license ever been suspended or revoked? If so, why?

EDUCATION

Circle the Highest Grade Completed:	High school 1 2 3 4	Graduate school 1 2 3 4
	College 1 2 3 4	Degrees:

	High school	**College**
Name of school, date entered, location		
Graduation date and grade point average		
List major and minor fields		
Scholastic honors		

Any academic or disciplinary probation? If yes, explain.

List extracurricular or athletic activities.

List part-time jobs.

How did you spend your summer vacations?

Are you proud of your college record? Explain.

WORK EXPERIENCE

1. From/Through/Most recent employer/May we contact?

Address   Phone

Current or final supervisor

Starting position and salary

How did you get the job?   Why did you leave?

What did you like the best about the job?

What did you like the least about the job?

2. From/Through/Employer before No. 1/May we contact?

Address   Phone

Current or final supervisor

Starting position and salary

How did you get the job?   Why did you leave?

What did you like the best about the job?

What did you like the least about the job?

_____

3. From/Through/Employer before No. 2/May we contact?

_____

Address   Phone

_____

Current or final supervisor

_____

Starting position and salary

_____

How did you get the job?   Why did you leave?

_____

What did you like the best about the job?

_____

What did you like the least about the job?

_____

Please summarize any relevant experience that uniquely qualifies you for this job.

REFERENCES

List three persons, not relatives or former employers, who have known you for the last five years whom we may contact.

| *Name* | *Address* | *Years Known* |

1. _____

2. _____

3. _____

_____

State your own personal definition of this position.

_____

Please tell us why you want this job and why you think you would be successful.

ACTIVITIES

Excluding religious or political groups, with what organizations do you now work?

What are your principal hobbies?

_____

What magazines do you regularly read?

_____

How many hours do you watch TV per week?

_____

What types of books do you read most often?

_____

Below are some of the reasons why some people want to join our company. Check four that are the most important to you and four that are the least important to you.

	Most	*Least*
The chance to be with a growing company.	_____	_____
The company's liberal pension policies.	_____	_____
The opportunity to be promoted.	_____	_____
The opportunity to sell.	_____	_____
The company's reputation.	_____	_____
The profit-sharing program.	_____	_____
Freedom from routine.	_____	_____
Job security.	_____	_____
The opportunity to travel.	_____	_____

What do you consider your most important accomplishment?

_____

What has been your most serious disappointment?

_____

Describe your most competitive situation and the steps you took to achieve success.

_____

What do you consider to be your three most important assets?

_____

In what three areas would you most like to improve?

_____

Are you willing to travel? To relocate?

_____

When can you start to work?

Sample Cover Letter No. 1

Melanie McFadden

19 Circle Street   (614) 555-1234
Columbus, Ohio 43216   mmcfadden@earthlink.net

April 10, 2004

Mr. James Ward
Director of Operations
Database International
5510 Mainway Drive
Los Angeles, CA 90086

Dear Mr. Ward:

I am a senior majoring in computer science and information processing at the University of Florida.

I have followed the success of Database International. You are recognized nationally as a leader in the industry and have a reputation for providing exceptional ongoing training programs for your junior programmers.

Enclosed is my resume outlining my academic, extracurricular, and work experience of the past four years.

If you would like to call me to set up a personal interview, I can be reached at (614) 555-1234. If I don't hear from you by April 29, I'll call you.

Thank you for your consideration. I look forward to hearing from you soon.

Sincerely,

Melanie McFadden

Melanie McFadden

Sandra Magioco

9 College Road, Baltimore, Maryland 21203   (410) 555-1776

February 5, 2005

Ms. Margaret Jimenez
XYZ Department Store
9 Financial Street
New York, NY 11351

Dear Ms. Jimenez:

I was recently speaking with Joanne Stewart, a manager with your store. Because she is familiar with my work, she strongly advised me to send a copy of my resume to your office regarding the opening as an assistant buyer in your sportswear department.

I feel confident that after reviewing my resume, you will see that I am a worthy candidate. Besides having a strong background in sales, I have worked closely with buyers for many years. Not only do I have skill in fashion display, customer service, and managing employees, I understand the demands of the retail fashion industry as a whole.

The opportunity to work with you is appealing. I look forward to your response and hope we can meet soon to discuss my resume and work history further. Thank you for your time and consideration.

Sincerely,

Sandra Magioco

Sandra Magioco
s_magioco@yahoo.com

Sample Resume No. 1

Jennifer Anderson

4332 Rookwood Street	(216) 555-3452
Cleveland, Ohio 44101	jennanderson@cox.net

JOB OBJECTIVE

Position as programmer with supervisory responsibilities.

EDUCATION

- B.A., University of Florida, 2003. Computer science/information processing major; liberal arts minor. GPA: 3.4.
- Junior semester abroad in Florence, Italy. Studied history, art, music, Renaissance literature, and Italian.
- Rotary scholarship finalist: May 1998. Alternate for one year of study in Fyfe, Scotland.

WORK EXPERIENCE

- *Anderson, Inc., 2003 to present.*
  Created computer programs using Java for privately owned company in Cleveland.
- *Tutor, Computer Science Center, University of Florida, 2002–2003.*
  Tutored freshman and sophomore students in math and computer science.
- *Borrans Corporation, Columbus, Ohio; summer intern, 2000–2002.*
  Programmer and operations trainee, responsible for training new employees and experienced employees in need of additional instruction.

ACTIVITIES/HONORS

- *Vice President, College Democrats: 2001–2002.*
  Recruited students to participate in city, state, and local campaigns.
- *Treasurer, Campus Achievers: 2000–2002.*
  Honorary student service society.
- *President, Student Union Activities Board, 2000–2001.*
  Coordinated activities from Parents' Day to spring break vacations.

References available upon request.

Sample Resume No. 2

George Rappaport
george_rapp@netstar.com

154 West 78th Street, New York, New York 10019   (212) 555-0030

JOB OBJECTIVE   Entry-level accounting position with medium- to large-sized public accounting firm.

EDUCATION   Bachelor of Science in Accounting with English minor, University of Maryland, 2004. GPA: 3.6.
- Dean's List, six semesters
- Junior semester in Mexico City, Mexico. Studied Spanish and Mexican heritage while living with a Mexican family.

WORK EXPERIENCE
- *Internal Auditor,* 2002–2004, HealthCare Insurance Agency, Baltimore, MD.
  Managed nine corporate accounts. Responsible for training and supervising staff of twelve.

- *Summer Intern,* 2003, Kenase Accountants.
  Experienced work in a small accounting firm first hand. Managed four of the company's ten largest accounts as well as eighteen long-term clients.

- *Summer Intern,* 2002, Business Management Legal Associates.
  Performed legal accounting and tax preparation for partners and associates.

ACTIVITIES
- Volunteer, Big Brother program, 2002–2004.
  Coached and served as "big brother" to two underprivileged teenagers.

- President, Blue Key (national senior honorary society), 2004.

- Scholarship Chairperson, Phi Kappa Psi Fraternity.

References available upon request.

Sample Resume No. 3

Gretl Pahane

gretlp@theriver.org

11 North Oracle Circle, Santa Barbara, CA 93103

(805) 555-9000

EDUCATION
- University of California, Santa Barbara—Bachelor of Arts in Oral History, May 2004.

MAJOR COURSEWORK
- Rhetoric, Religious Theory, PASCAL Programming, Political Science in the Modern Age, Squash.

EXPERIENCE

Tutor
- Dual Discovery Center, 800 Sproul Plaza, UCSB, Santa Barbara.

  Tutored socially disadvantaged high school students in various academic disciplines, with an emphasis in algebra and geometry.

Sales Associate
- The May Company, 1000 Maypole Lane, Primavera, CA.

  Marketed state-of-the-art organic disinfectants. Involved in all aspects of business, including cash and credit transactions, daily book- and record-keeping, and inventory.

Political Assistant
- Assistant to Representative Boris Bear, 8 Beach Front Bonanza Blvd., Bora Bora, CA.

  Performed administrative tasks including word processing, maintaining headquarter files, and telephoning constituents. Assisted door-to-door survey in reelection campaign; coordinated neighborhood voter registration drive.

Volunteer Work
- Adviser, Big Sister Program, Santa Barbara. Planned recreational activities for three inner-city teens.
- Pollster, Campaign to Re-elect Jerry Brown. Worked at midtown Los Angeles headquarters on voter survey phone bank. Solicited voter preferences through assertive phone skills.

PERSONAL
- Captain, UCSB Varsity Squash Team; UCSB Humanitarian Award (2003).

References available upon request.

John Rhies

2001 Northshore Drive, Detroit, MI 48231

February 25, 2005

Mr. Mark Nordbrach
Manager, Personnel Department
Wesley Manufacturing, Inc.
500 Sylvan Avenue
Redwood City, CA 94063

Dear Mr. Nordbrach:

I appreciate your taking the time to talk with me about entry-level management positions at Wesley.

I am especially interested in spending a day in the field with one of your division managers. I am eager to see the workings of the job you discussed—in progress.

If I don't hear from you by the end of the week, I'll call you on Monday morning, March 8.

Again, thanks for your time and consideration.

Sincerely,

John Rhies

John Rhies
john–rhies@interset.com
313-495-2501

Sample Thank-You Note No. 2

KEVIN SULLIVAN

3000 Sutro Boulevard, San Francisco, CA 94143 • 415-224-8966

April 8, 2004

Ms. Alison McCormack
National Recruiter
ABC Paper Products
9 Ellwood Avenue
San Francisco, CA 94142

Dear Ms. McCormack:

Thank you for taking the time to discuss with me the position of product manager with ABC Paper Products.

Though we didn't have a chance to discuss my part-time job, I believe it qualifies me for the position even more than my summer internships. Working ten hours a week over three years for the Reynolds Advertising Agency as a clerk gave me firsthand experience with designers and production artists. I was able to learn over an extended period the long-term ramifications of the wrong—and the right—paper decisions. This long-term view provided me with more insight than my three-month summer internship.

If I don't hear from you within the next week, I'll call you on Monday, April 19. I'm keenly interested in the position and the company. Again, thanks for your time.

Sincerely,

Kevin Sullivan

Kevin Sullivan
ksullivan@postnet.net

your third degree

The worst thing you can possibly do in a deal is seem desperate to make it. That makes the other guy smell blood and then you're dead. The best thing you can do is deal from strength, and leverage is the best strength you have. Leverage is having what the other guy wants. Or better yet, needs. Or best of all, simply can't do without.

—DONALD TRUMP, *THE ART OF THE DEAL*

L ike making a deal, there is a special art to interviewing," says Anne Marie Meyers, who coaches people on how to prepare for interviews. "You have to convince the prospective employer that they need you to work for their company. But to do that, you have to first convince yourself." Ninety percent of the interview, Meyers says, is based on the confidence and image you project.

So what's the worst that can happen during an interview?

When asked to describe how you function under pressure, you let out a high-pealed shriek, double over in your chair, and laugh uncontrol-

217

lably—so hard, in fact, that tears are rolling down your face, moistening your new suit. Unable to breathe, you gasp periodically. The recruiter, visibly frightened, buzzes the secretary at her outer alcove and asks for a box of tissues, which the secretary does not have and which she is asked, in an imperative panic, to *find* . . .

Or, in place of hysteria, you are stricken with amnesia

RECRUITER: Tell me about yourself.

YOU: Who?

RECRUITER: You . . . yourself. Tell me about yourself.

YOU: I don't remember.

RECRUITER: Well, Jim, thank you for your time. We'll be in touch.

YOU: Jim???

If the above scenarios seem unlikely, you can relax about interviewing for your first big job. The more typical ways of fouling up interviews—which everybody has, at some point, done—are far less embarrassing and much easier to correct.

be prepared

arah Greenspan's first interview is a good example of what can happen to an ace candidate who starts off unprepared. Sarah is a crackerjack. Hardworking, outgoing, smart as a whip, athletic—generally and specifically on the ball. The kind you'd love to hate if she weren't so nice.

Sarah's first choice was Xerox. The corporate headquarters were located on the East Coast, near her hometown. The company philosophy was one she admired, and the starting salary for sales reps was very attractive indeed. She was, in a word, psyched.

But, as you may have guessed, psyched was not enough. The problem was that Sarah was *too* psyched and *too little* prepared. Because she was uninformed, unrehearsed, and unprepared, the recruiter spent only fifteen minutes with her, despite her impressive credentials—top of her class, student body vice president, and employee at the Campus Copy Center.

What do I mean by "unprepared"? Back to Sarah.

XEROX INTERVIEWER: Sarah, I'd be interested to know a little about how you've overcome defeat.

SARAH: Well, um, let me think. I tend to be pretty successful when I put my mind to something. Um, I guess there was the time I was running for homecoming queen. I lost. And I mean, I was really busy, it was my junior year, I was student body vice president, I was working part time at a Campus Copy Center (we had Xerox machines, by the way) and I guess I didn't really have the time I would have liked to devote to promoting myself. I mean, I still think I could have won. But I got over it.

This was minute 7 of the interviewing process. By minute 14, Sarah was being thanked for her time and ushered to the door. What was wrong with Sarah's response?

First, Sarah was out of sync. She was still trying to sell her invincible being when the recruiter was specifically asking for a candid discussion of failure. She wasn't listening, a common problem of interviewees. Because she wasn't listening, the rest of her response sounded scattered and insincere. That wasn't the moment to plug Xerox—the recruiter had her resume; he could read; he knew she'd worked with their photocopiers and was familiar with the product. What he was looking for was Sarah's response to defeat. He wanted-ed to see her capacity to evaluate herself, under adverse circumstances, and do something constructive.

There are two obvious lessons to learn from Sarah's mistake. The first one is: When you are being interviewed, focus on what the interviewer is saying, then respond accordingly. The second lesson is even more to the point: Prepare answers in advance to common interview questions, like the one Sarah was asked. Back to Sarah, this time under better circumstances, in her interview with Gallo, where she was offered a job.

GALLO INTERVIEWER: How have you overcome defeat?

SARAH: Well, I very much wanted a university fellowship for a year's study abroad. I had been thinking about a career in international relations. I wanted to see Europe, and I knew I probably wouldn't have another chance to immerse myself in a foreign culture. I put all my eggs in one basket. I didn't apply for other study-abroad programs, and in April, after the second interview, I was nixed. Despite being seriously disappointed, I regrouped. I contacted the International Council on Economic Development and found out about volunteer programs in Latin America. I worked at the Campus Copy Center that summer, saving money, getting work experience, and taking my mind off what I didn't get. That fall I immersed myself in Latin American studies and applied to the Council's volunteer program in Bolivia. I was accepted, and the following May I was off. I think now that this was the best I could have hoped for. I was able to help other people and at the same time learned self-reliance. I found out about the world, and about myself.

Notice the difference in Sarah's response. She didn't try to dodge the question or reframe it to suit her agenda. She was clear, while showing a capacity for reflection and honest self-appraisal. She also showed that she has the ability to create value from failure, which is an asset in any job situation.

Further, Sarah was able to reveal a lot about herself without blowing her own horn. From her answer, the recruiter could also deduce motivation, tenacity, concern for others, and self-reliance. He could see, in short, complexity and capability from a response that used up a total of 90 seconds. He liked what he saw and made her an offer. (Sarah also received offers from Lever Brothers and Carnation.)

Let's look at another example. Alan King was extremely well qualified and well prepared for his interview with Shearson-Lehman. He had researched the company and the position; he had spoken with several employees and did an excellent job of communicating his background and his career aspirations. But when the interviewer wrapped up the conversation, he said: "Alan, you have excellent credentials and I'm sure you'll be very successful when you begin your career. However, I don't think you're what we're looking for."

Alan, thinking quickly on his feet, said: "If Shearson seeks employees who are quick starters, inquisitive, hard-working, dedicated, and committed to making things happen, then you should hire me. If you want an employee who won't be dissuaded by obstacles or excuses, and if you want someone who will continually lead others in finding new and creative ways to solve problems, I'm your candidate. If Shearson doesn't seek these qualities in their employees, then perhaps you're right. Perhaps I'm not what you're looking for."

The interviewer, who closes every interview with the phrase "I don't think you're what we're looking for," liked Alan because he overcame an objection with self-confidence and poise. He didn't take no for an answer. Shearson sought leaders—not complacent followers.

I routinely interview college graduates for positions as sales representatives. The more specific the applicants are about what they've done and about how those experiences have affected them, the more I'm convinced they'd be valuable employees. It's not enough just to say what you've done; you have to demonstrate that you've thought about how that experience has contributed to your personal or professional development.

To illustrate my point, I will briefly describe real interviews that I conducted with two applicants. The first applicant had all the right "canned" responses. He had obviously prepared for the interview by reading a book about interviewing, but he hadn't prepared by thinking through his responses to distinguish himself from all of the other applicants. He just didn't stand out from the crowd. He came across as rather ordinary and predictable. He also did not exude interest, enthusiasm, or confidence.

Toward the end of the interview, I gave him another chance to show some initiative: I gave him my business card and told him to call me if he had any questions about the position or about career opportunities within the company. Perhaps he could have redeemed himself if he had called later with specific questions. He could have written a follow-up note. I never heard from him again. Despite his high grades and work experience, we didn't call him back, either.

At the start of the second interview, I was skeptical because the applicant was a graduate of Yale. (I'm not a Yale grad.) This was an unreasonable prejudice, I realize. But it's a good example of a mind-set, which you will undoubtedly encounter from some interviewers in one form or another and will have to bulldoze your way past with confidence, preparedness, and authenticity.

I asked the second applicant, whose name is Ted, some of the usual questions. He responded with enthusiasm, imagination, and humor. He didn't strike me as someone who would be bored by the possibility of work. He'd played intramural sports, was involved as a class officer, had had a summer internship with clinical psychologists in the Bronx, and for two years had volunteered with the Big Brother program. He also had high aspirations. He asked about career track opportunities and my own career path within the company, and he talked about the future he envisioned for himself. Within the first five minutes, Ted managed to throw my prejudices right out the window. I asked him what some of his lifelong career goals were. He said: "I want to go into politics in the second half of my career. I want to be President."

We hired him. His determination, his track record, and his belief in his own ability made him a winner in my book. He'll succeed because he believes he can. By the way, if he does run for President at some point, he's got a campaign manager in me.

Back to prejudice for a moment. Perhaps you'll have to overcome a stereotype someone may have of people who did or did not attend your school, or a prejudice about the activity you did or did not join. You *will*, one of these days, have to overcome some kind of bias to get a job. Relax. Everybody else faces the same kind of situations. There were interviewers who were undoubtedly unimpressed by the fact that I had *not* gone to Oxford on a Fulbright, followed up by two years in Ethiopia with the Peace Corps, capped by a year in Paris at the Cordon Bleu, before my return stateside to pursue a career in marketing.

The trick is to be yourself. Doing so may win them over. However, if they know the real you and still aren't impressed, realize that you probably wouldn't have liked working there anyway. How could you be happy working for an organization that doesn't value your personality and abilities? Instead, determine to give the interview your best shot; be direct and professional. Identifying and overcoming objections, as well as bad attitudes, is part of being a pro at the interviewing process. It's also part of being a successful team player once you're hired.

your interview

Y ou've marketed yourself with your resume and cover letter. Now comes the big sell. You'll need to describe your experience so your interviewer knows you're prepared for the job. Rehearse for confidence. And, by all means, follow up after the interview. Here are some tips:

1. *Before the interview, do some research.* Check out the organization and the position. The better prepared you are for the interview, the more confidence you will project. Talk to people who work at the company or who hold similar positions for rival firms. Go to the library and research the company. Look in the Standard and Poor's Register of Corporations or the Moody's Manual. Check *Forbes, Fortune, Hoovers,* or other business magazines. Look for the organization's web page on the Internet. Learn the organization's history and the current climate. This is the type of knowledge that helps people at both ends of the interviewing

seesaw. Not only will your readiness impress your interviewer, it will also help you decide if the organization interests you. So develop questions about the company and the job ahead of time, then find the answers from your research.

2.   *Rehearse.* Before your interview, rehearse answers to questions likely to be asked. Ask friends to play interviewer and give them a list of questions to ask you. When you communicate effectively, your interviewer will be convinced of your abilities beyond your "paper" credentials. If you do not have someone to help you role-play, set up mock interviews at your career services center. You may even want to record a practice interview of yourself on a video camera and then play it back to see how you did. Without sounding arrogant, become comfortable and confident about your accomplishments. You want the interviewer to know that you are ambitious and self-assured.

Even after you've asked a friend to help you simulate an actual interview, continue to think and brainstorm about the really tough questions you're likely to be asked. For practice, go to all the interviews you're offered, even at companies you're not seriously considering. All the while, keep an open mind. The company you may be least interested in initially could be the very one that impresses you most.

3.   *Dress for success.* Your appearance says a lot about you, so invest in one good interviewing shirt, suit, and shoes. Have your hair cut and styled. Look neat, alert, and enthusiastic. Again, you're promoting yourself, so you want to present the best "you" possible. Don't take any shortcuts.

4.   *Relax.* If you've followed the first three steps, you have every reason to be confident as you walk into the interviewer's office. So relax, be yourself, and enjoy the experience.

Some Interview Tips

Now for a few tips from a combat veteran. Steve Kendall, a recruiter for Nabisco, appreciates interviewees who are animated, sincere, and forthright. "I want to see the applicant use examples to convince me of his or her qualifications and potential for success," says Steve.

"Let the interviewer set the pace," he continues. "The biggest turn-offs in job interviews are pat answers riddled with anxiety and interviewees who control the interview too abrasively in the first part of the conversation. Use the time in the last quarter of the interview to ask questions and gather information about the company."

Common Interview Questions

When Steve Kendall conducts an interview, two of his favorite questions are "Why are you interested in working for my company?" and "What are some examples of how you persuaded others to your way of thinking?" (How would you respond right now to those two questions?)

In addition, here are some of the most common questions interviewers ask college graduates. Use the sample answers as a starting point for figuring out answers of your own.

"Why should we hire you?" (Worst possible response: "Because.") This is a springboard from which to list the qualities that will make you a great employee. Be brief in giving your response and use specific examples to illustrate your points:

> I'm conscientious, tireless, and committed to going above and beyond what is expected of me. Last summer, as an intern with the New York Stock Exchange, I was always the first in to work and the last to leave at night. I made several excellent acquaintances, including the president of Merrill Lynch, who offered me a part-time job during the school year.

"Tell me about your education." (Worst possible response: "It's over.") This question is meant to find out how much emphasis you've put on your academic education. If you've made good or great grades, terrific. If you haven't, explain why: you worked twenty-five hours a week; supported yourself and your foster family of five completely; took eighteen units each semester; got your pilot's license; and so on. If you've learned a lot from taking demanding teachers, say so, but only if it's true. Never fudge in an interview. In addition to being unethical, padding your own story in an interview is painfully obvious to people who recruit for a living.

> Although my GPA is 3.2, I've made 4.0 for the last two academic years. I took serious classes, looked to my professors as mentors, and truly challenged myself. I'm proud of what I've learned during college.

"Tell me something about yourself." (Worst possible answer: "Taurus, Cancer rising, Moon in Sagittarius.") Like the first question, this is an open-ended query. Your interviewer is interested in seeing what you choose to include in your answers. Open-ended questions reveal a lot about who you are: Are you an achiever? Are you detail-oriented? Are you reliable? Are you a fast learner? Are you good at balancing several things at once? Would you have a cool head in a hot situation? What about the personal side of you? How are you perceived by others? Are you frequently available to help? Are you patient?

Your response to one open-ended query helps answer many questions at once. Notice how the applicant below manages to answer the question skillfully while letting her personality shine through.

> I'm an enthusiastic, determined, and highly self-motivated person. I take a great deal of pride in being successful in work and play. I've tried hard to develop my outside interests—some of which my friends and family consider crazy. I like to skydive, spelunk [crawl around in caves], and read science fiction. I also love organizing big groups of people—for outdoor park concerts, the annual summer Renaissance Festival, canoeing trips, and so on. My greatest weakness is that I have so many interests, I tend to take on too much at times.

By analyzing the responses to some of these questions, you can see how much you must "think on your feet" to answer questions in positive, concrete, and self-affirming ways. But the more responses to questions you've thought through and rehearsed, the better you'll be able to "close" your interview.

Here's an additional list of frequently asked questions for you to think about and rehearse. (You'll notice that some of these questions are similar to those in Chapter Two, on defining who you are.) Compare the answers from your freshman year to the answers to your interview questions. How have you changed?

- Tell me about a specific goal you have set and achieved, at school or at work.
- How much energy do you have? Describe a typical day and week.
- Describe any experience you have had that is relevant to this job.
- Where do you see yourself five years from now?
- Where do you see yourself ten years from now?
- What was your greatest defeat, and how did you overcome it?
- What is your greatest accomplishment?
- What do you do in your spare time?
- What is the last book you read?
- What book has had the greatest impact on you?
- What interests you most about this job?
- How would a previous employer or professor describe you?
- How would your friends describe you?
- What interests you most about this job and this organization?

how you will be evaluated

There are a number of different categories in which your interviewer will evaluate you. On a scale of 1 to 5, with 1 being the lowest and 5 being the highest, rate yourself in the following areas. Then think of one or more specific examples to support your rating and write the examples down in the spaces provided below:

- *Solving problems and setting priorities:* Able to understand and take action to solve even the most complex problems.

Number rating: _____

Example: _____

_____

- *Achieving goals:* Consistently sets and achieves goals; results-oriented.

  Number rating: _____

  Example: _____

  _____

- *Motivating others:* Effective at communicating a personal point of view to others.

  Number rating: _____

  Example: _____

  _____

- *Working well with others:* Works well with and gains the respect of co-workers.

  Number rating: _____

  Example: _____

  _____

- *Responsibility:* Follows through on commitments made to co-workers and clients.

  Number rating: _____

  Example: _____

  _____

- *Tenacity:* Determined to work well through even the most mundane parts of the job.

  Number rating: _____

  Example: _____

  _____

- *Detail-oriented:* Pays attention to even the smallest details while keeping the larger goals in focus.

  Number rating: _____

  Example: _____

  _____

- *Vision:* Envisions a mission beyond the immediate game plan; can see all the way to the championship.

  Number rating: _____

  Example: _____

  _____

- *Resilience:* Bounces back from defeat. Treats setbacks as stepping-stones. Explores other avenues despite the difficult nature of the situation. Consistently tests new ideas.

  Number rating: _____

  Example: _____

  _____

Other Criteria

Basically, most companies will evaluate you as Excellent, Good, Fair, or Weak on four points. They are:

1. *Personal qualities:* How do you come across? Are you strongly motivated or sluggish? Are you energetic or lazy? Do you have long-term goals or are you aimless? Are you articulate or shy? Friendly or boorish?

2. *Professional qualities:* Are you reliable? Are you honest? Can you inspire others? Are you able to juggle a number of projects at once? Are you decisive? Do you follow through?

3. *Accomplishments:* Can you describe your proudest achievements? What have they taught you? How have you grown from the challenges you've faced?

4. *Potential:* Do you consider the long term? Do you place high value on continuing your education and building new skills? Will you be a good investment for the company? Do you show signs of long-term interest in the industry, or will you be off to business school in one year?

MY TWO CENTS   *How Do I Apply It?*

Lennee Mozia, Duke University

I am from Denver, Colorado, and come from a culturally diverse background. My father was born and raised in Lagos, Nigeria, and my mother is an African-American woman from Lexington, North Carolina. My family and I spend a lot of time discussing a variety of issues from politics and religion to social trends. As a result of my environment, and the way I am in general, I have a very analytical mind and have learned to apply it in many areas of study.

Although many people (including my family) have suggested that my knack for discussion and observing issues would be best utilized in a courtroom, I realized in my time away from school that I am much better suited as a literature major than a law student (then again, things can and do change). My writing classes at Duke University gave me a chance to creatively express my opinions about themes in literature and how they relate to each other and the world. These were a key factor in helping me decide what I want to do with my education.

Surprisingly enough, Duke University is not where I received an education on how to properly approach an interview. Nobody interviewed me during my college application process, but the activity is very important for school and life in general. My first real interview came over summer break after my freshman year in college. I interviewed for a job at Victoria's Secret in hopes of becoming a sales associate.

The first thing I was asked to do after turning in my job application was to come to my interview in the company dress code, which was a black suit, a nice shirt, and professional black shoes. Many times the interviewer will not ask the applicant to dress in any particular way, but it is important to look put-together and professional when going to an interview. I am a firm believer in not judging people by the way they look or dress, but I do realize that one should really make an effort to dress well at an interview—not necessarily to convey a certain image or status, but to show the interviewer that he or she cares about the position enough to look well-groomed and professional.

My interview for the sales job at Victoria's Secret was the best kind of interview for me to begin with because sales is all about dealing with people, and that is exactly what I think an interview is all about. In the first half of my interview, the store manager asked me to step out on the floor and try to sell some underwear (this was not what I was expecting). After I tried to sell underwear to complete strangers, I felt a little more at ease about the second half of the interview, which was a series of questions I had to answer about my job experience and what I wanted to bring to the company.

The best advice I could possibly give to anyone going through an interview (which may be a little clichéd) is to say whatever feels appropriate, but natural. We often think the scripted answers to questions are the best, but if one does not believe or know what he or she is talking about, it really shows. I found in my interviews, as well as in my sales experience, that if I give my honest opinion about everything in a very respectful manner, people are very willing to listen to me because I am being myself and that creates a confidence that is reassuring to whoever is asking the questions. With this confidence, I have also been able to advance in my job at Victoria's Secret and become a beauty lead for the store. I am not saying that one should walk into an interview and just say whatever is on his or her mind, but that one should never just say what he thinks the person wants to hear. This attitude toward an interview can put anybody at ease, and the confidence that comes from that ease is one of the best things to have in any environment.

These are the kinds of questions interviewers have in mind when they sit down with you. You will find favor in their eyes if you can answer their questions with clarity.

a match made in heaven

The interview process is designed to make sure that the applicant and the organization are a good match. Therefore, as you diligently rehearse answers to an interviewer's questions, don't forget to prepare questions of your own. The answers you receive will help confirm whether or not the organization you're considering is the right one for you. To help you determine this, here is a list of questions you'll probably want to ask:

- *Job training:* What will be the job training procedure for my position?

- *Learning opportunities:* Does your organization provide an employee development program or other kind of learning opportunities?

- *Advancement:* What is the opportunity for advancement for someone who not only does his or her job, but goes beyond that?

- *Reporting structure:* What is the reporting structure for this position?

- *Facilities:* May I have a tour of your facility, especially the area this position occupies?

If you have other concerns or questions you want answered, by all means voice them during the interview. One word of caution, however. Inquiries about the number of vacation days, medical benefits, pension plans, and other nitty-gritty items should be saved until later. These issues are typically discussed when you are close to being offered the job, which rarely happens in your first interview. Although you have every right to know this information before you make a final decision to accept or reject the job, there's no reason to bring them up prematurely. Doing so will make it seem as if your primary concerns are about money and benefits, rather than making sure that your qualifications fit their needs. (The chapter that follows will discuss how to initiate a conversation about your employee package and how to negotiate a salary.)

Your career center is likely to have several books and videos on how to research companies and how to interview effectively. The career services office will also have information on companies that come to interview on campus. For example, most companies give the career services office large notebooks describing the history of the company and various positions available. Again, make sure that the company will be a good match for you and vice versa. Many career offices also link company home pages to their websites. You can make sure that a company will be a good match for you only if you have sufficient information. Get it. It will allow you to be savvy and well informed in your interviews.

handling rejection

At some point during the interview process, you'll have to deal with rejection. One way to handle it constructively is to call the employer and discuss the reasons you didn't get the job. What you learn from this discussion may help you in future interviews.

Another constructive means of handling rejection is to keep a positive attitude. Keep reminding yourself: "I will find a job." Commit yourself to that end. Believe in your capabilities and overcome all objections.

It was hard for Chris Nelson, who majored in economics. After graduate school, he searched for three years for a good banking job. He kept his head up, realizing that the perfect job was just around the corner. Finally he landed a job with First Boston. If you are talented and work hard, he says, the only other quality you'll need is perseverance.

some final points

No matter how the interview goes, be sure to send a thank-you note. You never know what's going on behind the scenes. The company's first choice may turn down the offer, or the person who was hired may not work out a month down the road. In that case, your last piece of correspondence may tip the scales your way. Always be ready for the unexpected. Eventually you'll succeed.

13

you're hired

The true objective is to take chaos as given and learn to thrive on it.

—TOM PETERS,
THRIVING ON CHAOS

Y ou did not laugh uncontrollably during any of your interviews. You did not misplace your identity. You were confident and authentic. We're talking home run.

Now come a few very important details. After each interview, write a thank-you note and then wait two weeks. If you still haven't heard from the company, call the interviewer to see if you're still under consideration. If so, request an appointment to see them again. If they don't grant you a second interview, ask nicely for a time frame on the decision process.

235

do they want you?

 t this point you'll have some indication of whether you're in or out. If you're still in, one or more of the following could happen:

1. *You spend a day in the office or in the field* to get a feeling for the job firsthand. If the interviewer doesn't propose this, request it. Seeing where you will spend a significant portion of your waking hours will help you further discern whether this job is really for you. Be observant and try to get a "feel" for the work atmosphere. Do the employees seem enthusiastic and friendly? Is the work environment safe, healthy, and pleasant? Checking this out before you accept the position could mean the difference between a job you like and a job you hate.

2. *You're invited to a dinner or lunch* so the prospective employer can observe you in a social setting. Two quick tips: Don't order alcohol, and avoid smoking if they don't smoke. Also, plan ahead about how you want to come across. Are you friendly or abrasive? Are you well-mannered or boorish? Do you spill your beverage on your future boss's white divan? Do you listen to others, or do you dominate conversations? Be sure to exhibit your star qualities of enthusiasm and graciousness.

3. *You could meet again with the interviewer,* in which case you will probably be introduced to others in the company. Meeting employees is a golden opportunity to learn more about the organization, even if all you have the chance to do is observe. Don't count on the recruiter alone to provide you with a composite picture of the company.

4. *You're flown to the home office.* This is optimal since it's in your best interest to know the philosophy and daily workings of the company. You will be introduced to lots of different people. Hold fast to your energy! You need to be as sharp and enthusiastic in your final introduction as you were in your first one. (After it's over, you will be able to wilt and take a much-needed break.)

5. *You take a series of tests*—analytical, verbal, logical, and so on—during your continued interview process. You may also be requested to complete a personality inventory.

These extra steps vary from company to company. The bottom line, however, is to remain poised, inquisitive, and attentive. Act as though you want the job—even if you haven't decided. After each interview, send an additional follow-up letter or note.

do you want them?

Once you've finished the second interview and talked with your "contacts," you will probably know if the job is right for you. If it's your only job offer, you may have to take it. That's okay. Give the job your very best shot. In the process, you may grow to like it more than you thought you would. If not, there's nothing to stop you from seeking out other positions.

Once you've decided that you want the job, you will need to find out about the *employee package,* such as salary range and benefits. As stated in the previous chapter, you need to use discretion about when to discuss these matters. Usually, the interviewer will bring up the employee package during the second interview. If not, you can open the conversation yourself in this way: "I am wondering about the salary range and benefits. Is it all right if we talk about this now, or will this be covered another time?"

Here is a list of what you'll need to know:

- What is the starting salary?
- Is there a bonus?
- Will you have the use of a company car?
- Is travel involved? If so, how much?
- What are the projected timetables for promotion?
- Is the job a "career track" position?
- Does the benefit program include medical and dental benefits?

- Is there a profit-sharing program?
- Is there a retirement plan?
- Is there a tuition-reimbursement program?
- Does the company cover travel and moving expenses?
- What kind of formal training will you receive?
- When can you start?

If you have several job offers, list the pros and cons of the company in which you are most interested. Here's an example:

ACME COMPANY EVALUATION SHEET

Pros	Cons
Company car	Relocation necessary
Bonus and salary	Too much travel
Interesting job	Will need to work overtime
Growth potential	Solitary job
Fortune 500 company	No formal training
Great co-workers	Six-month probation period

As I mentioned earlier, you'll meet more and more people as you progress through the interview process. Keeping up with so many names and faces can get confusing. To help you remember the important details, I suggest that you take notes. As soon as the introductions are over, and while the names are still fresh in your mind, write down what you want to remember about the people you've met. Below is a sample for you to follow.

PEOPLE I'VE MET AT THE COMPANY SO FAR:

Name	Date	What I Need to Remember About Him/Her

Here's what your notes might include:

Henry Jones	2/16/05	Vice President of Operations; plays golf; 4-year-old daughter takes karate lessons.

Here's space for you to jot down the real thing.

1. _____ _____   _____
   _____
   _____

2. _____ _____   _____
   _____
   _____

3. _____ _____   _____
   _____
   _____

4. _____ _____   _____
   _____
   _____

5. _____ _____   _____
   _____
   _____

6. _____ _____   _____
   _____
   _____

7. _____ _____   _____
   _____
   _____

8. _____ _____   _____
   _____
   _____

9. _____ _____   _____
   _____
   _____

10. _____ _____   _____
    _____
    _____

poising yourself for an offer

After you have all the answers to these questions, ask your interviewers if they have any more questions for you. If they do, answer the questions. If not, state that from all the information you have heard and all the information you've gathered, you would very much like to work for them. Personalize your closing conversation. Tell them what has impressed you about their company and be specific. Recount examples from the past few weeks or months that have led you to your conclusions. When you're finished, pause for a moment so that the interviewer has an opportunity to provide input. If the interviewer's comments seem vague and no job offer is forthcoming, then ask plainly, "What happens next?"

As the final stage of the interview process draws to a close, the interviewer may ask if you've interviewed with any other firms. Be honest, but be on your guard. Even if you're not as interested in the other companies, don't let them know that. You want to hold on to your bargaining power. If they think that they're the only company you are interested in or that is interested in you, they may make you a low offer.

If you're offered the position on the spot, *don't* accept. Tell the company you need some time to think it over, but make a commitment to call back with your answer. Then review the pros and cons list with your mentors, supervisors from your college jobs, professors, friends, parents, or other family members, such as your spouse or partner.

negotiating salary

When I accepted my first job out of college with the accounting firm of Touche Ross, I had two other offers from well-respected firms," says Donald Mason, who now works in Dallas for a private firm. "Because Touche Ross knew I was attractive to several employers, they offered me more money to start than the typical college grad."

In your first job out of college, you don't have tremendous bargaining power, but you do have some. So use it.

Employers never offer their highest or even their middle-range salary. They start low because they expect to negotiate with you. Push for a higher salary. Point out that you're more experienced than most people who have been out of college for two or three years because you gained four years of real-world experience during college. You're much more qualified and promising than the average college grad.

Don't push so hard that you alienate your new boss. But if you get $2,000 over the initial offer, terrific. If you haven't done anything in college to prove that you are better qualified than the rest of the pack of applicants, take what you're offered. On the job, you can prove that you're worth the best raises.

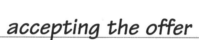

accepting the offer

When you accept an offer, do it gracefully. After you've ironed out the salary issue, accept with a positive, reaffirming statement, such as "I'm very pleased to be a part of your company."

This is your first official chance to bond with your new manager. You may want to take the initiative at the outset to ask about goals for your first year on the job. What defines minimum requirements? What sort of performance exceeds requirements? What do you have to do to be outstanding in your first year? Together, you and your manager may want to put some specific goals on paper so that you have something to refer to throughout the year. At salary review time, you will have something concrete with which to gauge your work, a contract of sorts between you and your manager.

tying up loose ends

Write thank-you letters to the companies you turned down. Thank them for their time. You may want to call those who gave you special attention. Expressing these courtesies leaves all doors open for the future.

MY TWO CENTS *How Do I Apply It?*

Jessica Ovitz, Saint Olaf College

Sometimes landing a job means taking risks and making short-term sacrifices in order to achieve the end goal. After graduating from college, I started working as an AmeriCorps volunteer for a nonprofit organization designing after-school activities for kids from low-income families. While I was enjoying the work I was involved with, the commitment with AmeriCorps was only for a year. I knew that it wouldn't be long until I would again be on the prowl for the ever-elusive "real world" job.

In addition to working with underprivileged youth, another passion of mine is writing. This is primarily why I chose my English major in college—because it allowed me the opportunity to do two of the things I absolutely love, reading and writing. I have always played "editor" to my friends and family throughout high school and college. For this reason, I have, over the years, entertained the thought of becoming a writer and editor.

When in pursuit of another career, it's helpful to be employed at the moment. So while I was holding down my AmeriCorps position I started to think of ways to explore this dream of mine. My AmeriCorps assignment was in Minneapolis, Minnesota, but I'm originally from Denver, Colorado. I had been thinking of returning home after my year with AmeriCorps to be closer to my family and I asked my sister, who's a student at one of the universities in Denver, if she knew anyone in her career services department who might be able to help me get started on a job search in the writing and/or publishing field in Denver. She gave me the e-mail address of a lady to contact and I sent off a letter expressing my interests and asking if she had any suggestions for my job search. In response, she gave me the name of a friend of hers, a publisher in Denver who'd worked with Prentice Hall for many years and had recently started her own publishing company. I was immediately intrigued, and knowing that I was headed home for Easter vacation, e-mailed my new contact hoping to set up an informational interview.

We ended up meeting over coffee and had a great talk about the publishing company she'd started, and I had a chance to ask her some of my questions about the business. The meeting exceeded my expectations in that she ended up asking me if I wanted to help her edit her next book. She was in the process of getting it ready for press and handed the manuscript to me and told me to run with it. Whoa! I was so surprised and a little nervous, but I knew that this was an opportunity I couldn't pass up.

I spent the next couple of months poring over the manuscript I'd been given. It was my first real "grown-up" job and I spent many hours after work making sure I went through the text with a fine-tooth comb. After completing my revisions for the book, I remained in contact with her via e-mail while continuing my work for AmeriCorps. When I knew I was moving back to Denver, I asked her to keep me in mind if she knew of any job opportunities either within her own company or elsewhere in Denver. It wasn't long after that she called me to let me know that her assistant would be leaving in the fall and if I was interested the position was open. I was exhilarated, not to mention relieved, that I had a job to return home to. So while I wasn't sure I had played "editor" correctly and I wasn't paid for my work at the time, I took a risk and my time and effort was rewarded with much more. Not only was I offered a job, but I was also asked to write the Afterword for the book I'd worked on. I was published! Sometimes you have to take a risk, even if you're not sure how it's going to turn out, in order to create possibilities for yourself.

You might also write thank-you notes to those who turned you down. You'll probably be qualified to work for them in the future. Maintain a favorable impression in their minds.

when to start

When should you start? That depends on how you're planning to celebrate finishing off college. If you've been waiting to backpack through Indonesia with your suitemates and have slept with a map of the South Seas above your pillow for three years running, don't forsake that for a briefcase and suit. The briefcase will be there when you get back, and student loans don't come due until six months following graduation. Take the time while you've got it. If, on the other hand, you can't wait to close in on that corner office, go for it. The job is yours. You can still see the world in two-week intervals during your paid vacations.

other incidentals

Y ou'll have to fill out insurance and benefit forms. You may also have some training, either "soft" or formal. Even if you are hurried right into your job with the minimum of instruction, don't worry. Ask questions. Solicit advice. Work hard. Learn all you can.

Starting your new job may scare you as much as starting college. Be patient with yourself. This period of adjustment will be easier and shorter than that of your peers who are less prepared for the real world. In the meantime, keep using all the techniques you learned in your internships and other jobs. Within about six months, you should feel like an ace who's been with the organization for years!

14

outlooks and insights

It is as though I had lost my way and asked someone the way home. He says he will show me and walks with me along a smoother path which suddenly stops. And now my friend tells me: "All you have to do now is find your way home from here."

—LUDWIG WITTGENSTEIN, *CULTURE AND VALUE*

I went to the woods because I wished . . . to front only the essential facts of life, and see if I could not learn what it had to teach, and not, when I came to die, discover that I had not lived.

—HENRY DAVID THOREAU, *WALDEN*

No matter what your first job after college happens to be, it marks a new beginning. It also marks a point of departure. If you started with the company and the job of your dreams, great. Your job right out of college might instead be less than terrific. But you have to start somewhere, building your skills, meeting people, and developing work habits. That's a positive, exciting challenge.

You may go through any number of changes at the outset of your career: from your new job to a string of promotions, to a better job with another company, to a smaller company, back to graduate school, or even to begin your own company. Your first job, however, is like a blank page. You fill it in as you go. And your possibilities are limitless as long as you pursue them.

games people play

In the working world, people measure personal success by all kinds of things—how much money they make, what their job is, how many people they know, how many dates they have, what kind of clothes they wear, what kind of car they drive, and how they balance career and family responsibilities.

Many of these things have to do with *appearances*, not *reality*. They reflect what people want others to think, not necessarily who they really are. Know the difference between the two and be true to yourself and your values. The best job in the world isn't worth much if you aren't happy. Similarly, no amount of money or possessions will make you any more satisfied with yourself if you aren't already content with who you are.

This book is about defining those things that are important to *you*, and you alone. So resist comparing yourself to those around you. That's a game you'll never win. There will always be people who are better off and people who are worse off than you. In college and in life, it's important to do what you believe is important and what you feel is right.

People may not always agree with you, especially if they feel threatened by your abilities. The going will often seem hard. That's okay. Preserve your integrity and don't let someone get the better of you. Your satisfaction will come from knowing that you took the high road.

President John F. Kennedy said it best in his 1961 inaugural address:

> For of those to whom much is given, much is required. And when at some future date the high court of history sits in judgment on each of us recording whether in our brief span of service we fulfilled our responsibilities to the state, our success or failure, in whatever office we hold, will be measured by four questions: First, were we truly peo-

ple of courage? . . . Second, were we truly people of integrity? . . . Third, were we truly people of judgment? . . . Finally, were we truly people of dedication?

character and ethics

You are working very hard to prepare yourself for a rewarding career. You are diligently studying, you are accomplishing goals, and you are honing your people skills. Without a doubt, the time and energy you're spending developing these qualities will not be in vain. However, of all the qualities you will need to succeed, one of the most easily overlooked is *character*.

By character, I don't mean your personality type. You could have an open, endearing, and charming personality, or a closed and not very fluid personality, but still have a lot of character. Some of the best leaders in their fields are introverts.

What I do mean by character is the ability to be *ethical*. Although ethics is somewhat hard to define, it's a human quality that's easy to spot. Usually ethics is marked by a concern for other individuals. Ethical people consistently exhibit a willingness to live up to the commitments they make, and they don't shrink from considering how their decisions affect those around them.

In your job, you'll face decisions that are difficult to make. When the answers aren't obvious, you can always seek wisdom by asking yourself the following questions: Would others approve of my behavior if they knew about it? Would I want someone else to behave similarly? Is what I'm doing right for the organization? Is what the company is doing right? If not, how will I handle it? What are my own personal standards, and how do I define them?

Here's a prime example of ethics at work. In journalism, the accepted, unwritten rule for quoting someone is that if the person says something to you but then adds, "Don't print that" *after* the statement was already made, then you are allowed to print it. But several journalists I've talked to said they would not print the quote if it was made by a "civilian," meaning a nonpolitician or anyone unfamiliar with the rules of the press. The reason? Plain fairness. That's the cornerstone of ethics. Begin thinking now about your moral views, especially as they relate to work. Particularly if you aspire to be a leader, character is crucial.

taking risks

A fter graduate school, Bob Kinstle took a job with a consulting firm in Virginia. The company's main business was in defense contracts, but the group's charter was to develop computer information systems for the commercial market.

One of his first assignments was to manage a project for a large bank in New York City. Over the next several months, the project team grew in size as he designed and implemented the system. At the end of the first year, the project began to wrap up, and the number of people assigned to it dwindled until there was just Bob. The company began to doubt its desire to penetrate the commercial market and prepared to abandon all future work with the bank. Bob, however, was certain that there was much more work to be done.

"I began to consider leaving the company and pursuing the bank as an independent contractor," Bob says. "The choice was difficult. I had a promising career with the company—I was the youngest associate manager, having been promoted to that level faster than anyone else in the company's history. Yet I longed for the freedom to set my own work schedule—to be my own boss," explained Bob.

"There really was no way to know the consequences of leaving the company," he continues. "Would they accuse me of stealing their client? Would the bank be willing to work with an independent consultant located in Virginia? What if the project really was over and no further work emerged? Could I find other contracts?

"After weighing the risks, I decided to make the change. I resigned from my position and notified the bank that I would be interested in continuing business with them. Largely because of the relationships I had developed over the previous year, the bank agreed to give me a small enhancement project related to our original work.

"This small project has grown over the ten years I have been a consultant for the bank. My office is located in my home. I connect to the bank's computers via modem. Trips to New York continue, although the frequency has decreased. The bank is satisfied, knowing that they can contact me twenty-four hours a day, seven days a week. And I am happy feeling free to pursue contracts that interest me, setting my own schedule for work, and designing systems that reflect my personality and preferences."

Pam Zemper has also experienced the advantages of risk-taking. She believes her professional growth came when she began taking risks that brought about positive results for her company. If you know yourself, your strengths and weaknesses, and you've learned to think critically, you will be able to make decisions that fulfill your dreams. Taking calculated risks can mean the difference between an outstanding career and an average one, between a zestful life and an ordinary one.

Throughout this book, I have encouraged you to:

- Apply yourself academically
- Gain work experience, both through part-time jobs and through internships
- Keep active in extracurricular activities

By following my suggestions, you should develop the inner resources to make these same kinds of critical career decisions when opportunities arise. Like Bob and Pam, you will be equipped to take risks that will lead you down a career path you'll love.

"All of us reach points in our lives when we can play it safe or walk into the unknown," says Bob Kinstle. "I'm not advising recklessness; however, after you've weighed the risks and rewards, you may still need to take a leap of faith to begin a new path."

calling it quits when it's time for a change

A t some point in your career life, you will leave your job for another one. When the time comes for you to hand in your resignation letter, you'll want to make sure that you leave on good terms. Career coach Joyce Lain Kennedy advises: "At any job level, act like a manager and resign gracefully. Don't burn bridges when you quit your job."

The reasons for leaving on good terms are evident. Making enemies could come back to haunt you in the form of poor references or a tainted industry reputation years later. To avoid these pitfalls, Kennedy offers some tips to help you bow out in style:

- *Avoid quitter's remorse.* Be sure that you really want to leave your present job.

- *Get the new offer in writing.* Make certain of your ground with the new organization before announcing your departure.

- *Write a cordial resignation letter.* Always give at least two weeks' notice, or whatever length of time your company requires. Never risk negative language in your letter. Simply note your new position and employer and the date you'll be leaving.

- *Meet with your boss.* Workplace courtesy requires that you let your boss know you are leaving before your co-workers, so set up a time to meet with him or her in private. Also, offer to help train your successor or otherwise ease the transition.

- *Don't boast.* Bragging about your higher new pay could create discontent in the workplace.

- *Don't bad-mouth the company or its employees.* Although you may have reason to complain, negative comments will get you nowhere. When pressed for the reason of your departure, simply point out that your new job is too good to pass up, which should be true.

being happy

It takes a strong commitment and hard work to maintain a healthy balance on the job and off. Being happy won't just happen. Like anything else, you have to work at it.

Once you've landed your job, take pride in what you do. Have concrete objectives that will guide and direct you. Concentrate not just on job success but on overall happiness. If there is any one point I want to make in this chapter, it's the importance of striking a bal-

ance between your personal life and your professional one. Remember, your job is only one
aspect of your life.

Kenneth Olsen, former CEO of
Digital Equipment Corporation,
knows all about making things happen on the job and off. In a
graduation speech to students at his
alma mater, MIT, Olsen reflected
on his thirty years of work since
graduating from college: "Running
a business is not the important
thing. Making a commitment to do
a good job, to improve things, to
influence the world is where it's at. I
would also suggest that one of the most
satisfying things is to help others to be
creative and take responsibility. These are
the important things."

"Your most precious commodity is not material," says Charles
S. Sanford, Jr., CEO of Bankers Trust New York Corporation. "It is
and always will be your time." If you keep work in balance with
other things in your life, Sanford urges, you can accomplish even
more on the job. "Read a little poetry, enjoy friends, and most of all,
don't take yourself too seriously. In the final analysis, whatever you
have accomplished won't be worth much unless you've had fun."

Okay, so the cynic in you cries: How much time did these CEOs
spend working in their twenties and thirties? Good point. They
probably spent a lot of time, but were they happy? How did all that
time at the office affect their families? You have to ask yourself, "Do
I want to be a CEO?" Some people would say "No thanks." I trad-
ed in the corporate life to run a small business that is part of a large
corporation. That was right for me and my life goals. You have to
carefully weigh the trade-offs of your long-term goals with what you
are doing—and enjoying—in the short term. Most of the working
population thrives quite happily in intermediate positions between
entry level and the top of the heap. They find a balance between
work they enjoy and spending time with their friends and family.

Maybe you won't have all the money in the world, but you will have time to enjoy those things that count the most when you're ninety—a job you liked, a lifestyle you enjoyed, and the opportunity to contribute to your own growth as well as that of others.

thoughts for the journey

I began this book with a personal anecdote, so I'd like to end with one. It has to do with becoming discouraged. And it's a story without which this book truly would have no closure.

About three months before I finished the manuscript for this book, I was exhausted. My job was quite tedious—not because the work itself had changed, but because my approach to it had shifted. I had little time to see my friends, and at night I just wanted to go to sleep early. Boring. In short, I was doing all those things I've said throughout my book never to do. Realizing that I wasn't being myself, and knowing for a fact that I wasn't having a good time, I decided to take a break to get back the perspective I knew was missing.

Egypt was the place for perspective. Why Egypt? It was exotic, distant, and vastly different from life as I knew it. Also, one of my interests is travel, and after my junior year in Spain, I made a personal promise to visit as many countries as I could. So off I went for the first time on a vacation by myself, leaving my "normal" life and my work behind me.

When I saw the age-old pyramids at dusk, a renewed energy and inspiration filled me. The pyramids symbolize balance, perfection, human achievement, and teamwork. Seeing the achievements of an ancient culture that have survived for thousands of years left me with a feeling of great awe and real humility. I wondered how many monuments from America's civilization would survive four hundred years, let alone four thousand.

Clearly, the Egyptians saw no limits to what they could accomplish. They saw things not in terms of what they were in the moment, but of what they could become in time. They looked to the possibility instead of the limitation. They made dreams into realities.

"Well, bully for Tut," you say, "but what has this got to do with college and careers and human potential?" The answer is that the pyramids helped me to recover my "edge"—my own potential. The tensions loosened inside of me and confidence took over.

My perspective restored, I was free to concentrate on challenges—including work, the book, and my personal life—with confidence and energy.

Throughout your life, the inspirations that motivate you will ebb and flow. You won't always feel inspired, and you won't always perform at peak. The important thing to remember when you reach an impasse is not to panic. Remove yourself from the ordinary—through reading *Don Quixote* or going to a concert or exhibit or taking a day trip by yourself. Maybe your most relaxing time is spent watching a football game or a weekly sitcom. That's fine. Just allow yourself time to unwind and replenish your own central energy source.

David Glenn, a division manager for Chevron for thirty years, reflects: "Live in the now—in the moment. It is easy to get so focused on a goal or destination that you forget to enjoy the journey. Every day in our jobs and families we are challenged to be of the moment with someone rather than too busy. Perhaps one of the benefits of becoming established is that we can enjoy the journey more."

the blue sky ahead

You have a lot to be proud of. If you're reading this book for the first time as a freshman, you get credit for getting this far and for committing yourself to making college and your career pursuit everything they can be. Good for you.

If you are reviewing this chapter for the last time and you have a job and are wondering how four years could come and go so fast, take time to pat yourself on the back. Look down from where you are now, realize how far you've come, and be proud of your accomplishments. The next peak you scale—your first job—is very similar to the challenges you've had in the last few years. Accept the challenges that are before you. In addition to doing a good or great job, give to the world something of what it has given to you—through your family, your friends, your activities, and your actions. Don't be typical. You are unique. Show the world the special gifts and contributions that only you can offer.

And so, here's to your unique success story. Here's to the ability you have to dream the dream and make it real. Go change the world! Good-bye and good luck.

afterword

aving graduated from college two years ago, I never thought I'd find myself wishing I could go back and do things over again. During those four years, I worked hard, studied abroad, and was involved in extracurricular activities. Having now read through these pages, I find myself feeling that I could have done so much more. If all this information had been available to me my freshman year, I sincerely believe that not only would I have milked the collegiate experience for all it was worth, but I would have a stronger sense of what my talents and interests are and how I could apply those in the "real world."

As a college graduate, I strongly encourage you to take the time to plot out what you want your college experience to amount to. When you approach the stage on graduation day, and the inevitable wave of nostalgia hits you, what are the memories you want flashing through your mind? Did you take the time to truly explore what you're about on a personal and professional level? What are the achievements you want to leave behind, and how have you positioned yourself for life after school? Make sure you take the time to investigate actively ways you can incorporate a variety of diverse experiences, in addition to your academic curriculum, that will not only enhance your understanding of yourself, but also make you more marketable to employers. It's important to ask yourself these questions, but it's vital that you move beyond simply questioning and test the waters.

Your time at college will be brief. Believe me, on graduation day you will think those were the fastest four years of your life. That is why it is so important to act now. With the tips and strategies offered in this book, I know I would have walked away from college feeling confident that I'd used the time to my advantage, and that I was walking into the next phase of life with a clearer picture of what it was I was going to bring to the world. If you've read this far, then I'm sure you've thought of some things you'd like to get involved with or something you'd like to research further. Do yourself a favor and start now! Only you have the power to put yourself in a position to succeed, so use the next four years to discover what you want that success to look like and I guarantee you'll feel much more confident when graduation rolls around. Good luck!

Jessica Ovitz
Graduate, Saint Olaf College

financial aid

This section will give you an overview of the financial aid system. If you wish to learn more go to http://studentaid.ed.gov.

aid eligibility

Eligibility for federal student aid is based on financial need and on several other factors. The financial aid administrator at the college or career school you plan to attend will determine your eligibility.

To receive aid from most programs, you must:

- Qualify for financial need (except for certain loans).

- Have a high school diploma or a General Education Development (GED) certificate, pass a test approved by the U.S. Department of Education, meet other standards your state establishes that the Department approves, or complete a high school education in a home school setting that is treated as such under state law.

- Be working toward a degree or certificate in an eligible program.

- Be a U.S. citizen or eligible noncitizen.

- Have a valid Social Security Number (unless you're from the Republic of the Marshall Islands, the Federated States of Micronesia, or the Republic of Palau).

- Register with the Selective Service if required (you can use the paper or electronic FAFSA to register, you can register at www.sss.gov, or you can call 1-888-665-1825 or 1-847-688-6888).

- Maintain satisfactory academic progress once in school.

- Certify that you are not in default on a federal student loan and do not owe money on a federal student grant.

- Certify that you will use federal student aid only for educational purposes.

The Higher Education Act of 1965 as amended (HEA) suspends aid eligibility for students who have been convicted under federal or state law of the sale or possession of drugs. If you have a conviction for these offenses, call the Federal Student Aid Information Center at 1-800-4-FED-AID (1-800-433-3243) or go to the FAFSA on the website, click on "Worksheets" in the left column, then click on "Drug Worksheet" to find out how this law applies to you.

Even if you are ineligible for federal aid, you should complete the FAFSA because you may be eligible for nonfederal aid from states and private institutions. If you regain eligibility during the award year, notify your financial aid administrator immediately. If you are convicted of a drug-related offense after you submit the FAFSA, you might lose eligibility for federal student aid, and you might be liable for returning any financial aid you received during a period of ineligibility.

How Will I Know What I'm Eligible For?

The information you reported on your FAFSA is used to calculate your Expected Family Contribution (EFC). The formula used to calculate your EFC is established by law and is used to measure your family's financial strength on the basis of your family's income and assets. The EFC is used to determine your eligibility for federal student aid and indicates how much money you and your family are expected to contribute toward your cost of attendance for the school year. If your EFC is below a certain number, you'll be eligible for a federal Pell Grant, assuming you meet all other eligibility requirements.

You can get worksheets that show how the EFC is calculated by downloading them from the website at www.studentaid.ed.gov/pubs. Click on the award year appropriate to you under "EFC Formula."

The amount of your Pell Grant depends on your EFC, your cost of attendance (which the financial aid administrator at your college or career school will figure out), and your enrollment status (full-time, three-quarter time, half-time, or less than half-time).

For other aid programs, the financial aid administrator at your college or career school takes your cost of attendance and then subtracts your EFC, the amount of a federal Pell Grant you are eligible for, and aid you will get from other sources. The result is your remaining financial need:

Cost of Attendance
– EFC
– Federal Pell Grant Eligibility
– Aid From Other Sources
= Remaining Financial Need

What Is a Cost of Attendance?

If you're attending at least half time, your cost of attendance is the sum of

- Your actual tuition and fees (or the school's average tuition and fees)
- The cost of room and board (or living expenses for students who do not contract with the school for room and board)
- The cost of books, supplies, transportation, loan fees, and miscellaneous expenses (including a reasonable amount for the documented cost of a personal computer)
- An allowance for dependent care
- Costs related to a disability
- Reasonable costs for eligible study-abroad programs

Costs unrelated to the completion of a student's course of study are not included in calculating that student's cost of attendance.

loan entrance counseling

About Direct Loans

Direct Loans are made to students attending school at least half time. The U.S. Department of Education is the lender, and you receive the loan money through your school. You may receive a Direct Subsidized Loan, a Direct Unsubsidized Loan, or both for the same academic year. A student qualifies for a Direct Subsidized Loan based on financial need, as determined under federal regulations. A student's need is not a factor in determining eligibility for a Direct Unsubsidized Loan.

Most of the provisions below apply to both the FFEL (Federal Family Education Loan) and Direct Loan programs.

Borrow Only What You Need   When your school determined your federal financial aid award, it used a standard budget to estimate the expenses you would incur while attending school. This expense estimate is referred to as your cost of attendance (COA). If you can reduce your expenses to an amount less than the school's estimated COA, you might not need to borrow as much as the school has awarded.

Interest Rates   The interest rate you are charged for both Subsidized and Unsubsidized Loans is variable and is adjusted once a year, on July 1, according to the formula on your promissory note. The rate will never exceed 8.25 percent. The interest on a Subsidized Loan is paid by the federal government while you are enrolled in school at least half time, or during grace or deferment periods. If you have a Direct Unsubsidized Loan, you are responsible for the interest from the day the loan is paid to you until you pay off the loan.

Loan Fee   The loan fee is another expense of borrowing a loan. The loan fee charged for Subsidized and Unsubsidized Loans is 4 percent of the amount you borrow. The loan fee is subtracted proportionately from each loan disbursement.

Promissory Note   Before you receive your loan funds, you must sign a promissory note. In past years, borrowers completed a separate promissory note for each new loan borrowed. Now, if you attend a four-year school or graduate school, in most cases, you will sign only one promissory note that will be used for all of your loans at a single school. This new note is called a Master Promissory Note (MPN). Direct Loan borrowers can now complete the promissory note online. FFEL borrowers should contact their private lender for promissory note guidance.

When you sign the Master Promissory Note, you are confirming your understanding that your school may make new loans for you for the duration of your education (up to 10 years) without having you sign another promissory note. You are also agreeing to repay your lender, the U.S. Department of Education, all loans made to you under the terms of the MPN. Therefore, it is very important that you completely read and understand all of the information on the MPN before you sign it.

You are not required to accept the amount that your school awards you. You should notify your school if you want to borrow a lower amount than the school has awarded you.

School Notification Your school must notify you in writing or electronically whenever it makes a loan disbursement. The notice must tell you the date and the amount of the loan disbursement, which loan funds are subsidized and which are unsubsidized, information about your right to cancel all or a portion of the loan, including the current loan disbursement, and procedures for canceling the loan.

FAFSA Information

Check out *FAFSA on the Web* (www.fafsa.ed.gov)—the way to apply online for student financial aid! Students who applied for aid last year may also be able to complete a Renewal FAFSA application online.

PIN The PIN is your identifier to let you access personal information in various U.S. Department of Education systems. You must have a PIN to file an online Renewal FAFSA or to make online corrections to your FAFSA.

Federal School Code Search Page Schools equipped for electronic communication with the Department of Education will receive your FAFSA information automatically. If you're filing a paper application, you can use the Federal School Code Search to look up codes for the colleges you are considering so that you can list them correctly on the FAFSA.

Leaving School Early   After you graduate, leave school, or drop below half-time enrollment, you will have a six-month "grace period" before you begin repayment. During this period, you will receive repayment information, and you'll be notified of your first payment due date. You are responsible for beginning repayment on time, even if you don't receive this information. Payments are usually due monthly.

The law requires that, when you withdraw during a payment period or period of enrollment (your school can define these periods for you and tell you which one applies to you), the amount of FSA Program assistance that you have "earned" up to that point is determined by a specific formula. If you received (or your school received on your behalf) less assistance than the amount that you earned, you will be able to receive those additional funds. If you received more assistance than you earned, the excess funds must be returned.

The amount of assistance that you have earned is determined on a pro-rata basis. That is, if you completed 30 percent of the payment period or period of enrollment, you earn 30 percent of the assistance you were originally scheduled to receive. Once you have completed more than 60 percent of the payment period or period of enrollment, you earn all of your assistance.

If you received excess funds that must be returned, your school can explain what portion of those funds must be returned.

loan exit counseling

When Do I Begin Repaying My Loans?

After you graduate, leave school, or drop below half-time enrollment, you have six months before you must begin repaying your loans. This is called the "grace period." Your repayment period begins the day after your grace period ends. Your first payment will be due within 60 days after your repayment period begins.

If you have Direct Subsidized Loans, you won't be charged any interest during your grace period. If you have Direct Unsubsidized Loans, you'll be responsible for the interest charged during your grace period. You may either pay this interest as it accumulates or have it capitalized when you start repaying your loans.

What Is the Interest Rate on My Loans?

The interest rate for both Direct Subsidized Loans and Direct Unsubsidized Loans is variable and is adjusted each year on July 1. The interest rate will be calculated differently depending on several circumstances.

The interest rate during the in-school, grace, and deferment periods is equal to the 91-day Treasury bill rate plus 3.1 percentage points (this applies to loans made on or after July 1, 1995).

For *all* Direct Subsidized and Unsubsidized Loans in repayment, regardless of the date the loans were made, the interest rate is equal to the 91-day Treasury bill rate plus 3.1 percentage points. By law, however, your interest rate can never exceed 8.25 percent.

Repayment Plans

Student Aid on the Web   Four repayment plans are available. If you do not select one, you will be assigned the Standard Plan.

- *Standard Repayment Plan.* With the Standard Plan, you'll pay a fixed amount each month until your loans are paid in full. Your monthly payments will be at least $50, and you'll have up to 10 years to repay your loans. The Standard Plan is good for you if you can handle higher monthly payments because you'll repay your loans more quickly. Your monthly payment under the Standard Plan may be higher than it would be under the other plans because your loans will be repaid in the shortest time. For the same reason—the 10-year limit on repayment—you may pay the least interest.

- *Extended Repayment Plan.* Under the Extended Plan, you'll still have minimum monthly payments of at least $50, but you can take from 12 to 30 years to repay your loans. The length of your repayment period will depend on the total amount you owe when your loans go into repayment.

This is a good plan if you will need to make smaller monthly payments. Because the repayment period generally will be at least

12 years, your monthly payments will be less than with the Standard Plan. However, you may pay more in interest because you're taking longer to repay the loans. Remember that the longer your loans are in repayment, the more interest you will pay.

- *Graduated Repayment Plan.* With this plan, your payments start out low, then increase, generally every two years. The length of your repayment period will depend on the total amount you owe when your loans go into repayment. If you expect your income to increase steadily over time, this plan may be right for you. Your initial monthly payments will be equal to either the interest that accumulates on your loans or half of the payment you would make each month using the Standard Plan, whichever is greater. However, your monthly payments will never increase to more than 1.5 times what you would pay with the Standard Plan.

- *Income Contingent Repayment (ICR) Plan.* This plan gives you the flexibility to meet your Direct Loan obligations without causing undue financial hardship. Each year, your monthly payments will be calculated on the basis of your Adjusted Gross Income (AGI), family size, and the total amount of your Direct Loans. To participate in the ICR Plan, you must sign a form that permits the Internal Revenue Service to provide information about your income to the U.S. Department of Education. This information will be used to recalculate your monthly payment, adjusted annually based on the updated information. For more information on this plan, visit the ICR definition site at www.ed.gov/DirectLoan/pubs/repabook/icr2.html.

companies with internship opportunities

Below is an abbreviated directory of internships, updated using *Internships 2003* (Peterson's, 2002) and other resources. Those internships with an asterisk (*) are listed in *Princeton Review's America's Top 100 Internships*. This list will give you an idea of some of the companies that offer internships, but remember this is only a very small sampling of internship programs. In addition to requesting more detailed information about the programs listed below, don't forget to contact businesses in which you are interested that don't advertise formal internship programs. Some of them will allow you to create internships to suit your individual needs. Also, many large corporations, such as General Mills and Hallmark Cards, offer internships in many different areas. For example, if you are interested in a specific company and have a background in marketing, check with that company to see if it has a marketing internship program.

Since this list is incomplete, be sure to investigate the many internship search sites online. The most complete would probably be Princeton Review's search at www.princetonreview.com/cte, which allows you to search in several different ways. To search for internships by region, try www.internships.com. If you want to run your search through an organization rather than a company, the National Society for Experiential Education's website at www.nsee.org/intern ships.htm is a good place to start.

Accounting Firm
Deloitte & Touche
10 Westport Road
Wilton, CT 06897

Adventure Travel Agency
Inner Quest, Inc.
34752 Charles Town Pike
Purcellville, VA 20132

Wilderness Inquiry
808 14th Avenue SE
Minneapolis, MN 55414-1516

Advertising Agency
American Association of
Advertising Agencies
405 Lexington Avenue, 18th
Floor
New York, NY 10174-1801

The Edelman Group
420 Lexington Avenue, Suite
1706
New York, NY 10170

Ocean City Advertising Agency
P.O. Box 1759
Ocean City, MD 21834

Architecture Firm
Gensler
One Rockefeller Plaza, Suite 500
New York, NY 10020

Shive-Hattery, Inc.
115 3rd Street SE, 9th Floor
Cedar Rapids, IA 52401

Art Gallery & Auctioneers
Christie's
20 Rockefeller Plaza
New York, NY 10020

San Francisco Art Commission
Gallery
401 Van Ness Avenue
San Francisco, CA 94102

Art Museum
*Metropolitan Museum of Art
1000 Fifth Avenue
New York, NY 10028-0198

Museum of Contemporary Art
220 East Chicago Avenue
Chicago, IL 60611

Athletic Club
National Basketball Association
645 Fifth Avenue
New York, NY 10022

PGA Tour, Inc.
100 PGA Tour Boulevard
Ponte Vedra Beach, FL 32082

Athletic Trainer
Amelia Wellness Center
869 Sadler Road, Suite 5
Fernandina Beach, FL 32034

Cornerstone Health & Fitness
Box 1308
Doylestown, PA 18901

Ballet or Theater Company
American Conservatory Theater
30 Grant Avenue
San Francisco, CA 94108

JFK Center for the Performing Arts
2700 F Street, NW
Washington, DC 20566

Bank
Federal Reserve Bank of Chicago
230 South LaSalle Street
Chicago, IL 60604

Federal Reserve Bank of New York
33 Liberty Street
New York, NY 10045

Botanical Gardens
Brooklyn Botanic Gardens
1000 Washington Avenue
Brooklyn, NY 11225

Denver Botanic Gardens
909 York Street
Denver, CO 80206

Camp Counselor
Camp Fire Boys and Girls
P.O. Box 3275
San Diego, CA 92163-1275

Trail Blazers
45 East 20th, 9th Floor
New York, NY 10003

Computer Company
*Apple Computer, Inc.
1 Infinite Loop, MS 84-3CE
Cupertino, CA 95014

SGI (Silicon Graphics, Inc.)
1600 Amphitheatre Parkway
Mountain View, CA 94043-1351

Consulting Firm
A. E. Schwartz & Associates
P.O. Box 79228
Waverley, MA 02479-0228

Hewitt Associates LLC
100 Half Day Road
Lincolnshire, IL 60069

Dance Studio
National Dance Education
    Organization
4948 St. Elmo Avenue, Suite 301
Bethesda, MD 20814

Defense Industry
Central Intelligence Agency
P.O. Box 4090
Reston, VA 20195

*Federal Bureau of Investigation
FBI Academy
Quantico, VA 22135

Design Center
American & International
    Designs, Inc.
900 South Avenue
Staten Island, NY 10314

Doctor's Office
*Center for Talented Youth
Johns Hopkins University
3400 North Charles Street
Baltimore, MD 21218

Drafting Firm
Minnesota Power
30 West Superior Street
Duluth, MN 55802

Engineering Firm
*The Boeing Company
P.O. Box 3707, MS 6H-PR
Seattle, WA 98124

Kimberly Clark Corporation
2100 Winchester Road
Neenah, WI 54956-0999

Environmental Law Firm
Kohn, Kohn and Colapinto
3233 P Street, NW
Washington, DC 20007-2756

Native American Rights
    Foundation
1506 Broadway
Boulder, CO 80302

Film Studio
Lighthouse Productions
120 El Camino Drive, Suite 212
Beverly Hills, CA 90212

Metro-Goldwyn-Mayer/United
    Artists
1350 Sixth Avenue, 24th Floor
New York, NY 10019

Group Counseling
Big Brothers/Big Sisters of
    Nevada
4045 South Spencer, Suite A-57
Las Vegas, NV 89119

Group Psychiatry Clinic
Gracie Square Hospital
420 East 76th Street
New York, NY 10021

Institute for Mental Health
    Initiatives
2175 K Street, NW, Suite 700
Washington, DC 20037

Hotel or Restaurant
Bonaventure Hotel & Suites
404 South Figueroa Street
Los Angeles, CA 90071

*Food Service Management
Internship Committee*
Lawyers Club Dining Service
551 South State Street
Ann Arbor, MI 48109-1208

South Seas Resort
P.O. Box 194
Captiva Island, FL 33924

*Human Resources/Customer
Service*
Hewitt Associates LLC
100 Half Day Road
Lincolnshire, IL 60069

Law Firm
American Bar Association
740 15th Street, NW
Washington, DC 20005

Office of General Counsel
1600 Defense, Pentagon
Washington, DC 20301-1600

Marketing/Sales
Lands' End
5 Lands' End Lane
Dodgeville, WI 53595

Mattel, Inc.
333 Continental Boulevard
El Segundo, CA 90245

Multimedia Firm
Gensys Multimedia Productions, Inc.
10850 Wilshire Boulevard, Suite 380
Los Angeles, CA 90024

*Lucas Digital LCD
P.O. Box 2459
San Rafael, CA 94912

Museum
Museum of Science
Science Park
Boston, MA 02114

The Museum of Television and Radio
25 West 52nd Street
New York, NY 10019

National Park
Denali National Park and Reserve
P.O. Box 9
Denali Park, AK 99755

National Parks Conservation Association
1300 19th Street, NW, Suite 300
Washington, DC 20036

Network TV Affiliates
ABC News Nightline
1717 DeSales Street, NW
Washington, DC 20036

CBS News, Inc.
524 West 57th Street
New York, NY 10019

Public Broadcasting Service (PBS)
1320 Braddock Place
Alexandria, VA 22314

Newspaper or Magazine
American Society of Magazine Editors
919 Third Avenue, 22nd Floor
New York, NY 10022

MAD Magazine
1700 Broadway
New York, NY 10019

Non-Profit Group
American Red Cross
8111 Gatehouse Road, 6th Floor
Falls Church, VA 22042

Clinical Directors Network, Inc.
54 West 39th Street, 11th Floor
New York, NY 10018

Nonprofit Financial Center
29 East Madison, Suite 1700
Chicago, IL 60602-4415

Outward Bound

Hurricane Island Outward Bound
    School–Southern Program
177 Salem Court
Tallahassee, FL 32301

Pharmaceutical Firm

Abbott Laboratories
College Relations
Department 39 K
Building AP51
200 Abbott Park Road
Abbott Park, IL 60064-6208

Merck Research Laboratories
Summneytown Pike, WP-42
P.O. Box 4
West Point, PA 19486

Photography Studio

Boston Photo Collaborative
67 Brookside Avenue
Jamaica Plain, MA 02130

Smithsonian Institution
Office of Imaging, Printing, and
    Photographic Services
American History Building
Room LB054
MRC 644
Washington, DC 20560-0644

Physical Therapy Center

Dr. Paul Schwann Applied
    Health & Research Center
3737 Wascana Parkway
University of Regina
Regina, Saskatchewan, Canada
    S4S 0A2

PR Agency

Brown-Miller Communications
1114 Jones Street
Martinez, CA 94553

Magnet Communications
110 Fifth Avenue
New York, NY 10011

Publishing House

The Boston Globe
135 Morrissey Boulevard
Boston, MA 02107

Houghton Mifflin Company
222 Berkeley Street
Boston, MA 02116-3764

Penguin Putnam, Inc.
375 Hudson Street
New York, NY 10014

Radio Station

The Westwood One Radio
    Networks
524 West 57th Street, 1st Floor
New York, NY 10019

WLRN Public Radio and
    Television
172 Northeast 15th Street
Miami, FL 33132

Real Estate Agency

Pennsylvania Real Estate
    Investment Trust
200 South Broad Street
Philadelphia, PA 19102

Record Label
Naxos of America, Inc.
416 Mary Lindsay Polk Drive, #509
Franklin, TN 37067

*Sony Music Entertainment
550 Madison Avenue
New York, NY 10022

Recording Studio
S.O.S. Productions, Inc.
753 Harmon Avenue
Columbus, OH 43223

Wall Street Music
28545 Greenfield, Suite 200
Southfield, MI 48076

Research & Development Firm
Performance Research
25 Mill Street
Queen Anne Square
Newport, RI 02840

Procter & Gamble Company
Miami Valley Laboratories
Box 538707
Cincinnati, OH 45253-8707

Science Lab
Brookhaven National Laboratory
Building 438
Upton, NY 11973-5000

Toxikon
15 Wiggins Avenue
Bedford, MA 01730

Whitney Laboratory
9505 Ocean Shore Boulevard
St. Augustine, FL 32086

Social Service
American Cancer Society
1626 Locust Street
Philadelphia, PA 19103

Break the Cycle
P.O. Box 64996
Los Angeles, CA 90064

Sports Physician
Memorial Health and Lifestyle Center
111 West Jefferson
South Bend, IN 46601

Summer Opera
Metropolitan Opera Guild
Education Department
70 Lincoln Center Plaza
New York, NY 10023-6593

San Francisco Opera
301 Van Ness Avenue
San Francisco, CA 94102

Symphony Center
Carnegie Hall
881 Seventh Avenue
New York, NY 10019

Teaching Assistant
International YMCA
Go Global
5 West 63rd Street, 2nd Floor
New York, NY 10023

Manice Education Center
68 Savoy Road
Florida, MA 01247

American Conservatory Theater
30 Grant Avenue
San Francisco, CA 94108

Theater Company
Denver Center Theater Company
1050 13th Street
Denver, CO 80204

Zoo
Baltimore Zoo
Druid Hill Park
Baltimore, MD 21217

JFK Center for the Performing
    Arts
2700 F Street, NW
Washington, DC 20566

The Minnesota Zoo
13000 Zoo Boulevard
Apple Valley, MN 55124

Theatrical Set Designer
Alley Theater
615 Texas Avenue
Houston, TX 77002

Also look for these books:

The Internship Bible 2004, Princeton Review, 2004.

Scoring a Great Internship, Natavi Guides, 2002.

The Back Door Guide to Short-Term Job Adventures, Ten Speed Press, 2002.

Internships for Dummies, For Dummies, 2001.

Internship Success: Real-World, Step-by-Step Advice on Getting the Most Out of Internships, McGraw-Hill/Contemporary Books, 1998.

I'll Work for Free: A Short-Term Strategy for a Long-Term Payoff, Holt, 1994.

books for further reference

ACADEMIC ADVICE

Navigating Your Freshman Year, Natavi Guides, 2003.

Scholarships, Grants & Prizes 2004, Peterson's Guides, 2003.

2003 Guide to Federal Government College Financial Assistance Information (CD-ROM), Progressive Management, 2003.

The New Dictionary of Cultural Literacy: What Every American Needs to Know, Houghton Mifflin, 2002.

Fishing for a Major, Natavi Guides, 2002.

10 Steps in Writing the Research Paper, Barron's Education Series, 2001.

You Are Here: College Internet Guide, Yahbooks Publishing, 2001.

College Majors and Careers, Ferguson Publishing, 1999.

INTERVIEWS

Knock 'Em Dead 2003, Adams Media Corporation, 2003.

201 Best Questions to Ask on Your Interviews, McGraw-Hill Trade, 2002.

Job Interviews for Dummies, For Dummies, 2000.

60 Seconds & You're Hired, Penguin USA, 2000.

Best Answers to the 201 Most Frequently Asked Interview Questions, McGraw-Hill Trade, 1996.

The Complete Job Interview Handbook, Perennial, 1994.

Sweaty Palms: The Neglected Art of Being Interviewed, Ten Speed Press, 1992.

RESUMES AND COVER LETTERS

The Resume Handbook, Adams Media Corporation, 2003.

The Resume Makeover, McGraw-Hill Trade, 2003.

Resumes That Knock 'Em Dead, Adams Media Corporation, 2002.

Winning Resumes, Wiley, 2002.

The Overnight Resume, Ten Speed Press, 1999.

Winning Cover Letters, Wiley, 2002.

Cover Letters That Knock 'Em Dead, Adams Media Corporation, 2002.

The Perfect Cover Letter, Wiley, 1997.

CHOOSING A CAREER

What Color Is Your Parachute 2004, Ten Speed Press, 2003.

Job Hunting A to Z: The Wet Feet Insider Guide to Landing the Job You Want, Wet Feet Press, 2003.

The Five Patterns of Extraordinary Careers, Crown Publishing Group, 2003.

Jobs Related Almanac, Barricade Books, 2002.

Career Guide to America's Top Industries, Jist Works, 2002.

Guide to Internet Job Searching, 2002–2003, McGraw-Hill/Contemporary Books, 2002.

The Harvard Business School Guide to Finding Your Next Job, Harvard Business School Press, 2000.

Discover Your Passion: An Intuitive Search to Find Your Purpose in Life, Tomlynn Publications, 2000.

Great Jobs series, McGraw-Hill/Contemporary Books, 2000.

The American Almanac of Jobs and Salaries (2000–2001 edition), Avon, 2000.

Best Jobs for the 21st Century, Jist Works, 1998.

How the Real World Really Works: Graduating into the Rest of Your Life, Berkley Books, 1997.

JOB ISSUES FOR MINORITIES

Vault Guide for Conquering Corporate America for Women and Minorities, Vault Reports Inc., 2003.

Cool Women, Hot Jobs, Free Spirit Publishing, 2002.

Pathways to Career Success for Minorities, Ferguson Publishing, 2000.

Job Search Handbook for People with Disabilities, Jist Works, 2000.

Learning a Living: A Guide to Planning Your Career and Finding a Job for People with Learning Disabilities, Attention Deficit Disorder, and Dyslexia, Woodbine House, 2000.

College and Career Success for Students with Learning Disabilities, McGraw-Hill/Contemporary Books, 1996.

SUCCEEDING ON THE JOB

How to Sell Yourself, Career Press, 2002.

Competitive Strategy, Free Press, 1998.

Nichecraft: Using Your Specialness to Focus Your Business, Corner Your Market and Make Customers Seek You Out, HarperBusiness, 1996.

Work with Passion, New World Library, 1995.

Getting Things Done When You Are Not in Charge, Fireside, 1993.

What They Still Don't Teach You at Harvard Business School, Bantam Books, 1990.

graduate school: applying and getting in

should you stay or should you go?

It may surprise you that the median age for graduate students in business and law is now twenty-seven. That means that with a graduate degree at twenty-four, you'll be competing with people who have five years of work experience. To increase your odds, why not get some work experience after graduation before applying to graduate school? You can earn money, establish your independence, and then return to school with a new perspective. (Besides, many companies pay for their employees' graduate work. You could take courses at night and earn your degree over four or five years.)

Exception to the Rule

If you want to become a professor, go directly to graduate school. Do no pass Go; do not collect $200. Academia is competitive on terms of its own, and "real world" experience does little to improve your chances.

Applications

If you plan on going straight to graduate school, you'll have to take entrance exams and fill out applications for prospective schools.

Entrance Exams

If you've decided to seek another degree beyond your B.A., you might have to take one of a battery of tests: the GRE, GMAT, LSAT, or MCAT, to name a few. Your performance on these tests is one of the factors weighed in the admissions process.

A good place to start is with the test itself, because your score will help you decide which schools you have a good chance of being admitted to.

A breakdown of the various tests follows.

GRE: Graduate Record Examination   This test is designed to measure general analytical, quantitative, and verbal abilities, as well as knowledge and understanding of the subject matter of specific graduate fields. It is required for admission into many graduate and professional schools. There are two parts to the GRE: the General Test and the Subject Test. The General Test consists of three sections. The analytical writing section is a 75-minute writing section that tests your ability to articulate your opinion and to analyze an argument. The two parts of this section are scored on a scale of 1 to 6. The two other sections, one verbal (30 minutes) and one quantitative (45 minutes), are similar to those sections on the SAT. Scores for these sections are reported on a scale of 200 to 800. All testing centers in the United States are now Computer-Based Testing (CBT), so make sure you familiarize yourself with the test format. Downloadable software is available to help you with this.

The eight different Subject Tests (which are administered in biochemistry/cell/molecular biology, biology, chemistry, computer science, literature in English, mathematics, physics, and psychology) are intended for students who have majored in each subject in college and are now seeking an advanced degree. They last for two hours and 50 minutes each. Subject test scores are reported on a scale of 200 to 990. The General and Subject tests may be taken on two different dates. Scores are usually reported within two to six weeks.

The computer-based GRE General Test is offered year round at CBT centers. Registration is on a first-come-first-served basis, so schedule early for the date you would prefer. Subject Tests are offered three times each year in November, December, and April. Registration for tests is due about one month before each test date.

Computer software and practice tests are available. Further information, practice tests, and registration forms can be obtained through the GRE website at www.gre.org, by writing to GRE-ETS, P.O. Box 6000, Princeton, NJ 08541-6000, or by calling GRE at (609) 771-7670.

GMAT: Graduate Management Admission Test   Required for students applying to business schools, the GMAT contains two 30-minute analytical writing sections and two 75-minute verbal and quantitative sections. These last two sections consist of problem-solving math questions (not much harder than the SAT), data sufficiency (regular math concepts posed in more confusing formats), reading passages (three in order of difficulty), grammar (basic concepts tested in "What is wrong with this sentence?" format), and analysis of situations (logical reasoning). Scores are usually mailed out about five weeks after the test date.

The GMAT is administered throughout the year at CBT centers. Again, register early to secure your seat on your desired day. Test centers are located throughout the United States and Canada and in many foreign locations. For further information, practice tests, and registration forms, visit www.mba.com, contact ETS by mail at Educational Testing Service, Rosedale Road, Princeton, NJ 08541, or call (609) 921-9000.

LSAT: Law School Admissions Test   The LSAT consists of four 35-minute scored sections, as well as a 30-minute writing sample and two unscored experimental sections. The four sections consist of facts and rules (containing outcome and factual questions), arguments (making distinctions between conclusions and assumptions), reading passages (very difficult—simply read for the main idea and refer back for specific questions), and games (involving diagramming problems), followed by a writing sample (this is sent to law schools, but it's rumored that they don't use it in making decisions). One distinguishing feature of the LSAT is that no points are subtracted for errors, so lucky guesses can raise your score. Scores are reported within four to six weeks and are on a scale of 10 to 48.

The LSAT is given four times a year, in February, June, September, and October; be advised that most law schools require that the LSAT be taken by December to qualify for admission the following fall. Again, there are test centers throughout the United States and in some foreign countries. For more information or to apply, call (215) 968-1001 or visit www.lsac.org.

MCAT: Medical College Admissions Test   The MCAT is designed to test a student's knowledge and understanding of the biology, chemistry, and physics designated as prerequisites to the study of medicine. This material is usually that covered in first-year college science courses. The test also evaluates basic analytical ability in solving medically relevant problems. The daylong MCAT (8:30 to 6:00) is divided into four sections: science knowledge (separate biology, chemistry, and physics sections), science problems (the three disciplines combined in problems), skills analysis–reading (passages followed by comprehensive questions), and skills analysis–quantitative (questions involving quantitative material). A recent addition to the test is an expository essay section. Scores are given for each of the six sections, on a scale of 1 to 15; they are reported within 45 days.

The MCAT is given in April and September, and registration is usually due about a month before the test. For registration information, write to MCAT Program Office, P.O. Box 4056, Iowa City, IA 52243, call (319) 337-1357, or email mcat_reg@act.org.

In addition to the MCAT, there are other medical tests, designed to measure general academic ability as well as science knowledge. These include the following:

- AHPAT: Allied Health Professions Admissions Test. Required for admission into allied health schools—those that offer programs in such fields as chiropractic, dental technology, midwifery, social work, physical therapy, and many other medical professions. Call The Psychological Corporation at 1-800-622-3231 or visit www.tpcweb.com/pse/index.htm for more information.

- OAT: Optometry Admissions Test. Required for those seeking admission into schools and colleges of optometry. For further information, visit www.opted.org/info_oat.cfm#5 for an online application, write to Optometry Admissions Testing Program,

211 East Chicago Avenue, Suite 1846, Chicago, IL 60611-2678, or call (312) 440-2693.

- PCAT: Pharmacy College Admissions Test. Required for admission to colleges of pharmacy.
- VCAT: Veterinary College Admissions Test. For those seeking admission into colleges of veterinary medicine.

For the PCAT and the VCAT, contact The Psychological Corporation using the information listed above.

NTE: National Teachers' Exam   The NTE tests are standardized exams that measure the academic achievements of students who wish to join, or are already admitted to, teacher education programs. There are three types of exams: Core Battery Tests, the nationwide Specialty Area Tests, and the statewide Specialty Area Tests. The first of three two-hour-long Core Battery tests is the Test of Communications Skills, which examines listening, reading, and writing skills. The second, the Test of General Knowledge, tests understanding of literature and fine arts, mathematics, science, and social studies. Finally, the Test of Professional Knowledge assesses the student's aptitude for the types of decisions required of beginning teachers. The scores for this section, however, are not added into the final score.

Tests are given in the following subjects: art education, audiology, biology and general science, business education, chemistry and physics, early childhood education, education in the elementary school, education of the mentally retarded, educational administration, English language and literature, French, German, home economics, industrial arts, introduction to the teaching of reading, library media specialist, mathematics, music, education, physical education, school guidance and counseling, social studies, Spanish, special education, speech communication, and speech-language pathology. There are also state-sponsored Specialty Area Tests in other subjects not covered in the nationwide tests. A single score is reported for each test; for the Core Battery Test there are three scores, on a scale of 600–695. Specialty Area scores are reported on a scale of 250 to 999. Scores are usually mailed out within four to six weeks.

Core Battery Tests are usually administered in October, March, and June, while Specialty Area Tests are given in November, March, and July. Registration closes about one month before each test date. The Core Battery and Specialty Area Tests are taken on different days; you may take one, two, or three of the Core tests on the same day and up to two Specialty Area Tests during a special double session given once a year. For further information, call ETS at (609) 771-7395 or visit the ETS website at www.ets.org/praxis/index.html.

Test Preparation Services

Whether you like them or not, standardized tests are an important part of the graduate school admissions game. They provide an efficient way for admissions officers to discriminate among hundreds of faceless applicants. Fortunately, studying for these tests can improve your scores tremendously.

Many organizations, on and off campus, offer courses that include subject reviews and practice tests as well as strategies to help students "beat" each test. Some test-takers swear by these methods, while others hesitate to invest so much money in preparing for the exams. (The classes can run upwards of $500.) Below are descriptions of two of the most popular courses offered nationwide.

Stanley Kaplan   The Kaplan course is for the student who thrives on self-paced study. Students are given review materials to study at home on their own time. Kaplan has also developed online courses and review materials for PDAs. Students also have the use of the Kaplan Study Center. The center is filled with people taking practice tests, listening to audiotapes, and questioning tutors. You can come and go as you please. For more information, go to the Kaplan website at www.kaplan.com.

Princeton Review   How is Princeton Review different? First of all, the course caters to the student who desires a structured classroom setting. Pupils who display similar weaknesses are grouped together. During weekly lectures, techniques and concepts are taught. Workshops may be attended for further practice. Private tutoring is available, as are online courses. Find out more about Princeton Review courses at www.review.com.

Deciding Where to Apply

Once you know which field you'd like to do graduate work in, it's a good idea to consult the *Graduate School Guide* (School Guide Publications, 1-800-433-7771) or GraduateGuide.com (www.grad uateguide.com). You can purchase this book, check it out at the library, or borrow it from your school's career services office. It contains a list of all the universities in the United States and indicates which degrees each offers.

There are other online services that can help you find a graduate school, depending on what your specific criteria are. These include www.gradschools.com, www.petersons.com, and http://grad.stu dentsreview.com. For other advice on graduate schools, read *Graduate Schools in the U.S. 2004* (Peterson's Guides, 2003) and *The College Board Index of Majors & Graduate Degrees 2004* (College Board, 2003).

As with your college search years ago, you'll need to make a list, contact the schools, find out their requirements, apply, and interview.

What Else Determines Admission?

Test scores, college grade point average, activities, work experience, recommendations, and essays are all factors in the selection process.

Let's be realistic. No applicant is strong in all areas. As you complete your application packet, emphasize your strengths and minimize your weaknesses (don't deny them). Begin your applications early and make sure that you give recommenders plenty of time (at least one month). Remember, things always take longer than planned . . . especially things of quality.

Scholarships

You may be eligible for local and national scholarships. Some highly competitive scholarships, like the Rhodes or the Fulbright, require recommendations, interviews, high grades, work experiences, and athletic achievement. But there are hundreds of other grants available through your school's scholarship office. Check them out.

In addition to searching for scholarships, you can also apply for federally funded scholarships, grants, loans, and work through the Free Application for Federal Student Aid. Apply for FAFSA money online at www.fafsa.ed.gov. If this is your first time using FAFSA, register for a PIN number first so that you can speed up your application process and return to a saved application to make changes. If you have used FAFSA before, fill out a renewal application because FAFSA saves much of your information from previous years (see Appendix A).

In addition to applying for scholarships and federal money, you might also want to check out these books for more ideas: *Cash for Grad School* (HarperResource, 2004), *Getting Money for Graduate School* (Peterson's Guides, 2002), *The Graduate School Funding Handbook* (University of Pennsylvania Press, 2002), *Dan Cassidy's Worldwide Graduate Scholarship Directory* (Career Press, 2000).

Also look for these books:

Graduate Admissions Essays, Ten Speed Press, 2000.

How to Write a Winning Personal Statement for Graduate and Professional School, Peterson's Guides, 1998.

The Grad School Handbook, Perigee, 1998.

How to Get into the Right Business School, McGraw-Hill/Contemporary Books, 1998.

Getting What You Came For: The Smart Student's Guide to Earning a Master's or a Ph.D., Noonday, 1997.

continuing your education once you graduate

Graduated does not mean educated.

—HARRY EDWARDS, *THE STRUGGLE THAT MUST BE*

The real university is a state of mind.

—ROBERT M. PIRSIG, *ZEN AND THE ART OF MOTORCYCLE MAINTENANCE*

I f a well-rounded college education is a combination of academic work and real-world experience, then the best education outside of college comes both on the job and off.

Chances are that once you graduate, you will, at one time or another, be transferred to another city. Keeping busy and meeting new people will become a primary concern. The following suggestions should help.

Taking Classes

"Now that I'm out of school officially, I can concentrate better on the details when I take classes at night," says Scott Freuner, who tries to take courses as much as he can. "I'm in retail and I don't get to stretch my mind academically at work. In the evenings I take subjects like creative writing or Western civilization. It's fun, it keeps me alert, and because I'm motivated to learn, I'm remembering more than I did in college."

Many people continue their education formally by enrolling in one class every semester. Some may even earn their master's degree through evening courses over a period of years. Others may take classes that don't apply to a degree. A class on Chaucer or immigrants in urban America will help you remember that there is a world outside your nine-to-five job. It will challenge your mind in ways that are different from your challenges on the job. The contrast is key.

Try taking courses outside a college or university, such as ballroom or salsa dancing, Chinese cooking, or pottery making. Seminars are typically sponsored in every city. You may want to take a Saturday course in public speaking or how to use software. Even if your company will not pay, you many want to participate.

Museum and Library Lectures

"Once a month on Tuesday nights, a friend and I go to a yearlong series of lectures at our local library," says Hank Sands, an architect. "Last month the lecture was by a professor on the tropical rain forests, about which I knew little before I attended. After the talk, I went and checked out a book the lecturer recommended. I may never be an expert on any of these subjects, but over time I'll know a little about a lot of things."

Most museums and libraries offer free or affordable lecture series on topics ranging from extraterrestrials to creative writing to the life cycle of vampire bats. Professionals in the field give the lectures. Usually the people in the audience are interesting too.

Weekend Seminars

"My weekend seminar on management training was more like a mini-vacation," says Adele Hayward, who manages an employment agency for temporary personnel. "We broke into several different groups and discussed key issues in management: how to hire the best people, how to keep them motivated, how to give people constructive criticism. I met many interesting people, including someone who made me a job offer two weeks later."

There are seminars every weekend on topics ranging from wine tasting to finance and accounting. Some of the seminars are in retreat areas and are both educational and recreational.

Book or Writing Clubs

In every city there are informal groups where books or writing are discussed. This is a great way to make friends. You may want to form your own reading/dinner clubs to discuss classics you never read or current literature.

"My book club is like an extended family," says Margaret Maillor, a freelance photographer, who formed a club with her friends three years ago. "We've read everything from *The Origin of Species* to *The Bonfire of the Vanities.* It's been fascinating to learn different things about your friends through their interpretations of each book. We all refrain from being judgmental, although sometimes it's hard. We get into some pretty rigorous debates at times."

Outdoor Clubs

These clubs offer a variety of activities, such as hiking, canoeing, camping, sailing, and skiing. Sometimes weekend group trips are available to your favorite mountain or resort.

Pat Sullivan's membership in the Audubon Society led her to a career. Because of her affection for waterfowl, Pat often joined the Society for excursions to rookeries along the Atlantic cost. On one of these trips she met a researcher from a prestigious midwestern zoo. After they had spent the weekend together, she offered Pat a job. Six months later Pat was in Cincinnati conducting ornithological research.

Computer Groups

If you have a computer and an Internet connection, you can hook it up and exchange information and play games with other computer buffs across the country. You may also want to try your hand at co-authoring a software program.

Free Concerts

Most cities feature free concerts or plays in the summer. You can pack a picnic and a blanket and relax while listening to Verdi's *Aïda* and gazing up at the stars. If your city doesn't have a series of park concerts, check the churches and synagogues. They often feature classical music concerts.

"Summer wouldn't be summer without concerts at Wolftrap," says Richard Harrin, a congressional aide in Washington. "Music under the stars, a picnic on the grass, and wine with your friends is one of the best ways to spend a Saturday night. It's a close second to a night at the ball game."

a look at the world of work

B elow is an analysis of numerous jobs compiled from *Occupational Outlook Handbook* (VGM Career Books, 2000) and *Occupational Outlook Quarterly* (Vol. 46, No. 1, Spring 2003). While not every job is represented nor every aspect of a job analyzed here, this will give you an idea of what certain occupations require, which is always helpful when you are taking steps toward a career.

For more detailed information on any of these jobs, you may go to the Bureau of Labor Statistics' Occupational Outlook website (www.bls.gov/oco/). Here, just as below, jobs are grouped by types. Additionally, each occupational overview ends with suggestions for sources of additional information, including membership associations for each occupation. You should also be sure to investigate the books in Appendix C listed under "Choosing a Career" for even more information.

Administrative Support Occupations, Including Clerical

	Job Requirements								Work Environment					Occupational Characteristics			
	1. Leadership/persuasion	2. Helping/instructing others	3. Problem-solving/creativity	4. Initiative	5. Work as part of a team	6. Frequent public contact	7. Manual dexterity	8. Physical stamina	9. Hazardous	10. Outdoors	11. Confined	12. Geographically concentrated	13. Part-time	14. Median yearly earnings (in thousands of dollars)	15. Employment growth	16. Number of new jobs, 2000–2010 (in thousands)	17. Entry requirements
Bank tellers					●	●					●		●	17.2	D	–59	
Bookkeepers & accounting clerks				●	●						●		●	23.2	–	39	
Computer operators		●		●	●	●					●			25.0	D	–33	
Data entry keyers				●	●	●					●			19.2	D	–32	
Legal assistants			●	●	●									32.8	F	62	
Postal service workers					●		●		●					35.0	D	–4.5	
Receptionists & information clerks	●				●	●					●		●	25.6	F	256	
Reservation & transportation ticket agents & travel clerks	●				●	●				●				11.8	A	28	
Secretaries & administrative assistants				●	●	●								24.5	S	265	
Shipping, receiving, & traffic clerks		●		●	●									22.5	S	83	
Stenographers & court reporters			●	●	●	●								25.4	A	3	
Teacher assistants	●	●			●	●	●						●	15.8	F	301	

Agricultural, Forestry, & Fishing Occupations

Occupation													
Agricultural workers	●	●	●	●	●	●	●	●	●	●	23.2	S	37

Construction Occupations

Occupation													
Boilermakers						●			●	●	38.4	−	.6
Bricklayers & stonemasons		●	●	●	●	●			●	●	35.2	A	21
Carpenters		●	●	●	●	●		●	●	●	28.7	S	98
Carpet, floor, & tile installers		●	●	●	●	●	●	●	●	●	26.5	A	22
Concrete masons & terrazzo workers		●	●	●	●	●		●	●	●	26.9	S	5
Construction & building inspectors	●	●		●		●		●	●	●	37.5	A	11
Drywall workers & lathers		●	●	●	●	●		●	●	●	29.9	S	17
Electricians		●	●	●	●	●		●	●	●	35.3	A	120
Glaziers		●	●	●	●	●		●	●	●	26.4	A	7.2
Insulation workers		●	●	●	●	●		●	●	●	25.5	A	7.2
Painters & paperhangers		●	●	●	●	●	●	●	●	●	25.1	A	99
Plasterers		●	●	●	●	●		●	●	●	29.4	A	6.4
Plumbers & pipefitters		●	●	●	●	●	●	●	●	●	34.7	A	59
Roofers		●	●	●	●	●		●	●	●	25.3	A	31
Sheet-metal workers		●	●	●	●	●			●	●	28.0	F	51
Structural & reinforcing metal workers		●	●	●	●	●		●	●	●	32.9	A	20

D = Declining employment, − = Little/No change, S = Slower than average, A = Average, F = Faster than average, N/E = No Estimate Available

Engineers, Surveyors, & Architects

	Job Requirements									Work Environment				Occupational Characteristics			
	1. Leadership/persuasion	2. Helping/instructing others	3. Problem-solving/creativity	4. Initiative	5. Work as part of a team	6. Frequent public contact	7. Manual dexterity	8. Physical stamina	9. Hazardous	10. Outdoors	11. Confined	12. Geographically concentrated	13. Part-time	14. Median yearly earnings (in thousands of dollars)	15. Employment growth	16. Number of new jobs, 2000–2010 (in thousands)	17. Entry requirements
Architects		●	●	●	●	●								47.7	A	19	
Surveyors	●	●	●	●		●	●		●					37.6	A	20	
Engineers																	
Aerospace engineers		●	●	●					●					67.0	A	7	
Chemical engineers		●	●	●										64.8	S	1.4	
Civil engineers		●	●	●										53.5	A	24	
Computer hardware engineers		●	●	●										52.2	F	15	
Computer software engineers		●	●	●										52.2	F	664	
Electrical & electronics engineers		●	●	●										62.7	A	31	
Industrial engineers		●	●	●										52.6	S	12	
Mechanical engineers		●	●	●										58.0	A	29	
Mining engineers		●	●	●										56.1	D	–1	

Occupation			
Nuclear engineers	71.3	–	.3
Petroleum engineers	74.3	S	–.6
Executive, Administrative, & Managerial Occupations			
Managers & Administrators			
Education administrators	60.4	A	61
Financial managers	55.1	A	122
Medical health services managers	N/E	F	81
Management Support Occupations			
Accountants & auditors	37.9	A	181
Human resources, training, & labor relations specialists	49.0	A	116
Inspectors & compliance officers, except construction	36.8	D	–11
Purchasing agents	41.8	–	12
Underwriters	38.7	–	2.1
Wholesale & retail buyers	36.5	S	111
Health Diagnosing & Treating Practitioners			
Chiropractors	63.9	F	13
Dentists	110.2	S	8.8

D = Declining employment, – = Little/No change, S = Slower than average, A = Average, F = Faster than average, N/E = No Estimate Available

Health Diagnosing & Treating Practitioners, continued

	Job Requirements									Work Environment				Occupational Characteristics			
	1. Leadership/persuasion	2. Helping/instructing others	3. Problem-solving/creativity	4. Initiative	5. Work as part of a team	6. Frequent public contact	7. Manual dexterity	8. Physical stamina	9. Hazardous	10. Outdoors	11. Confined	12. Geographically concentrated	13. Part-time	14. Median yearly earnings (in thousands of dollars)	15. Employment growth	16. Number of new jobs, 2000–2010 (in thousands)	17. Entry requirements
Dietitians & nutritionists	●	●	●	●	●									35.0	A	7.4	
Occupational therapists	●	●	●	●	●	●								48.2	F	27	
Optometrists			●	●	●	●	●							68.5	A	5.9	
Pharmacists	●	●	●	●	●	●								66.2	F	53	
Physical therapists		●	●	●	●	●	●							56.6	F	44	
Physician assistants		●	●	●	●	●								47.1	F	31	
Physicians	●	●	●	●	●	●								164.0	A	107	
Podiatrists		●	●	●	●	●								79.5	A	14	
Recreational therapists	●	●	●	●	●	●			●					27.8	S	2.5	
Registered nurses		●	●	●	●	●	●	●						40.7	F	561	
Respiratory therapists		●	●	●	●	●	●							34.8	F	38	
Speech pathologists & audiologists	●	●	●	●	●									43.1	F	40	
Veterinarians	●	●	●	●	●	●	●	●	●					51.0	F	19	

Health Technologists & Technicians

Occupation			
Clinical laboratory technologists & technicians	32.4	A	53
Dental hygienists	45.8	F	54
Diagnostic medial sonographers	32.9	F	8.6
Dispensing opticians	22.4	A	13
Emergency medical technicians	20.3	F	54
Licensed practical nurses	26.9	A	142
Medical record technicians	20.6	F	66
Radiological technologists	32.9	F	39
Surgical technicians	25.8	F	25

Machine Operators, Tenders, & Setup Workers

Occupation			
Metalworking & plastic-working mach. operators	24.2	S	74
Printing press operators	27.7	S	12

Fabricators, Assemblers, & Handworking Occupations

Occupation			
Precision assemblers	29.1	S	171
Welders & cutters	25.8	A	97

Marketing & Sales Occupations

Occupation			
Cashiers	10.7	A	488
Insurance sales workers	36.5	S	13

D = Declining employment, − = Little/No change, S = Slower than average, A = Average, F = Faster than average, N/E = No Estimate Available

Occupational Characteristics / Work Environment / Job Requirements

	Job Requirements									Work Environment				Occupational Characteristics			
	1. Leadership/persuasion	2. Helping/instructing others	3. Problem-solving/creativity	4. Initiative	5. Work as part of a team	6. Frequent public contact	7. Manual dexterity	8. Physical stamina	9. Hazardous	10. Outdoors	11. Confined	12. Geographically concentrated	13. Part-time	14. Median yearly earnings (in thousands of dollars)	15. Employment growth	16. Number of new jobs, 2000–2010 (in thousands)	17. Entry requirements
Marketing & Sales Occupations, continued																	
Manufacture & wholesale trade sales workers	●	●	●	●	●									36.5	S	111	
Real estate agents & brokers	●	●	●	●	●								●	28.0	S	41	
Retail sales workers		●	●		●				●				●	10.7	A	510	
Securities & financial services sales workers	●	●	●	●	●								●	48.1	F	82	
Travel agents		●	●		●									23.0	S	4.3	
Mechanics & Repairers																	
Vehicle & Mobile Equip. Mechanics & Repairers																	
Aircraft mechanics & engine specialists			●	●	●		●	●	●			●		38.1	A	28	
Automotive & motorcycle mechanics			●		●	●	●	●	●	●				27.4	A	151	
Automotive body repairers			●				●	●	●	●				27.4	A	23	
Diesel mechanics			●		●		●	●	●	●				29.3	A	40	
Mobile heavy equipment mechanics			●				●	●	●	●				31.5	S	17	

Electrical & Electronic Equipment Repairers

Occupation										
Computer, automated teller & office machine repairers	•					•		29.3	A	24
Electronic equipment repairers	•	•	•			•		35.6	S	15
Electronic home entertainment equip. repairs	•	•	•		•	•		23.5	D	−6.6
Radio & telecommunications installers & repairers	•		•	•	•	•	•	43.7	D	−7.5

Other Mechanics & Repairers

Occupation										
Equipment repairers	•			•	•	•		N/E	A	6.1
Heating, air-cond. & refrig. mechanics	•	•	•	•	•	•		29.2	F	54
Home appliance & power tool repairers	•	•						26.0	S	2.7
Industrial machinery repairers	•	•	•	•	•			31.8	S	75
Line installers & cable splicers	•		•	•	•	•		42.6	F	54
Vending machine servicers & repairers	•		•	•	•		•	23.3	A	6.8

Natural Scientists & Mathematicians

Computer & Mathematical Occupations

Occupation					
Actuaries	•	•		•	65.6	S	.8
Computer programmers	•	•	•	•	47.6	A	95
Computer systems analysts	•	•	•	•	52.2	F	554

D = Declining employment, – = Little/No change, S = Slower than average, A = Average, F = Faster than average, N/E = No Estimate Available

Natural Scientists & Mathematicians, continued

	Job Requirements									Work Environment				Occupational Characteristics			
	1. Leadership/persuasion	2. Helping/instructing others	3. Problem-solving/creativity	4. Initiative	5. Work as part of a team	6. Frequent public contact	7. Manual dexterity	8. Physical stamina	9. Hazardous	10. Outdoors	11. Confined	12. Geographically concentrated	13. Part-time	14. Median yearly earnings (in thousands of dollars)	15. Employment growth	16. Number of new jobs, 2000–2010 (in thousands)	17. Entry requirements
Mathematicians		●	●											49.1	D	–.1	
Statisticians		●	●											48.5	–	.5	
Physical Scientists																	
Atmospheric Scientists		●	●	●										54.4	A	1.2	
Chemists		●	●											46.2	A	18	
Geoscientists		●	●	●					●			●		53.9	F	21	
Physicists & astronomers			●	●										73.2	A	1.1	
Life Scientists																	
Agricultural scientists		●	●	●					●					42.3	S	1.5	
Biological scientists		●	●											46.1	F	30	
Foresters & conservation scientists	●	●	●	●			●	●	●					42.8	S	2.2	

Production Occupations

Precision Production Occupations

Occupation			
Bookbinding workers	20.7	S	8.5
Dental laboratory technicians	25.7	S	2.7
Food processing	20.4	S	23
Jewelers	23.8	–	.6
Machinists	28.9	S	39
Photographic process workers	21.6	–	1.6
Prepress technicians & workers	43.7	D	–13
Tool-and-die makers	37.3	–	2.8

Plant & System Operators

Occupation			
Stationary engineers	38.3	D	–.8
Water & sewage treatment plant operators	29.7	A	16

Service Occupations

Protective Service Occupations

Occupation			
Correction officers	28.5	F	145
Firefighting occupations	31.2	S	2
Guards	16.2	F	393
Police & detectives	48.7	F	174

D = Declining employment, – = Little/No change, S = Slower than average, A = Average, F = Faster than average, N/E = No Estimate Available

Service Occupations, continued	1. Leadership/persuasion	2. Helping/instructing others	3. Problem-solving/creativity	4. Initiative	5. Work as part of a team	6. Frequent public contact	7. Manual dexterity	8. Physical stamina	9. Hazardous	10. Outdoors	11. Confined	12. Geographically concentrated	13. Part-time	14. Median yearly earnings (in thousands of dollars)	15. Employment growth	16. Number of new jobs, 2000–2010 (in thousands)	17. Entry requirements
Food & Bev. Preparation & Serv. Occupations																	
Chefs & cooks			●				●			●			●	15.6	A	645	
Waiters & waitresses			●		●	●	●						●	12.5	A	1,156	
Health Services Occupations																	
Dental assistants	●			●	●	●	●							22.6	F	92	
Medical assistants	●			●	●	●	●	●						20.7	F	187	
Nursing, psychiatric, & home health care aides	●			●	●	●	●	●					●	16.6	F	623	
Cleaning Service Occupations																	
Building cleaning workers							●						●	15.3	A	461	
Personal Service Occupations																	
Barbers, cosmetologists, & related workers						●	●			●			●	15.2	A	90	

Childcare workers	15.7	A	127
Flight attendants	13.7	A	23
Social Scientists, Social Workers, Religious Workers, & Lawyers			
Lawyers		A	128
Social Scientists & Urban Planners			
Economists	48.3	F	34
Psychologists	48.1	A	33
Social scientists	39.0	A	2.6
Urban & regional planners	42.9	A	4.9
Social & Recreational Workers			
Recreation workers	16.5	F	118
Social workers	30.6	F	141
Religious Workers			
Protestant ministers	N/E	N/E	N/E
Rabbis	75.0	N/E	N/E
Roman Catholic priests	N/E	N/E	N/E
Teachers, Counselors, Librarians, & Archivists			
Adult & vocational education teachers	24.8	A	47

D = Declining employment, – = Little/No change, S = Slower than average, A = Average, F = Faster than average, N/E = No Estimate Available

	1. Leadership/persuasion	2. Helping/instructing others	3. Problem-solving/creativity	4. Initiative	5. Work as part of a team	6. Frequent public contact	7. Manual dexterity	8. Physical stamina	9. Hazardous	10. Outdoors	11. Confined	12. Geographically concentrated	13. Part-time	14. Median yearly earnings (in thousands of dollars)	15. Employment growth	16. Number of new jobs, 2000–2010 (in thousands)	17. Entry requirements
														Occupational Characteristics			
			Job Requirements							**Work Environment**							
Teachers, Counselors, Librarians, & Archivists, continued																	
Archivists & curators		•	•	•										31.8	A	2.6	
College & university faculty	•	•	•	•	•									46.6	F	315	
Counselors	•	•	•	•	•		•							38.7	F	120	
Librarians	•	•	•	•	•		•							38.5	S	10	
Teachers—Preschool, kindergarten, elementary, middle, & secondary														35.0	A	571	
Technologists & Technicians, Except Health																	
Engineering & Science Technicians																	
Drafters				•		•				•				32.4	A	42	
Engineering technicians		•		•		•								36.0	A	62	
Science technicians		•		•		•								31.0	A	34	

Other Technicians

Occupation			
Air traffic controllers	64.9	S	1.9
Broadcast technicians	25.3	A	12
Library technicians	21.7	A	21

Transportation & Material Moving Occupations

Occupation			
Aircraft pilots & flight engineers	91.8	A	11
Bus drivers	24.4	A	88
Construction machinery operators	25.0	S	34
Truck drivers	26.0	A	589

Handlers, Equip. Cleaners, Helpers, & Laborers

Occupation			
Construction laborers	14.5	A	135

Writers, Artists, & Entertainers

Communications Occupations

Occupation			
News analysts, reporters, & correspondents	26.5	S	2.2
Public relations specialists	34.6	F	49
Radio & TV announcers & newscasters	17.9	D	–4
Writers & editors	36.5	F	80

Visual Arts Occupations

Occupation			
Artists & related workers	31.7	A	29

D = Declining employment, – = Little/No change, S = Slower than average, A = Average, F = Faster than average, N/E = No Estimate Available

Writers, Artists, & Entertainers, continued

	1. Leadership/persuasion	2. Helping/instructing others	3. Problem-solving/creativity	4. Initiative	5. Work as part of a team	6. Frequent public contact	7. Manual dexterity	8. Physical stamina	9. Hazardous	10. Outdoors	11. Confined	12. Geographically concentrated	13. Part-time	14. Median yearly earnings (in thousands of dollars)	15. Employment growth	16. Number of new jobs, 2000–2010 (in thousands)	17. Entry requirements
				Job Requirements						Work Environment				Occupational Characteristics			
Designers			●	●	●	●								29.2	D	104	
Photographers & camera operators			●	●	●	●							●	20.9	F	11	
Performing Arts Occupations																	
Actors, directors, & producers			●	●	●	●	●					●	●	27.4	F	42	
Dancers & choreographers			●	●	●	●	●					●	●	21.4	A	4.3	
Musicians			●	●	●	●	●					●	●	30.0	A	45	

D = Declining employment, – = Little/No change, S = Slower than average, A = Average, F = Faster than average, N/E = No Estimate Available

where to find help

The strongest people are not the ones who never have trouble, they are the ones who seek out help when they do encounter troubles. Remember that whatever you have experienced and whatever shame or guilt might be associated with it, the brave thing to do is to find ways to work through your fears. A great many resources exist for students and others who are facing these issues, so be sure you find the help you need. Above all, remember that you are not alone and that there are many people willing to help you.

Groups with local chapters have not been included (AA, Planned Parenthood, etc.), but check your phone book or any one of the referral numbers listed below for how to get in touch with these groups. Also remember that your school's counseling center is there to help you. Make an appointment with a counselor and start getting help.

EATING DISORDERS

National Eating Disorders Association (NEDA)
1-800-931-2237
www.nationaleatingdisorders.org

Anorexia Nervosa and Related Eating Disorders, Inc. (ANRED)—
    Affiliated with NEDA
541-344-1144
www.anred.com

Eating Disorder Referral and Information Center
858-481-1515
www.edreferral.com

Also look for these books:

Fighting the Freshman Fifteen, Three Rivers Press, 2002.

Bodylove: Learning to Like Our Looks and Ourselves, Gurze Books, 2002.

Over It: A Teen's Guide to Getting Beyond Obsessions with Food and Weight, New World Library, 2001.

Making Weight: Healing Men's Conflicts with Food, Weight, Shape, and Appearance, Gurze Books, 2000.

Binge No More: Your Guide to Overcoming Disordered Eating, New Harbinger Publications, 1999.

SUICIDE AND MENTAL HEALTH

Hope Line Network—Provides listings, by state, of other help line numbers
1-800-SUICIDE (784-2433)

TeenLine Hotline Help Center
1-888-747-TEEN (8336)

The Trevor HelpLine—Provides suicide prevention for gay and questioning youth
1-800-850-8078

Mental Health Referral Service
1-800-THERAPIST (843-7274)

National Mental Health Association Information Center
1-800-969-NMHA (6642)

Also look for these books:

College Student Suicide, Haworth Press, 1990.

Women and Anxiety: A Step-by-Step Program for Managing Anxiety and Depression, Haterleigh Press, 1998.

Unmasking Male Depression, Word Publishing, 2001.

ASSAULT, ABUSE, AND VIOLENCE

Rape, Abuse, and Incest National Network (RAINN)
1-800-656-HOPE (4673)
www.rainn.org

Sexual Assault Crisis Line
1-800-643-6250

National Domestic Violence Hotline—As well as helping victims of domestic violence, NDVH also provides information and help for those people who think they might be abusers.
1-800-799-7233 (Spanish Available)
www.ndvh.org

National Center for Victims of Crime
1-800-394-2255
www.ncvc.org

Also look for these books:

> *It Happened to Me: A Teen's Guide to Overcoming Sexual Abuse*, New Harbinger Publications, 2002.
>
> *The Rape Recovery Handbook: Step-by-Step Help for Survivors of Sexual Assault*, New Harbinger Publications, 2003.

DRUG AND ALCOHOL ABUSE

National Drug and Alcohol Line—Provides information on alcohol and drug abuse, as well as advice on local treatment options
1-800-662-HELP (4357)

Alcohol and Drug Information–Prevention Online
www.health.org

Alcohol Treatment Referral Hotline
1-800-252-6465
www.adcare.com

Also look for these books:

> *Kill the Craving: How to Control the Impulse to Use Drugs and Alcohol*, New Harbinger Publications, 2001.

Alcohol Abuse: Straight Talk Straight Answers, Ixia Publications, 1999.

STDS, HIV, AND AIDS HELP AND SERVICES

National Sexually Transmitted Disease Hotline
1-800-227-8922

AIDS Hotline
1-800-252-6465
www.adcare.com

HIV/AIDS National Resources Center
1-800-362-0071

AIDSinfo
1-800-HIV-0440 (448-0440)
www.aidsinfo.nih.gov

PREGNANCY COUNSELING

Planned Parenthood Hotline
1-800-230-PLAN (7526)

Teen Pregnancy Referral Hotline
1-800-522-5006

DEBT RECOVERY AND FINANCIAL HEALTH

Look for these books:

The Complete Idiot's Guide to Beating Debt, Alpha Books, 1999.

The Complete Idiot's Guide to Managing Your Money, Alpha Communications, 2002.

Cliff's Notes: Managing Your Money, Hungry Minds, 2001.

The Debt Free Graduate: How to Survive College without Going Broke, Career Press, 2000.

BEREAVEMENT COUNSELING

AARP Grief and Loss Toll-Free Support Line—AARP offers grief support by trained volunteers who themselves have experienced the death of a loved one. Family members, friends, and co-workers who have lost a loved one are encouraged to call this line for support with their grief.
1-866-797-2277

UCLA Bereavement Hotline
1-800-445-4808

Try checking with your local hospitals to see if they offer community bereavement groups or personal bereavement sessions.

Also look for these books:

How to Go on Living When Someone You Love Dies, Bantam Books, 1991.

I Wasn't Ready to Say Goodbye: Surviving, Coping and Healing After the Sudden Death of a Loved One, Champion Press Limited, 2000.

travel abroad options

A chieving your goal of traveling overseas might seem difficult if you don't think you have the financial resources to go as a tourist. All the information listed below is to help you achieve your dream with minimal expense to you. Not only do organizations try to help students find discounted travel opportunities, but many organizations, companies, and groups offer work and volunteer travel experiences for students and young people. While you might find that some of these opportunities do cost something to you, usually your room and board are free and you receive financial compensation for your work.

Also in this appendix, you will find a list of funding and fellowship opportunities. While some of these opportunities, such as the Rhodes, the Fulbright, and the Rotary, have some specific requirements (e.g. applicants are beginning graduate work or are proficient in a language) don't let that discourage you from your funding search. Many scholarships are specifically for college students traveling overseas. For other funding opportunities and all other information, be sure to visit your school's study abroad office. If your school does not have a study abroad office, other, larger schools welcome questions from people who are not students at their university, so check with them.

Search for student travel discounts:

www.studentuniverse.com

www.statravel.com

www.istc.org

BEYOND THE PEACE CORPS—VOLUNTEER AND WORK ABROAD

Transitions Abroad

www.transitionsabroad.com

This magazine was "created as the antidote to tourism . . . with the specific goal of providing information that would enable travelers to actually meet the people of other countries, to learn about their culture, to speak their language, and to 'transition' to a new level of understanding and appreciation for our fascinating world" (www.transitionsabroad.com/information/media/history.shtml). *Transitions Abroad* also has a comprehensive website where you can investigate various ways to travel and do so cheaply.

International Student Travel Confederation

www.istc.org

ISTC, established in 1949, combines "more than 70 specialist student travel companies [who] work through the not-for-profit member associations of the ISTC" to make travel affordable for students through flight, insurance, ground transportation, work exchange program, and identity card benefits (www.aboutistc.org).

Council on International Educational Exchange

http://us.councilexchanges.org

Search for opportunities to work, volunteer, and teach abroad; learn about global service projects and hosting opportunities; or join an international student exchange.

GoAbroad.com

www.goabroad.com

This site provides "comprehensive international education and alternative travel databases. . . . In addition to some of the largest directories of their kind on the internet, GoAbroad.com provides extensive additional information . . . travel guides, currency converter, and embassy directories" (www.goabroad.com/about.cfm).

Service Civil International (SCI)

www.sciint.org

SCI "aims are to promote peace, international understanding and solidarity, social justice, sustainable development, and respect for the environment. SCI believes that all the people are capable of living together with mutual respect and without recourse to any form of violence to solve conflicts." SCI has U.S. and Canadian branches through which people can volunteer for various opportunities and workcamps around the world.

Global Volunteers

www.globalvolunteers.org

Global Volunteers is a private, non-profit, non-sectarian organization offering volunteer vacations worldwide. It mobilizes some 150 service-learning teams year-round to do volunteer work in 19 countries on six continents.

United Nations Volunteers

www.unv.org

The United Nations Volunteers (UNV) program is the volunteer division of the United Nations. The UN General Assembly created UNV in 1970 to serve as a partner in development cooperation as help is requested by UN member states. This organization supports human development globally by promoting volunteerism and by mobilizing volunteers.

BUNAC

www.bunac.com/usa

BUNAC offers U.S. students and youth work/travel programs to Britain, Ireland, Australia, New Zealand, and Canada and a volunteer program in South Africa. Each program offers a unique insight into life in a completely new culture and a chance to spend extended time working and traveling overseas.

Camp Counselors USA

www.campcounselors.com

CCUSA is a worldwide organization that provides youth with the opportunity to travel, work, and earn money. Over the past 16 years CCUSA has recruited and placed more than 95,000 participants from more than 60 countries in camps and with employers around the world.

Idealist

www.idealist.org

Idealist is a project of Action Without Borders, which is independent of governments, political ideology, or religion. Idealist's website will let visitors search or browse by name, location, or mission over 36,000 nonprofit and community organization in 165 countries. It lists thousands of volunteer opportunities in local communities and around the world and organizations that can help to get you abroad.

Cross-Cultural Solutions

www.crossculturalsolutions.org

Since 1995, Cross-Cultural Solutions has brought more than 2,500 participants to countries around the world. Their commitment is to international volunteer work, while their mission is to operate volunteer programs around the world in partnership with sustainable community initiatives. They are an international not-for-profit organization with no political or religious affiliations.

European Internships

www.europeaninternships.com

European Internships designs and delivers customized programs for individuals and groups who want to learn about other cultures by studying or working abroad. It was born in the USA and created by bilingual people who have worked in the study and work abroad industry for a long time. Their goal is to help participants fully immerse themselves in another culture, so each program is structured to help students learn about the language, customs, and lifestyles of the local people.

International Rescue Committee (IRC)

www.theirc.org

IRC is the leading non-sectarian, voluntary organization providing relief, protection, and resettlement services for refugees and victims of oppression or violent conflict. Employment and volunteer opportunities are listed for all over the world in all job areas.

Habitat for Humanity International

www.habitat.org/hr/intl.html

Habitat for Humanity International works with people who are committed to Habitat for Humanity's work of providing families with simple, decent shelter. Although assignment terms may vary, Global Assignee positions typically are for three-year periods. Positions in most countries require a willingness to communicate and affirm the Christian roots and principles of Habitat for Humanity.

NEED MONEY? FELLOWSHIP AND FUNDING OPPORTUNITIES

Fulbright Scholarships

www.iie.org.fulbright/us/ and www.fulbright.org/scholarship.htm

The U.S. Congress created the Fulbright Program to foster mutual understanding among nations through educational and cultural exchanges.

Rotary Ambassador of Goodwill Scholarships

www.rotary.org/foundation/educational/amb_scho/prospect/index.html

Some Rotary Clubs offer Ambassadorial Scholarship opportunities to increase international peace and understanding through graduate study abroad. Please refer to the club in your home district to find out whether it sponsors ambassadorial scholarships.

Rhodes Scholarships

www.rhodesscholar.org

Rhodes Scholarships enable outstanding students to pursue a degree from the University of Oxford.

U.S.–Ireland Alliance Fellowship
www.mitchellscholar.org

The George J. Mitchell Scholarship is a national post-graduate fellowship awarded for one year of study at an institution of higher learning in Ireland or Northern Ireland.

Finding Funders
www.fdncenter.org/funders/

The Grantsmanship Center
www.tgci.com/intl/

The Ford Foundation
www.fordfound.org

The David and Lucile Packard Foundation
www.packfound.org

The Robert Wood Johnson Foundation
www.rwjf.org/index.jsp

W. K. Kellogg Foundation
www.wkkf.org

MacArthur Foundation
www.macfdn.org

The Andrew W. Mellon Foundation
www.mellon.org

The Starr Foundation
www.fdncenter.org/grantmaker/starr/

The Rockefeller Foundation
www.rockfound.org

The Annie E. Casey Foundation
www.aecf.org

Charles Stewart Mott Foundation
www.mott.org

The Robert W. Woodruff Foundation
www.woodruff.org

The Annenberg Foundation
www.whannenberg.org

Also look for these books to give you some travel abroad ideas:

Alternatives to the Peace Corps, Food First Books, 1999.

Volunteer Vacations: Short-term Adventures That Will Benefit You and Others, Chicago Review Press, 2003.

Work Your Way Around the World, Globe Pequot Press, 2003.

How to Live Your Dream of Volunteering Overseas, Penguin USA, 2002.

The International Dictionary of Voluntary Work, Globe Pequot Press, 2003.

Get Outside: A Guide to Volunteer Opportunities and Working Vacations in America's Great Outdoors, Falcon, 2002.

International Job Finder: Where Jobs Are Worldwide, Planning Communications, 2002.

Work Worldwide: International Career Strategies for the Adventurous Job Seeker, Avalon Travel Publishing, 2000.

Peterson's Overseas Summer Jobs 2002, Vacation-Work, 2002.

Taking Time Off, Princeton Review, 2003.

Abroad and Beyond, Cambridge University Press, 1988.

Other Success Books by Carol Carter

The following books are available through Prentice Hall Publishers.
Visit www.prenhall.com (search by keywords "keys to").

The following books are available through LifeBound. Visit www.lifebound.com.

Do You Have Advice?

If you would like to send me your comments on what you did and didn't like about the book, I would greatly appreciate it. Or, if you have a story of your own that you think would illustrate an important point, please write it down here or on a separate sheet of paper. I'll use your comments and suggestions as I revise the book for future editions.

1. This book gave me a clearer focus on my college goals and plans.   Ⓨ   Ⓝ

2. I like the various opinions and attitudes that the book reflects.   Ⓨ   Ⓝ

3. This book made me feel more comfortable about the future.   Ⓨ   Ⓝ

4. I would improve the book by (check one):
   ○ Adding more examples
   ○ Having fewer examples
   ○ Other

5. I would recommend this book to my friends.   Ⓨ   Ⓝ

6. How I found out about this book (check one):
   ○ I saw it in a bookstore.
   ○ My teacher assigned it.
   ○ It was a gift.

Thank you for your suggestions. Mail or fax the form to:

Carol Carter
LifeBound   Fax: (303) 436-0938
1600 Broadway, Suite 2400
Denver, CO 80202

Your name: _____

Address: _____

Phone: _____

E-mail: _____

Do we have permission to quote you?   Ⓨ   Ⓝ

Do we have permission to contact you?   Ⓨ   Ⓝ